D1238253

PHIL A. KOURY

Yes, Mr. DeMille

G. P. Putnam's Sons   New York

To Mary

Contents

Part I

AMONG THE LILLIPUTIANS

1.

OUR first meeting was in the winter of 1946.

There was nothing epic in his manner. His voice did not sound like thunder from Mount Olympus. He stood at the door to his office, a foot propping it open, with a warm, interested, almost shy smile.

"Please come in."

It wasn't what one might have expected by way of greeting, no outburst ripping open the gates of Hollywood or flaying the souls of extras. A warmth filled the visitor, a feeling that he was the most important person DeMille was to see that day. Was this the legendary DeMille, the bruising, blistering Alexander of the sound stages, who practiced deliberate cruelties on players and his staff out of sheer love of exhibitionism? Was this the cinematic disciple whose fervor for the Bible had sent him shinnying like an enraged Crusader up the walls of a cardboard Antioch; whose Biblical dramas woven with human passion were once described as "a fraud that enabled immorality to hide behind the protection of the Holy Book"?

His office was not a small-scale model of the Roman Colosseum. No gladiator or thick-set Thracian toting a lead shield was in evidence nor even one assistant chained to the wall. Nothing in his meticulous dress or manner would have sent Caesar to his knees.

The office was in total disarray—sketches, pictures, clippings, books, small-scale models, assorted statuary, occupied the chairs, leather couch and the immense desk. The walls of satiny walnut

11

were bulletin boards. Thumbtacks held up more sketches, pages out of old books, memos scribbled to himself. Newspaper cartoons gave evidence of his fight against the union for banishing him from radio for refusal to pay a "one-dollar political assessment"—a controversy that had become one of the severest emotional upheavals of his life.

Everything in the room pointed to the production then in preparation. "We are calling it *Unconquered,* the story of Fort Pitt and the beginning of Pittsburgh." He gestured toward the walls. "Those are little aids that help us put together a mammoth production. We spend fortunes just finding out about the era of our story—little things that make a story authentic. Did you know that Pittsburgh was once in Virginia? Ah, you didn't, did you? I thought so. Those are things you don't find in the little red schoolbook. Did you know that a Scottish regiment lifted the siege of Fort Pitt, after marching through the forests and encountering Indians? Think of it—a Scottish regiment fighting Indians in America. Only time it ever happened. Those are the things we get for $100,000 of research. Now, the critics won't believe it. They'll see the Scottish Black Watch marching through the forest, with Indians sniping at them from behind trees, and they'll go back to their offices and write that DeMille is nuts, that any fool school kid can tell you there was no Scottish regiment at the mouth of the Ohio in 1763."

He paused. His eyes narrowed in open appraisal and one could feel their power and penetration.

He said slowly: "They say I have nothing but yes men around me. A yes man can do me great harm. I don't operate that way. I like to pick a man's mind. I know what I know, so I'm interested in what you know. If you don't tell me what you think, if you yes me, the picture is hurt. If you tell me what you think, we'll have no problems. I had a man here once who decided he would never say yes. He kept saying no to everything to prove to everyone that he wasn't a yes man. Then I once had a very agreeable fellow in your job. I finally had to tell him for God's sake wait until I finish talking before you say yes."

He turned next to a source of much sorrow, a major battlefield in his life.

"I guess you know I don't get along with the movie critics. They don't like my pictures. The public seems to like them but not the critics. Every time I make a picture the critics' estimation of the American public goes down ten degrees. When I did *The King of Kings* I showed Jesus paying off the Roman head tax with gold taken from the mouth of a fish. A woman critic on a Chicago newspaper threw up her hands. She wrote that only DeMille could do anything so ridiculous as pulling a fish out of water with gold in its mouth. I sent her a friendly note saying she might like to check the Book of Matthew. I was happy to have the Savior of Mankind as my authority."

He was smiling again, softly. "Do you think you will like your work here?"

"Yes, Mr. DeMille," I said.

2.

DeMILLE'S home sat on a ledge near the top of the Laughlin Park hill sector, a few blocks behind the crowded Hollywood business area. It was joined by a glass-enclosed passageway to another home, equally imposing, the former residence of Charlie Chaplin. The latter housed, beside the family projection room and storage area, the offices of Cecil B. DeMille Productions, Inc.

Until its dissolution in 1952 the family-owned company managed DeMille's varied and substantial investments, principally real estate, oil and race horses. These multimillion-dollar interests were in the care of the "staff up at the house," as we referred to it with some awe. It was abundantly clear that the "house staff" was on the policy-making level as to both movie and outside interests. We of the "office staff" were not a part of this charmed circle. The house staff called the office staff by their first names; the studio staff addressed key house-staff members only as "Mr. so-and-so" and "Miss so-and-so." The real power was up on the hill; as an office-staffer put it, "the difference between Mount Olympus and an anthill."

The late W. C. Fields lived for a time in a large gray stucco home, a level or two below the twin DeMille mansions. The red-nosed comic was not regarded as a chatty neighbor, least of all when DeMille was heading his powerful open-air tonneau to the studio. At this time of day Fields was apt to be just stirring himself from a highly bibulous funk. One night there were raps at his door. It was during World War II, and a blackout was in progress.

Fields was not aware of the blackout, and there was some authority for the belief he was not altogether certain of the existence of the war. Fields, feeling little pain, glared at the figure outside his door. It was Cecil. It was obvious Fields did not relish a call from a man whose two homes looked down on his one, and whose chauffeurs, limousines and far-flung interests had been evening-long targets of the little band of cronies who regularly gathered at the Fields home for drinking bouts of very high amperage.

"I'm Cecil DeMille."

Fields burbled slightly.

"There's a blackout on."

"A what!"

"Don't you know we're having a blackout!" snorted DeMille, right in his neighbor's crimson nose.

"A blackout!" Fields shouted back, broadcasting 100-proof fumes.

"Yes, Mr. Fields, a blackout. Turn off your lights and fill your bathtub."

The offhand reference to emergency storing of drinking water struck Fields in another light.

"My God, Cease," he cried, "can't we have a blackout without one of your bathtub scenes?"

The first phase of DeMille's day was usually devoted to company affairs at the house office. These concluded, he departed for the studio. The distance was roughly two miles, negotiable by a prudent driver in ten minutes. DeMille made it in less, often as little as five minutes—an element that was important to us because of the ceremony attendant upon his arrival at Paramount. The home-to-studio run was noted with precision by the secretaries at either end; at the moment DeMille headed his car down the winding private roadway a call was made to the studio—"Mr. DeMille is on his way."

Apart from giving the staff a chance to steel itself for the imminent arrival, the information served other purposes. Subordinates could be summoned from nearby coffee shops or sound stages. In the event DeMille had sent word in advance that he wished to see a staff member "this morning," it was imperative to know the exact moment of arrival.

"This morning" meant only one thing—"instantly upon arrival." This nervous selectee seated himself outside DeMille's door, DeMille nodding him in as he strode into the chambers.

Too, Mr. DeMille's progress from garage to his office was unimpeded, the staff being extraordinarily solicitous. The street door to the bungalow was propped open, an assistant taking a stand at the garage entrance across the street to seize Mr. DeMille's inevitable valise as he stepped from the car.

The small boxlike, single-story building sat with quiet dignity in a corner of the vast Paramount studio grounds, safely removed from the secular activities in other parts of the lot. They called it "the bungalow," for no apparent reason, perhaps, other than that its severe white stucco exterior was softened into a measure of amiability by climbing roses and rows of trim hedges. Our offices, most of them quite small, opened into a narrow hallway that ran the length of the building. At the far end, like a jeweled crown on a stick, were Mr. DeMille's quarters.

In Hollywood, differences in position or influence were reflected with great sensitivity in the décor and furnishings of one's office. It might be generally said that paneled walls began on the assistant-producer level, though a number of what were nimbly called "top" writers enjoyed similar appointments. In the bungalow, however, below DeMille, all was equality. There were titles among us, but these were apt to fade in the common assault upon everyday problems. The dozen men and women who comprised Mr. DeMille's personal staff had daily, if not hourly, communication with him, lunched with him and at least two or three nights a week sat beside him in the projection room at his home to see movies for pleasure or business.

Life flowed down the corridor past our cubicles toward the fount of authority. Everything that was important moved in that direction, and we were wont to gauge the importance of a visitor by the degree of his penetration down the corridor. My office as "personal representative" was at the entrance to the corridor, across from the writers' conference room, and thus occupied what might be charitably described as a lower level in the hierarchy. A visitor whose mission stopped at that point was not likely to arouse more than passing curiosity, but the temper of studio life being what it was, it appeared a matter of some necessity to ascertain the identity of those individuals who achieved audience with Mr. DeMille. While little of this daily commerce would directly affect a staff member, one had to reckon with the fact that permanence in a movie studio could hinge rather heavily on knowing who was seeing whom and, if possible, what was said. It seemed that a good part of our time was devoted to speculating on what so-and-so was doing in so-and-so's office. A DeMille visitor naturally set into motion resourceful and subtle inquiries designed to elicit the

critical information from one of Mr. DeMille's corps of secretaries, dutiful, tight-lipped sentries outside his door.

Doors to the staff's single-room offices, opening into the
corridor, were usually ajar to enable the occupants to perceive
the flow of life toward Mr. DeMille's office. There were draw-
backs to this fish-bowl existence, yet it had an important advantage. Being addicted to leather heels, Mr. DeMille broadcast
his approach down the wooden corridor and sent us into pos-
tures of deep thought or sudden industry. His strident walk also
alerted the staff that the moment was at hand to present a
particular piece of work, perhaps long overdue. When bent on
some mission, Mr. DeMille did not stop even briefly at any
cubicle, so an assistant with a pressing problem would have to
follow in his wake across the studio lot, stepping lively to keep
up, and fading away like a dive bomber when the matter was
settled, whereupon the next assistant in hot pursuit would leap
forward to his side—thus enabling us to get quite a bit done *in
transitu.*

This column of people on the march was the subject of much
fascinated comment around Paramount, and secret jesting. Visitors were alerted to watch for it and usually were on hand at
luncheon time to observe it in full flower. Mr. DeMille cus-
tomarily arrived at his studio offices shortly before noon, having
breakfasted late. On most days it was well after 1 o'clock when
he began his luncheon trek to the studio restaurant. It was an
unwritten rule that all staff members were expected to sit at
the DeMille table—his writers, executive assistants, field secretary (as distinguished from his "stationary" secretaries) and
business agent.

As time wore on, the hungry staff grew fretful waiting for
the click of DeMille's heels or the sharp rap on their door. When
at last it was heard, the staffers were on their feet, one by one,
falling in behind DeMille as he pounded down the corridor,
sparks flying from his heels. Should one of the doors be closed,
it was DeMille's custom to rap it violently, calling out, "Lunch-

eon," startling visitors within and bringing the conferences to an abrupt end. With the restaurant close at hand, there have been occasions when DeMille was seen entering the restaurant as the "tail" of the entourage was just leaving the building—in haste to be at the luncheon table on time. When DeMille stopped, the retinue stopped, and when he started, the line moved, it being considered improper, if not imprudent, to reach the DeMille table in advance of the master.

The late DeWolf Hopper, a frequent observer of the ceremonial procession, once recoiled at the thought of DeMille's "obsequious staff of servitors, required to anticipate his every wish without putting him to the distressing necessity of voicing it." Hopper saw a subtle nuance even in DeMille's frowns— "one may signify more salt, and to the casual observer both contractions of the eyebrow may seem identical, but to the apprehensive eye each is eloquent and ominous."

3.

OUR relations with Mr. DeMille were marked by a sense of uneasy deference, largely because his attitudes were unpredictable and his reactions often explosive. A secretary a few years ago met Mr. DeMille at the bungalow entrance, umbrella in hand, when she observed him hurrying through a sudden shower. "Some rain," he remarked, whereupon the secretary replied, almost guiltily, "I'm so sorry, Mr. DeMille."

He looked upon his aides in much the same way a baron might look upon loyal retainers, and felt they depended on him. "I cannot consider retirement," he said when the subject was broached by Hedda Hopper a few years ago. "I have built up something here that I just can't walk out on. What would happen to the people who work for me?"

He was inclined to preen his feathers when introducing staff members to visitors, and would credit us with having charge of some enormously vital function, leaving the inference that no man under DeMille could be anything less than the head of a powerful, complex department. This curtsy to eminence was one we were happy to acknowledge, and quite gravely, too. As befit persons suddenly given a weighty stewardship, we listened intently, spoke infrequently, and then only with the greatest care in the selection of words and intent, at the same time glancing at the boss to observe what effect, if any, our comment had in that ever-important quarter.

The presence of some high government official or captain of industry often brought out the generalissimo in the boss. He issued soft but crisp orders, first to one, then another, tilting his head slightly to his right, which was the signal for the ever-present field secretary to jot down what he was about to say. We always fell in with his real intent on these occasions—the boss marshaling and commandeering his forces—and were careful not to interject remarks that might spoil the performance, even though he might be issuing an order on something long since accomplished. Observing this flow of orders, warnings and sage comments, with the rest of us quietly making notes or nodding, the visitor sat in openmouthed awe before a demonstration of the sort of efficiency a fellow can have when he puts his mind to it.

In the absence of guests, our luncheons were much less formal, though one might hesitate to describe any of them as relaxed. Their mood was set by Mr. DeMille, the staff having achieved a most admirable resiliency that enabled it to laugh with Mr. DeMille, be angry when he was angry and, with virtually no notice, bestir feelings of grave concern. His intense spirit and preoccupation were such as to make it unnecessary to point out that staff luncheons were never in the nature of a revel. It was up to us, like cautious beavers emerging from earthen cells, to sniff the air for signs of trouble and make adjustments accordingly.

Until a few years ago the workers on the Paramount lot referred to the DeMille luncheon table as "the throne." It was so called because it had for years sat on a foot-high platform with DeMille's heavy, ornate armchair rising regally above it, affording a full view of the large dining room filled with assorted artists, mercenaries and studio workers. DeMille gave up the chair, taking a smaller model, and eliminated the platform in compliance with a gentle suggestion tendered by the front office. It had become apparent that press correspondents were diverted by the sight of DeMille and staff on the higher plateau, with consequent loss of publicity to other studio stars.

The bungalow contained a compact little autocracy with a part in it for those who observed the rules. To work successfully for DeMille, one had to suffer when suffering was required. It was important to realize that here was a unique system of his own careful making, stamped with his temperament and geared to it. If help was brought in from the outside, it was only on his terms, and he drew into his orbit anyone capable of contributing to the objective.

There was one pitfall among many into which partly awake staffers occasionally stumbled. A newcomer had been apprised of the danger in advance, so one day when DeMille posed the question, he was ready.

Samson and Delilah had been in release two or three years, and the newcomer had just seen a rough preview of *Greatest Show on Earth*.

DeMille remarked that in his opinion the Bible picture was greater than the circus picture.

"Impossible," the newcomer said quickly. "I vote for *Greatest Show*."

Any other answer would have brought on complications; DeMille's latest picture was always his best. He had said so with each production—seventy in a row—going back nearly half a century. "This is my greatest," he would tell the press, the Barnum in him assuming confident command. One picture was never included in these calculations, *King of Kings*. He felt the Christ story was a "different thing that cannot be compared with any other picture."

On occasion we would find ourselves compelled to take a position contrary to the boss's judgment, a tack which, though dangerous, might bolster a badly sagging ego. A letter was received one day from a poor, elderly widow with a $5 bill enclosed. She wished to invest the money in Mr. DeMille's "wonderful company that has given me so much pleasure for nearly forty years." She was hopeful that "the investment will give me a little income for my old age."

DeMille, charmed by the sentiments, sent the letter over to Paramount accountants with instructions to figure out how much in dividends would be accumulated by the $5 investment in five years—the time it takes for the average film to repay production costs and yield a profit.

The amount came to something under $4.

"We'll send the woman her five dollars plus the dividend, and we'll send it to her *now*. She won't have to wait five years like I have to," DeMille said excitedly. "Then we'll release a story to the press, so the public will understand what this movie business is all about. How many firms are able to wait five years for a return on their money?"

A properly sentimental letter was prepared, advising the widow of her windfall, and noting with regret that no shares in the DeMille company were publicly held.

"Now let's prepare the news release," the boss said, "and we'll incorporate the letter right into the article. It should go out to all the major newspapers."

An assistant suggested that a press release might have unsavory repercussions. What will the public say when it reads that Cecil DeMille, a man of power, influence and charitable instincts, is sending a little old lady three or four dollars in return for an investment which she hopes will yield a pension in her old age?

The boss appeared unconvinced. "I cannot agree with you. Write the story and let me see it."

He rejected the first draft, then a second. The third was not returned. It was not released to the press or ever mentioned again—a tacit pat on the back!

The staff rarely caught him off base on the essentials, whether in publicity, music, costuming, set decoration or what not. He amazed studio technicians by his grasp of the mechanics. They long since had learned that he was certain to be at their side when the time came for their contribution to a DeMille picture. He sat with the man who dubbed in sound, or "mixed" the various background noises of the final sound track, or supervised the musical score. He marched into the laboratories of Paramount, set up quarters, and remained a frightening force in the lives of the technicians for weeks, long after the trial and turbulence had ended on the sound stages.

This versatility penetrated even the refinements. And sometimes it went far beyond, with DeMille charting a new path for experts in their own field. One such experiment embroiled a gentle yet proud musical director at Paramount.

The musician had been ordered to help compose the music for *Samson and Delilah.*

For the tent scene, in which Samson is set upon by the seductive Delilah and shorn of his hair, DeMille wanted "very, very soft music."

"Give me some idea," pleaded the nervous musician.

"Harps."

"Harps?"

"Yes, harps," purred DeMille, simulating a soft strumming.

The man went away and a few days later he paused at

DeMille's luncheon table, but before he could speak, DeMille uttered one word: "Harps!"

"Impossible," said the man, shaking his head sadly.

The next day it was the same.

"He doesn't like harps," DeMille told us, when the composer had gone. "I like harps. He says he can't do the scene with harps only. I say he can do the scene with harps only, and what is more he *will* do the scene with harps."

For weeks the composer worked with a group of harpists, reported frequently to the boss that everything was going badly, that he feared the results would not please him. The boss retreated not an inch, voiced his confidence that it would be a fine scene and the harp music would be lovely, probably the best in the picture.

Two months later DeMille sat with the musician as the harp music was dubbed into the tent scene. De Mille was right; the music was lovely, soft as an opiate. The musician heaped congratulations upon the boss, who smiled shyly and thanked the man for having put it all over so beautifully.

For *The Sign of the Cross* back in 1932 DeMille hired twenty-five lions at $25 a day each, a lot of lions for a depression year. Word went out for the scenes to be shot as quickly as possible. The animals were to bound up some nearby steps preliminary to entering the arena and "devouring" Christians kneeling in the sands. The cameras were set and the lions herded into a heavily wired enclosure. Instead of rushing up the steps, they calmly lay down.

DeMille turned to one of the trainers. "Listen, this is costing a frightful lot of money. When are those lions going up?"

"Oh," said the trainer, "lions don't know anything about that; they don't go up stairs."

"Well," announced DeMille, "these lions are going up stairs!"

He took a chair in one hand, an ax handle in the other, and entered the cage. Shouting, jumping up and down, he made several false charges at the startled beasts, who looked at DeMille as if to say, "Where are the trainers? Why don't they protect us from this man?" With DeMille's antics rising to a fearsome crescendo, they scampered up the steps, casting frightened glances behind them.

Peter Calvin, one of DeMille's grandsons, having seen the picture a number of times through the years, contends the lion prodding was picked up by the soundtrack. "If you listen closely you can hear Grandfather in the background yelling, 'Goddamn it, get going!'"

The *Sign of the Cross* era was a natural for DeMille. The filmland Savonarola, approaching it with a fervor bordering on orgiastic joy, depicted quite a number of Nero's cruelties and sinful indulgences. Indeed, the great malefactor would have been proud of DeMille's re-enactment of Christian martyrdom in the arena.

To handle the lions DeMille hired a lad named Melvin Koontz, then a raw youth of twenty, but who since has become a prominent supplier of Hollywood wild life. DeMille needed thirty lions for the several arena sequences in order to show just how perilous life was for Christians who clung to the faith. A lion trainer will shy away from putting males and females together, particularly when they are not used to each other. Koontz was not able to find thirty of one sex. An enterprising youth, eager for a DeMille credit on his record, he commingled hostile males and high-spirited females, with interesting results. There were several bloody border scraps among the herd, including an assault by a mean lioness. She reached out of a chute and clawed Koontz severely.

Another critter, a male, was moved to ignore the DeMille script. In one of the scenes, three lions are cajoled into supping on a Christian (a dummy with pockets stuffed with savory meat chunks dipped in fresh blood). Suddenly the bold male takes out after Koontz and with one swipe bats him off a wire enclosure, up which the plucky trainer was energetically shinnying.

The 350-pound assassin happened to be an aged codger with only one good eye. He flopped down on the prostrate Koontz, almost smothering him under his saggy belly. Koontz was saved by his own presence of mind. He thrust his arm to the elbow into the animal's tuskless mouth. This almost up-ended the lion, whereupon he sat back with something closely resembling a foolish grin.

Another male, conceded to be no fool, was called upon to leap upon Koontz, who was dressed for the moment like a Christian and kneeling in suppliant and final prayer. But something else caught the lion's attention—a lightly clad girl, tied to a post and judiciously garlanded with flowers. Amid dead silence, the animal sniffed at the shackled beauty and might have loitered in the vicinity indefinitely had not Koontz leaped to his feet and chased the amorous beast into a cage with a pick handle.

After all this, Koontz began goading the animals into action. Several young males, strong of loin, showed some resentment— perhaps distrust, though students of this animal say it is not distrust at all but a basic contempt for human beings. Be that as it may, not even the robe of Christianity was sufficient to dissuade this knot of snarling cats from committing a most antisocial act. At least a dozen players came within the orbit of their spray. A wrathful DeMille, stalking Koontz on the dampened sands, thundered: "This is an outrage! Those goddamn lions of yours are urinating on my Christian martyrs!"

The difficulty of communicating ideas caused Mr. DeMille indescribable agonies. Department heads would construct a red barn with a slanting roof when what he actually wanted was one with a flat roof. "I have to deal with sixty-four departments and if I tell them I want a red barn they'll come up with sixty-four different red barns." To banish the problem, he took to hiring an artist or two at the start of each picture. They produced numberless sketches. Like the writers, the artists suffered through one rejected sketch after another, and only those with Mr. DeMille's initials in a corner were official. These were handed to department heads, and woe to him who departed in the smallest detail from the approved sketch!

Few were held in greater esteem by the bungalow than the late Gordon Jennings, special effects expert. Jennings, an engineer, was the wizard behind many an awesome DeMille episode—the train wreck in the circus picture, siege of Fort Pitt in *Unconquered,* and his most monumental, the crash of the 17-ton Minoan god, Dagon, in the collapsing-temple scene in the Samson story.

A part of a temple was built in full scale on a back lot at Paramount, with electrical push-button controls that enabled Jennings to set off small charges of dynamite hidden in the structure. The huge plaster idol had to fall in a certain way, in order to bring down first the right wall of the temple, then the left.

DeMille instructed Jennings at great length on the demands of the script.

It was not DeMille's habit to remain away from a scene of this magnitude, but on this occasion he told Jennings to go ahead alone. The engineering and construction had taken almost a year, costing $100,000.

Four or five cameras were stationed on the temple set when Jennings pressed an electrical button. Muffled powder blasts sent the idol forward with a groan, its right shoulder coming to rest on a temple column, and there it stopped.

Nothing else happened.

Two cameras had obtained a small amount of usable footage of the movement of the 40-foot-high idol, but little else.

The first attempt had failed.

Rebuilding of a portion of the set took four weeks and $40,000 more.

For the common good it was fortunate that DeMille had elected to remain away from the shooting. His jaw had a firm set to it as Jennings explained their new approach—adjusting the percussive force of the dynamite and increasing the number of charges.

The staff expected a cyclonic outburst from DeMille, directed at Jennings. But we also expected an ultimatum from the front office, too. It was footing the bill. Jennings confided that he was approaching the second test with the feeling of a magician facing execution if he did not raise his subject from the dead. "I've got armor plate under my shirt. I'm ready for the Great White Father," Jennings grinned, employing a reference to the boss popular with some of the older studio workers.

In the second attempt the temple-collapse went off perfectly, leaving Jennings in nothing short of a transport of joy. There was some comment around the lot as a result of DeMille's strange behavior, for not in the memory of the most grizzled veteran had a blunder of this magnitude escaped his wrath. The talk reached DeMille. "I hear I am getting soft," he said to the staff one day. "Old DeMille has lost his fire. Well, well." He was about seventy then; his manner and the look in his eyes told us there was absolutely nothing to the rumor.

He brought a letter written by a Paramount official to the luncheon table one day, smiled mysteriously as he held it up before the staff, saying he would read it before the meal was over. Little stratagems of the sort appealed hugely to the boss's sense of drama.

In an hour or so, he opened the letter slowly and began to read midway in the text:

> "These are a few of the many dazzling facets among the gems of your accomplishments—reverberating throughout time and destiny, the rectitude of your stand for justice and the true principles of Americanism during a period when much of the time you walked the pioneer's trail of solitude. The beacons you have lifted for all to see are no less significant than those hung in the Old North Church by Paul Revere, the immortal words on the walls of Belshazzar's Court, or the magnesium-glow flame of TRUTH in a mind divinely illuminated."

He looked at us, a smile playing at the corners of his mouth.

"I will not ask for comments but those who wish to express an opinion are free to do so."

Not a word from anyone. In a matter as ticklish as this, a mere suggestion of a smile was at least heretical, if not openly defiant. This was one of those rarest of moments—the boss refusing to take an accolade seriously. "I don't seem to find any sympathy here," he said, pocketing the letter with mock resignation.

Mr. DeMille's memory was poor in later years, at times driving him to almost indecipherable commands. Once he pointed exasperatingly at an actress standing a short distance away. "That girl over there, what's her name?"

It was his daughter Catherine.

His top secretaries, Misses Cole, Mosk and Rosson, wrestled with such references as "What was that man's name who came here with his little girl four years ago?" or "Remind me to put that thing back in the other scene before we get too far along." When they became even more vague, a daily log was kept, starting in 1944, of every telephone call from an outside source, along with a notation as to whether it was put through to DeMille, and, if possible, the gist of the conversation. It provided ready replies for queries like "When did I speak to Louie

Mayer last?" or "Have I ever talked on the phone to Herbert Hoover?"

Virtually every move was documented. One could, for example, ascertain the name and cast of a movie screened at Mr. DeMille's home on any night for years back. This in itself was a hefty record. He saw an average of 150 films a year over a period of seventeen years, this being almost his only relaxation in the last decade or two before his death.

Though a small core of loyalists remained with DeMille through the years, many departed within a relatively short time, while others faded after sincere effort to survive the rigors of life in the bungalow. At the peak of his buccaneering, in the 1920–30's, the mortality among his workers was forbiddingly high. DeMille would not tolerate skill without stamina, and those that possessed only skill soon disappeared. There were moments when DeMille deeply regretted this lack of perseverance and durability among the mortals that came to his bungalow. He hoped they would see the kind of life they had to live from then on, accept it for what it was, perhaps even embrace it, bravely and resolutely like a forest Druid, and become one of its determined champions. Alas, too few felt the call. He once exclaimed, having just banished a couple of workmen from the sets, "They know when they come here how DeMille works. Why does God send me the curse of the child mind?"

These turbulences through forty years made him chary of staff loyalty. He had crushed too many who did not have the stamina to rise up smiling. He watched for little changes of attitude among his aides, in time developing an extraordinary sensitivity; he could detect a defection in its incipient stage. He secretly worried when an assistant turned churlish or moody, just as he was delighted by little gestures of affection, whether by way of a compliment or merely an anniversary card.

At Christmas time for several years the wife of a staff member had baked DeMille a fruitcake, and each year he grandly eulogized the little offering.

One Saturday the husband did not appear at the studio, probably unaware the company was shooting that day. The boss himself, in a stampeding mood, called the home and finding the husband was away, delivered a ringing assault on the missing man's intelligence and wound up with a proposal that the couple might wish to pack up their bags and return to their home town. The little woman was in tears when the husband reached home. He called the studio, had DeMille summoned to the phone and proceeded to lambast his employer in a manner that brought a sudden halt to the wife's tears, so stunned was she by the incongruity of it all, like watching a pygmy beating on the chest of a giant.

The conversation lasted fully a half-hour; at the end the two were engaged in an earnest appraisal of a production problem, the tension gone completely. Though few have had the courage to practice it, the assistant became a rabid proponent of the "fight back" school of philosophy and tried without much success to persuade other staff members to stand up to DeMille, with clenched fists if necessary.

The husband may have forgiven the boss for browbeating his wife in a fit of anger, but the wife did not forget. The following Christmas she baked no fruitcake. Its absence under the DeMille tree, a glittering sentinel keeping watch over stacks of expensive gifts, was noted by DeMille. It worried him for weeks but he said nothing until one day at luncheon. Served a piece of fruitcake, he looked at the delicacy and, in a wistful voice, reminisced, "I am very fond of the fruitcake Mary always baked for me at Christmas time," then sadly, "but this year I did not hear from her."

4.

WRITERS and staff members flunked out of the bungalow in large numbers through the years—a mortality that was heaviest among the men. In time, women became the core of his organization. "I had a mother that won my admiration," he once explained, "and I have liked women ever since. We seem to strike a note of understanding. And I like fighting with them and enjoy their reactions."

For years his all-female team—secretaries to film editor—was the envy of the industry. This extraordinary dedication reached a high note during the big quake of 1933, a DeMille secretary leaning out of a second story window when the tremors were at their worst and calling down to her boss, "I have completed the notes on the interview, Mr. DeMille. I will come down now."

There was only one major woman director in the film industry and no women producers in the late 1920's. Editing, cutting and decorating of sets were the tasks of men. Not so in the DeMille organization.

This was the period of "the nine women." Only one of them was married—Mrs. DeMille. The others were wed to their work, spending their days at the studio and their week nights at the mansion on DeMille Drive in Laughlin Park. The staff luncheons were an institution even then. The women scheduled no social engagements during production, never lunched off the lot. At night they accompanied the boss to his home for dinner, spent the evening looking at "rushes" or movies important to casting.

Jeanie Macpherson, Bessie McGaffey, Emily Barrye, Ella King Adams, Anne Bauchens, Gladys Rosson, Dorothy Griwatz, Florence Cole and Constance Adams (Mrs.) DeMille—names

31

that spanned his career and proved his faculty for inspiring in women a desire to devote their lives to his work.

Bessie McGaffey, his researcher, remembered that he once gave her a trained nurse for a Christmas present "to help me get well after an operation." She found him "soft-hearted and hot-headed, quick as lightning and absent-minded. He has an annoying habit of swooping down on me at the most unlikely moment in search of a script. No, he doesn't remember who wrote it or who was in the cast. It seemed to him there were lions in it. Perhaps there were tigers. Come to think of it the scene was set in France, or maybe it was a farm in Alaska. Anyway, there was a baby in it, and by this time I ought to know the script that he has in mind and would I please locate it at once?"

His script girl, Emily Barrye, confessed she had lost some of the best husbands in the world in order to keep her job—"There was that banker from Dubuque, that broker from New York." They were careful to note that he liked women to be feminine even during working hours, but that he "hated red fingernails, bleached hair, too much lipstick or rouge."

On the day of his death, three of the old guard were at their desks. Anne Bauchens, who began with him forty-three years before, was turning her attention as film editor to his next project, a saga of Boy Scouts. Florence Cole, his No. 1 studio secretary, was noting down the next day's appointments. She had joined the select DeMille circle thirty-one years ago. The third was Berenice Mosk, his "girl Friday," grave, soft-spoken, intellectual.

Berenice Mosk held the most difficult job in the DeMille secretariat, at once secretary, memory jogger, technical expert and clearinghouse for a vast variety of items important to the production. She first joined DeMille some twenty years ago, left for a short while, then returned to remain with him until his death.

In its nontechnical moments, "Bernie's" job consisted in never being beyond the beckoning power of a whisper when DeMille walked abroad from his office. She was always at his side whether he was lunching, editing a film, screen testing a player or haranguing authors.

She had the two requisites for her part in the bungalow's daily drama, an agile mind and rocklike stability. Sooner or later souls in torment went to her, to her shockingly small office midway down the long corridor, where they found her smiling like a benevolent icon behind stacks of books and papers. We sat with her, chatting until small hours of the morning. The weak sought her counsel, and the afflicted her comfort.

Probably no story conference with the boss had been held in the past ten years without Berenice Mosk. She took copious notes, said nothing. Her inscrutability was amazing, even during those moments of crisis when the mountainous waves of the boss's anger threatened to wash away the bungalow. She revealed neither censure nor approval, no inkling of how she felt on the merits of a situation that had provoked an outburst from the boss. Soon, however, the harassed functionary would hurry to Miss Mosk's office, muttering, "Wonder what Bernie thinks about it?"

To all who examined the DeMille office, Miss Mosk became a fascinating detail. She stood for hours on the set, a huge black binder-type book in her arms, noting virtually every DeMille word and action. Her book contained endless memos —*Find out the name of the character woman we saw in a restaurant today. Has a good face. Good type for circus audience. . . . No yellow costumes should be used for circus in front of yellow backing. Send wires to circus about costume plates.*

There were other types: *Have the swimming pool filled. . . . Get little Jody a toy. . . . There are 28 million telephones in the United States—21 million of them in homes.*

Miss Mosk's famous black book contained a full script of the film being made, with hundreds of marginal notes. Some were references made months ago by DeMille bearing on a future scene, descriptions of "pieces of business," camera angles and lines of dialogue. It was her duty to bring the correct memo to DeMille's attention on the right set at the right moment. On the first day's shooting on *Samson and Delilah* the book weighed ten pounds.

During production Bernie was put at her physical best to keep up with her boss's activities—viewing the "dailies" (the film shot on the set the previous day), editing, checking the first rough cuts, recording lines, dubbing and scoring. She figures she has seen each picture about 150 times. A sturdy soul, she was in the audience when *Samson and Delilah* had its first public showing. "That was for entertainment," she recalls.

The great personal worth of Berenice Mosk to DeMille the Director was indicated in his frequent reference to her as "my right arm and memory." She kept a daily log during the periods of filming on the sets. The chronicle sparkles with Bernie's own observations, as well as the wit of others, all of it showing her enthusiasm and durability in the most difficult stage of a DeMille production.

The cast and crew were at Sarasota in the winter of 1951, filming the circus picture, when Bernie made the following notes, taken at random from her log.

This morning Art Concello pulled a DeMille by going up and trying the 50-foot trapeze fall first. He landed in the pit—full of water, of course—and was really dunked. Some of the crew standing around watching, said, "He won't pay any attention to that—he's a trouper."

One of the writers in a lather today because we'd shot a scene he hadn't written yet.

Saw our first day's dailies. This is really exciting stuff to see on the screen. Color is gorgeous—soft and true. Betty Hutton looked completely at home up there on the trapeze.

Gloria Grahame got a nice hand when she rode through on the elephant's trunk.

While Hutton was up on the trapeze doing a difficult stunt— the camera was at a high angle shooting down—Charlton Heston was to jump out of a jeep and run into position below her. Here was Hutton knocking herself out, after a third take! when Heston jumps out of the jeep, trips on a ring-curb and sprawls on the sawdust. Picking himself up in great embarrassment, he takes off his hat and apologizes.

After two weeks under the Big Top at Sarasota, Bernie noted: *Everybody is so tired, edgy and groggy and everything this day kept going wrong. We need a vacation—from each other.*

Today Hutton did her favorite stunt—flying, for which she got another DeMille "medal."

This was Cornel Wilde's day. He went up and hung by his knees, holding Betty Hutton for several takes. And with no visible effort on his part. A great relief to the whole company when it was over. Betty at one point said she thought she was getting too heavy to hold, whereupon Cornel, the perfect gentleman, replied, "Why you're light as 120 pounds of feathers."

The notes recorded moments when tempers were short, with more than the usual amount of feuding between principal players.

The gals are at it again—Hutton and Lamour. Each claims she's never been so insulted!

A woman came up in back of the Boss and touched his shoulder. She said she just wanted to be able to say that she had touched him, and now, she said, she is ready to die. Imagine!

The great Hutton-Wilde feud flared up today. I heard both sides. It started with Betty having eaten garlic last night—great preparation for a love scene! Wilde quipped, "That's all right. I swallowed an Airwick."

Attention publicity: DeMille wants to talk to you about photo taken of him, fat man and midget. Boss thinks it entertaining.

In all the years I've been with Mr. DeMille today was the first time I've ever been scared. During the big boom shot, following Brad driving the caterpillar, Mr. DeMille got caught between the boom going forward, and the jeep coming toward the camera. Everybody got panicky, except the Boss of course, who ordered the take to proceed. Mr. DeMille insisted he wasn't hurt, and later John Crawford who was driving the jeep came over and apologized. Mr. DeMille was very gracious. John said, "I didn't know whether to kill the director or spoil the scene." And Mr. DeMille replied, "Always kill the director."

Gladys Rosson was his confidante and advisor. "She rules my home and my office," he would explain to vistors. He once related how Mrs. DeMille, upon learning that he and Gladys were going to New York by plane for the first time, exclaimed, "Oh dear me, suppose something should happen to Gladys!"

Gladys' management of affairs penetrated almost every level of activity at the company offices in Laughlin Park as well as in the studio bungalow. Who, besides herself, would accompany Mr. DeMille on major trips were mainly her decisions, naturally awaited by the staff with much anticipation. On trips she doubled as valet, usually selecting the shirt, tie and ring to match that he would wear the following day, setting the articles out neatly the night before. She strove as much as possible to preclude the necessity of his lifting a finger.

The high mark in this solicitude was reached in the course of preparations for a trip to London, where we had intended to premiere *Unconquered* until the British Government instituted its dollar-freeze program. In orderly 1-2-3 fashion, Gladys listed the chores which each staff assistant would perform during the entire journey, including the responsibility of arranging for deck chairs aboard ship.

One assignment, for the public relations director, read as follows:

On arrival at any city, get off the train before it stops, obtain names of persons waiting to greet Mr. DeMille.

The recipient of this agile requirement never quite lived it down, the staff needling him relentlessly. In time he referred to himself as "the man in the DeMille organization who gets off the train before it stops."

For years it was Gladys Rosson's job to invest the money made by DeMille Productions. She decided, as she once put it, "whether there's any money to be made in oranges, oil wells or fancy birds," adding, "C. B. dislikes indecision. He expects me to use my judgment and is willing to abide by it."

The day before the crash of '29 DeMille instructed her to sell some stocks that were off a quarter of a point. "I thought he had merely asked me to get a price on them," she recalled. "The smash came. The stock dropped 20, 50, then 100 points and we lost a small fortune. I was terrified but C. B. never broached the matter. He knew what I was suffering."

He once referred to her as "my extra brain," and through the 18-hour workdays found her to be "a merry, chatty feminine human being one moment and an efficient machine at the sign of work."

Gladys Rosson's death a few years ago ended more than thirty years of scrupulous, unwavering loyalty in a lifetime that knew virtually no outside interests save her employer's.

Probably no staff member was as little known on the outside as Anne Bauchens, dean of the DeMille servitors. Gentlest of women, with a twinkly little smile set off by bright blue eyes and pure white hair running riotously to ringlets, she spent her professional life in that most horrid of academic chambers—the cutting and editing room—and all of those years in DeMille's employ.

Of the facets of the DeMille hierarchy, Anne was the most paradoxical. Who would guess, seeing this kindly, unobtrusive woman, that it was she who edited DeMille's throbbing, two-fisted movies? She is oldest in point of service among the colony's film editors, and like all good practitioners of the craft Anne suffered much mental torture in the task of tightening, mending, pruning and generally improving the narrative values of thousands of feet of film which directors like DeMille tossed into the cutting room after intense and oftentimes erratic days on the sets.

Anne joined DeMille during the early period of organizational growth, a mere sprite of a girl. She helped him film by day and edit by night. She recalls that the first *Ten Commandments* took ten years off her life. "The boss used sixteen cameras and shot enough film for ten pictures, more than 100,000 feet."

Anne reduced it to 12,000, a task that can "lead you to one of three things—fame, drink or the nearest psychiatrist."

Hollywood has acknowledged her work as one of the major undisclosed reasons behind DeMille's success. At the 1940 Academy Awards Darryl Zanuck handed her an "Oscar" for her editing of *Northwest Mounted Police*, the first woman to receive the honor.

Applying the shears to scenes that seem to limp and drag took courage, particularly in an unpredictable and strident atmosphere. Anne learned that a shell of objectivity is a good safeguard when dealing with human nature in Hollywood. With stoic-like patience she was able to weather the storms that swept out of the bunaglow, reserving the tears after particularly hard days for the intimacy of her room. She had not one such day but many during the troubled period of *The Greatest Show on Earth* but, as she explained it, "when C. B. kissed you on the cheek the next morning and smiled in that shy way of his, you were just apt to forget the trials of the day before."

5.

IT was DeMille's custom to spend weekends at Paradise, his famous hideaway near a crest of the Sierra Madres, about twenty miles from Hollywood. The staff was certain that he sat on a peak and looked down into the valley like Napoleon watching the tide at St. Helena, brooding over the numerous deficiencies of his staff. Here he gained new strength for the fresh assaults on Monday morning, making innumerable little notes to himself as he spent the weekend reading the material prepared for his approval.

The road to Paradise ranch led over a series of concrete aprons rising from the beds of mountain streams. The aprons allowed for traction in the winter when water roared down the mountain, at times reaching radiator high to Mr. DeMille's powerful cars.

Before buying the land about 1920 he sent a man to investigate.

The report was aggressively negative:

"It's all rocks and hills and you can't grow a thing on it. There aren't any people within miles, and it would cost a fortune to install a phone. If the lower road is blocked, there would be no way on earth to get a message to you except by dropping it from an airplane. It's terrible. Loneliest spot I ever saw in my life."

DeMille's eyes danced as the man talked. "Great!" he said. "I'll buy it."

The main ranch house, consisting of sleeping quarters for

guests and a 50-foot square living room, sported a sort of rustic and Indian motif, derived from a scattering of log and bamboo furnishings, as well as a full-size ornate totem pole. Walls held a moose head from Canada and the bust of a grizzly shot by DeMille near the dwellings. In a corner stood a pipe organ, its sonorous pipes carved with Aztec inscriptions. A pool table, standing unobtrusively at one end of the immense room, was for the pleasure of weekend house guests carefully chosen and royally entertained. Mr. DeMille himself slept in a private stone cottage just below, and out of sight of, the ranch house. His first act upon arising was a plunge into the spring waters of a small pool, totally obscured by trees to protect his nude caperings from chance visits. Few guests could summon the courage to try the icy water; a prudent toe-test usually sent them into full retreat.

In the area of the ranch DeMille owned some 700 acres and leased substantial parcels of adjoining preserves belonging to the Government.

On this rocky hill terrain he consistently refuted the best local advice on practical agriculture by raising self-supporting crops of apples, grapes and alfalfa. Then in 1929 he decided to try his hand at a pheasantry. Not something ordinary but a model institution of its kind. There was an expanding market for pheasants in enough states to intrigue a person not given to sidelines that did not pay. Quickly the pheasant population rose to 4,000. Neat rows of 12-by-25-foot pens were set up, their approach beautifully landscaped. These contained the rarer specimens—Manchurian, silver, golden, black neck and Lady Amherst pheasants. There were also African crowned cranes, Abyssinian gruven fowl, blue Australian goura pigeons, blue and white pea fowl, and forty white doves. The doves appeared in scenes of the crucifixion in *The King of Kings* (later pensioned for life for their efforts).

In later years he turned to turkeys, with somewhat less commercial success. A Christmas turkey from DeMille graced the board of many a player and technician at Paramount. One year he sent a bird to Bosley Crowther, the good-natured, erudite film editor of *The New York Times*—the first such gesture to a film critic. When the two met in New York a short time later at the premiere of a DeMille picture, Bosley thanked the producer for the gift, added with a smile, "You're the only movie producer in America with the courage to send a turkey into New York in advance of his picture!"

A DeMille turkey was a gift to each staff member at Christmas time, carefully selected by the office to be of uniform weight and size so that it could not be inferred that Mr. DeMille was favoring this or that worker. Larger birds went to studio executives, a giant specimen being reserved for Y. Frank Freeman, Paramount studio head. It was Mr. DeMille's fond desire on those occasions to choose a bird from his flock that was too big for the Freeman oven, an affable sort of contest that went on year after year.

On Thanksgiving, it was suggested to the staff members that they might wish to *purchase* a DeMille bird, and most of us did, the price being the same as that at the local markets, with the added advantage that it placed us in the somewhat exclusive position of inviting friends and relatives to partake of "one of Mr. DeMille's turkeys." They were excellent birds with, we always thought, more white meat and whiter white meat than the coarse, unpedigreed type sold on the outside.

Persons high in rank or wealth were the natural objects of Mr. DeMille's benefactions at Paradise. Entry was restrictive. "Anyone less than an ambassador would have to have a gun," an older staff man once remarked. The social thermometer was extremely sensitive in other respects: *all* guests were not given the full treatment. But those so favored were permitted a moderate dip into DeMille's stock of 50-year-old bourbon. These ancient spirits were once part of the store aboard the DeMille yacht *Seaward*, a 106-foot schooner-type vessel.

DeMille used to steal away and cruise up and down the coast in the *Seaward* with the help of a crew of eight. Uninterrupted by studio workers or others, he leisurely read stacks of story manuscripts. On occasion he would board his writers and set sail. For weeks the *Seaward* cruised about, in touch with the studio by radio while the party devoted long hours to knotty script problems.

One day unexpectedly, while the boss was at the studio, federal officers flashed aboard the *Seaward,* arrested its captain for illegal possession of liquor—eighty gallons of 50-year-old bourbon! In a choleric rage DeMille denounced the raid with the air of a man struck in the face by the Bill of Rights. He arranged for defense of the captain, assured him he was the victim of foul play, then gave voice to a legal theory on which the defense would advance its case, namely, the *Seaward* was the captain's home and therefore was entitled to have liquor on it.

The captain forfeited a $2,000 bond for failure to appear at a subsequent hearing. The fate of the bourbon became veiled in some mystery. It was in bottles aboard the *Seaward*. The 50-year-old bourbon at Paradise turned up in small wooden casks—the only hint of the connection between the two was DeMille's remark to an assistant a few years ago that "this bourbon was once in danger of being taken over by government lackeys who did not know the difference between public and private property."

DeMille counted on gentlemanly restraint on those occasions when a cask of the ancient spirits was produced for his guests, the restraint to be in inverse proportion to the guest's personal prestige.

The staff for years knew of the boss's pride in the age and bouquet of his bourbon; actual sampling was beyond their social ken. It did come about by a concourse of circumstances that a staff man spent a night at Paradise as a guest, and did sample the bourbon.

It started with the review of DeMille's *Unconquered* that

appeared in the Denver Rocky Mountain *News*. It was not a good review. It ridiculed the story, chided the producer and took exception to certain performances. Such criticism was old hat at the bungalow. We held to DeMille's belief that the greater the critical disgust the greater the box-office return. What did catch our attention, however, was an editorial in the *News* a few days later. The writer, Lee Casey, referred to his newspaper's unfriendly review of *Unconquered*, then praised the picture in charming classical prose. We felt that his logic was excellent.

DeMille was elated. "If that man ever comes to Hollywood I'll invite him up to Paradise," delivering the ultimate tribute to Mr. Casey's social acceptability.

Some time after, Mr. Casey came to Hollywood and was ushered into the boss's presence. There were warm greetings all around. Here was a pro-DeMille editor, a species not too numerous. Casey let drop a bit of information that caused Mr. DeMille to raise a promising, almost ecstatic, eyebrow. Casey said he liked good bourbon. In this respect, the boss had a fine surprise in store for the sage journalist.

Indeed, the late Mr. Casey *was* a lover of fine bourbon, as the boys around Denver will attest; but how ardent a lover was yet to manifest itself to DeMille.

A dinner of lavish proportions over, DeMille disappeared like an aging gnome into the earth below the cabin. He emerged a few minutes later, blowing honorable dust off one end of a small steel-banded oak cask, which he clasped tightly to his breast.

He drew an amount into a water glass, savored the bouquet for a moment, then thrust it grandly toward Casey.

By now Casey's gastric juices were like a rampaging mountain stream. To DeMille, who rarely imbibed deeply, the speed with which the journalist unloaded nearly half a glassful of the antique stimulant was startling in the extreme. Nor had Casey paused to savor the bouquet. On his face was a look comparable to the beneficiary of a vision at Lourdes. The journalist knew he had in a sense tasted something unusual. Presently, he returned to the cask and poured himself a glass. The move caught us by surprise, and of course there was nought that could be said—understandably Casey's long and gentlemanly acquaintance with bourbon proved a pawn to Mr. DeMille's hospitality. He made other visits to the cask, liberally priming his innards, being careful not to corrupt the elixir with a mix. Eventually we came down out of the hills to return Casey, with some assistance, to his hotel room.

We received a wire from him a few days after the visit, stating in part: ABSTAINED FROM FOOD FOR TWO DAYS SO AS NOT TO DISTURB ETHEREAL 50-YEAR-OLD GLOW OF DEMILLE BOURBON. I BOW TO WORLD'S GREATEST PRODUCER OF MOVIES AND BOURBON.

DeMille received the compliment with a smile of paternal warmth, noting that the demolition of such an extraordinary amount of rare liquor was warranted by Lee's deed of newspapering courage. He continued to admire Casey's strength as a journalist even though he may have deplored his capacity as a tippler.

Weekend parties at Paradise in the years after World War I were not out of keeping with the spirit of the times. The partying vigor of the 20's found a lot of eager participants in Hollywood. Some had the time, place and money to toss elaborate displays of refined orgy. The social expressions at Paradise were produced by a man who prided himself on an ability to film a first-class revel. A number of DeMille pictures clearly demonstrated his skill with this sort of gaiety. In fact, these screen parties on occasion got out of hand. A hero of one of his more memorable high-society movies was observed on his knees, snapping like a giddy terrapin at clusters of grapes festooned around the shapely hips of a party girl. It was made in DeMille's pre-Biblical days, and other producers were making sparkling efforts along the same line. It was then that public sentiment within the industry began to take over. Enough was enough. The producers wrote a morality code, then vowed to honor it. DeMille naturally chafed under some of the provisions, conflicting as they did with a policy which he has reflected so often in directions to his writers: "Hit sex hard!"

The parties at Paradise were regarded by the best elements of the film colony as high-spots of the social season. At the plates of feminine guests DeMille placed a perfume called "Paradise," especially prepared for him from blossoms growing on the ranch. Fine brandies and wines graced the table in their proper turn. The salt sticks even boasted a pedigree: they were prepared by DeMille's cook who once made them for Emperor Franz Joseph. At no point were we tempted to conclude it was just another decorative detail dreamed up by a master showman. Weeks later someone complimented the cook on his connection with the Emperor's salt sticks. Mystified, he said he was born in Austria, to be sure, but he had never made salt sticks for Franz Joseph or any other ruler.

Women guests brought their evening clothes for the weekend affairs but the men were requested to bring only their trousers. Three Russian shirts—red, white and black—hung in the closet of each bedroom, and a male completed his costume by choosing one of the shirts. As an adornment he had the choice of a gold or silver chain.

"Only one guest, a well-known playwright and screenwriter, is reported as ever having refused to subscribe to this masquerade, and he was shortly thereafter dismissed from DeMille's employ," Ring Lardner once related.

On Saturday nights an additional ceremony took place at cocktail time. As Lardner described it, "A valet carries in a three-tiered basket lined with crumpled black velvet and full of costume jewelry, French perfume, gold compacts, and other similar gifts. The women are permitted to examine these items before dinner, but forbidden to touch any of them. Just before eating, they gather at the billiard table and roll the balls according to a prescribed set of rules to determine the order in which they may choose their gifts. Later, when dinner is over, each takes her turn at examining the display, once more, this time more closely, and experimenting with possible selections before a mirror, while the others stand by watching and hoping that their own choices won't be taken before their turn comes. DeMille, who makes a hobby of collecting jewels, has been known to toss in a pigeon-blood ruby or other unset gem worth far more than the whole basket, and revel in the fact that no one chose it over the gaudy baubles. It seems to put women in their proper perspective for him."

6.

THE barbs hurled at DeMille's pictures by what he called "big city critics" were many and varied. They sent him into reflections of such bitterness that a deep caution was bred in all of us. A newcomer to the staff learned immediately of the existence of this cold war. He was told it was risky to schedule an interview without knowing in advance something about the visitor's background, politics and, if possible, his attitude toward DeMille. The warning signals always went up when a correspondent asked to talk to DeMille about his Biblical pictures. We knew he had been stung most by editors from metropolitan papers who took a dim view of his claims to a unique ministry —that sent the Biblical word to far corners of the earth.

Too often we faced the ordeal of handing DeMille a clipping of a story twitting him for, in one critic's phrase, "coining sexy dollars off Holy Writ." DeMille was able to handle the enemy at press interviews, and quite graciously, but it was up to us to identify members of the so-called anti-DeMille clique. A worrisome duty, but one that had to be faced if we were to avoid the sly implication that perhaps there was something amiss in our relationship with the press. It was up to the staff, he said philosophically at luncheon one day, "to protect me from the madmen who are at large. Some of them write for newspapers."

For proper ears, DeMille went to great pains to prepare lively interviews. He had a way of weaving into the conversation subtle blows against some of the popular heresies urged against him—polite efforts calculated to convert the cynical visitor. DeMille had pat answers to certain recurring questions: "Have you ever changed the Bible for your stories? . . . Was your father a minister? . . . Who influenced you most as a young man?" And if the interviewer was bold: "How do you feel about the fact you have never won an Academy Award?"

DeMille was ever on the alert for latent, mischievous motives. Interviews often drew forth his hidden resentments. He delivered hard, direct blows to shatter myths that had clung to him through the years and which he felt were now out of keeping. He was nothing if not a consummate showman and, understandably, made some of his dreams come through at these interviews. It was part of his showmanship to take fate by the hand in order to reveal to a visitor the unerring and predestined route that led to his present high estate. He lined up the facts of his life, like peaks in a well-plotted story, and sent them to a surging climax. He never stopped trying to put to rest distortions about himself, and freely assigned colorful roles to otherwise meaningless events in his life.

As a showman, it was easy for DeMille to recoil from the humdrum. Any man whose life and work influenced millions ought not to be saddled with a lackluster genesis. Better for him to be born full blown on his twenty-first year. DeMille's pride of ancestry was much too strong for anything of the sort. It happened that Cecil's brother, William, did not concur with Cecil's story of their early youth. Perhaps William's memory was faulty; in their young days many exciting episodes moved the family along a path aimed toward Cecil's ultimate rise in the film world. Numberless little gems of wisdom influenced and shaped the budding career. Where, indeed, was William when their father read a chapter of the Bible and American history each evening at bedtime? Cecil vividly remembered his brother and himself at their father's knees. But not William, the soft-spoken, pipe-smoking scholar who early fled from film making to a university professorship. How was it William did not recall those nights at the paternal knee beneath the flicker of candles? Nor did he know anything about the family crisis that was destined to shape the future Cecil, when, after much ado, their mother persuaded their father to abandon his ideas about becoming a mininster and to devote himself to playwriting on Broadway. And Bill should have observed these things because he was older.

Cecil fluently recalled all of them. True or not, what harm could be done in giving these events their proper and fateful place in history? Here again, it was DeMille the showman, responding to an intuitive faculty for drama, the kind of drama the public wants, and, more important, having those things accepted that pleased and edified him most.

In the fall of 1951 DeMille was visited by a European writer whose mission was to obtain material for a book on important Americans. Much planning took place, and we sat for hours in DeMille's office as he rehearsed replies to questions we were certain the visiting writer would ask. It was a perfect occasion to banish a lot of doubt in the minds of staff members. We were never quite certain whether the facts in the last interview were final or official, changing as they did from time to time. So it was somewhat risky to send out press releases based on previous interviews. Some releases returned to haunt us—usually by a demand from "up front" as to where we had gotten such facts.

The interview with the European consumed the better part of two days. A secretary took the talks in shorthand, an arrangement we viewed with great secret joy. Now the record was there, in DeMille's own words, thus diminishing the possibility of accusations that staff members were "going about changing the facts of my life."

DeMille was in princely form that day.

You have mentioned that your father's ambition was to become a minister. Is this correct?

Yes, Father studied for the Episcopal ministry, and he was a professor of English at Columbia Grammar school, I think it was, before the University was founded. It was in the 1870's and he met my mother, who was a teacher of English at Lockwood's Academy in Brooklyn and she persuaded him, at least she told him, that he would have a much larger congregation to which he could deliver his message if he turned to the theater instead of the church—that in the church he might be able to speak to thousands—through the theater he might be able to speak to hundreds of thousands—and then when I came along the mantle fell upon my shoulders in a new form which was the motion picture, and I was able to reach hundreds of millions.

Is it fair to assume, Mr. DeMille, that you inherited your great interest for Biblical themes as the result of your father's great devotion to his faith?

Yes, that's true. My father used to read every night to us boys a chapter of the Old Testament, and a chapter of the New Testament, and a chapter of history. American history first, then we went into French history, English history, and he would read classics to us—you see there was no diversion then in the evening. No motion pictures, no television, and it was all centered around the father. I remember we did not have electric light then in our home and I can see now the yellow lamplight falling down over this central figure who was reading. . . .

Did she, your mother, coin phrases?

No. She was a good writer, and incidentally, a little incident in connection with that: My father and Belasco when they wrote their first play which was called *The Wife*—it was the first of the American social plays that I recall. They couldn't afford a stenographer. The first manuscript of those plays that went to Dan Frohman was written in my mother's handwriting.

Was he a disciplinarian—your father?

Yes—but never in a violent way—he would explain what you had done that was wrong, and if you couldn't offer a rather good explanation for it, you felt rather foolish.

Are you emotional, Mr. DeMille?

Perhaps more than he. I am yes, I have to be for the work I do to get dramatic effects. I can be moved by a great scene, and I can be made to cry by a great piece of acting, by a high point in heroism or patriotism. I can stand before the Lincoln Memorial at night alone and be deeply moved.

Mr. DeMille, did your father ever suggest to you what you should choose for your career?

No—never—I was pretty young when he died and on his deathbed, he said to my mother, "Make the boys butchers or grocers or candlestickmakers or anything, but keep them away from the stage." So naturally we both made a beeline for the stage.

I want to ask you, Mr. DeMille, if—

Let me continue a second in the answering of that question you asked me—if you mean did he ever *influence* me—I would say yes, strongly. Because he was a very great playwright—a very successful one and I grew up in that atmosphere—I absorbed it. The family used to assemble every night after he and Belasco had finished their day's work and Father would read to us what they had written that day and we were asked to comment on it.

I want to ask you, Mr. DeMille, if you have ever done something against your father's explicit desire, but now that you mention that his wish was, on his dying bed, that you should rather become a butcher it seems to me that you went explicitly against his wish.

No, I don't think he meant it even. The stage has, of course, great disappointments as well as great triumphs, and I think there was a touch of humor perhaps in his suggestion.

On his dying bed?

Yes—in his suggestion. Incidentally, on his deathbed, I remember very well that he would read—not from the book, but from his memory, chapter after chapter of the New Testament —of the Bible. He repeated the church services.

Would you describe the scene of his dying bed? Did you see him?

Yes—it was something that was very painful to me because he sent for me and he saw the family one at a time—it was in our house at Pompton, New Jersey—and he asked me a question. And I couldn't answer because I was choked and I couldn't answer—I did not know that he was dying—I didn't know how sick he was even. I was a little boy, but something prevented my talking because my throat was tight as you are when you're about to cry—so I couldn't answer and he waited for a few minutes and he said, "Well, run along and play." I've never forgotten that and I never could get it from my mind—that he couldn't understand that I wanted to—I'm sure that he did—but he couldn't understand at the time what I wanted to tell him—I wanted to express my love and affection for him but I couldn't. I couldn't speak. I was nine or ten at the time.

Did your father have some maxim—some precept—some philosophy which he handed down to you—to the family?

Honesty, respect, morality, propriety—I don't think there was any single thing. He kept on his desk a saying of Dion Boucicault's—PLAYS ARE NOT WRITTEN, BUT RE-WRITTEN. It served me well, because I don't think anybody rewrites more than I do.

What was his favorite pastime? Let's see—hunting, fishing or playing cards—racing—

No, he didn't go in for racing or anything of that sort. He went through the Civil War as a boy and he used to hunt a little bit—I don't think he ever killed very much—and he used to be fond of walking. I remember in Echo Lake, New Jersey, there was a big rock up on a hill called Fourth Act Rock because he and Belasco used to walk up to that and that's where they got the idea for the fourth act of the play *The Charity Ball,* which was a well-known American play, and that rock was always known to us as Fourth Act Rock. But he did not go in for sports of any sort.

Was he a pessimist or an optimist, your father, Mr. DeMille?

He was an optimist, I would say, hundred per cent optimist. But not a stupid optimist. Reason dominated him first.

Could you describe his attitude toward money?

His attitude toward money? Well, he never had very much because at the end of the Civil War, the family was entirely ruined and I remember that I wore Bill's clothes after he had outgrown them and Bill wore my Uncle John's clothes after *he* had outgrown them. Then when Father became a successful playwright, we began to have money, but he just treated it as a means to an end. I don't think money interested him at all.

Mr. DeMille—I noticed in these four days I had the pleasure of being with you that you are dressed meticulously and every day differently.

Well, with me, I think it's probably vanity. When you get to be seventy years old, the only way you can make an impression probably is by being well dressed.

You mentioned the other day, Mr. DeMille, that he was a Democrat—your father. Was he ever active in politics?

No, he was never active in politics, except as he influenced people; coming from the South right after the Civil War—anybody that came from the South alive after the Civil War was a Democrat.

Were your parents well-to-do people, Mr. DeMille?

No, they were not. Father made a very small fortune with his plays. When he died, Mother was left with three children, a home, and $20,000 life insurance, and whatever value the plays might have.

You never enjoyed an allowance from your family, Mr. DeMille?

As a boy I got ten cents a week.

That would make a dollar today probably. Do you give an allowance to your own children?

Yes, yes I have. I don't suppose my mother had a day until I brought her out here—a day from the time my father died until I brought her out here—that she wasn't worried about money.

Are you religious, in the sense that you observe rituals?

Well, I don't think I am religious in the true ritual. If faith in God and belief in Divinity is religion, I don't think that the practice of forms is necessary in religion, and I think it is very apt, in many instances, to deprive thought of its religious value, if it is presented in a definite form that you repeat over and over again every day of your life. I think the importance of contact with a Supreme Being or a Supreme Mind is well. I think Jesus of Nazareth covers it more thoroughly probably than any being—any Divine Being—that has ever visited the earth. He gives a very careful method of approaching contact with the Supreme Being and he was against form most of the time. He went into the Temple and threw form out, because form had led to money values and it had gotten as far away from religion, if religion means, as I believe it does, the contact of the human being with the Divinity. Form is not necessary . . . it all depends on the individual. You asked me whether I have gone by form—I have not. My father went to church always, and followed form, but never taught form. He tried to teach the meaning of the forms, and if you can absorb the meaning of the forms, then forms will not be harmful, but beneficial. But if they are just forms and the meaning of the form does not reach you, then they are harmful because they stop your own individual thinking and your own individual contact with the Supreme Being.

Insofar as Mr. DeMille's career and reputation ever became an issue, it was the staff's task to keep a nice balance between pride and public relations. What the boss loved to hear about himself might be injurious—if it caused the public or press to react badly. He expected us to be alert to such things, and not hesitate to tell him when he was about to commit an inadvisable act. "I can't watch out for everything," he often reminded us, "and there's one thing I won't stand for, and that's for DeMille to look foolish." It was his way of saying we had better be careful that *DeMille* did not say anything reflecting discredit on DeMille.

One of the staff people most concerned about this was a tall, deep-chested Swiss named Henry Noerdlinger, who withstood with remarkable poise the burdens of conducting research for DeMille. Around the lot they called him the sad Swiss, but the principal strength that endeared him to his close friends came from the fact that Henry did not fall prey to the mesmerism within the bungalow. Born and educated in Switzerland, Henry was a monument of intellectual honesty, innately kind, and fearless in leaping the hurdles set up by the boss.

Henry's office was within earshot of DeMille's office, thus facilitating communication. The process was one of the most familiar in the bungalow—DeMille opening his office door and in a voice that boomed down the corridor and into every cellular office—"What is the Taj Mahal made of?" The rest of the staff didn't stir; when the sentence ended with a question mark we knew it was Henry's to worry over. Henry kept an academic tongue discreetly in his cheek when the boss split the air with such historical teasers as, "Henry, did the women in Samson's days wear a bra?"

It was often a matter of regret that Mr. DeMille would insert into the script customs and events of a bygone era without first checking with Henry. Of course Delilah had to be shown in a bra and it was up to Henry to look into the books for something that would justify decking out the girl so fetchingly.

Himself an old hand at research, the boss would not take no for an answer when he had his heart set on showing how something *really* happened back in the darkness of history.

Henry felt he could not wrongfully hypothecate history, so having produced evidence in a dozen books that did not support the boss's position, it was up to the boss to make his choice. Faced with the weight of evidence against him, DeMille had been known to settle for a single reference in a single volume, aware as he was of the vagaries of historians and of the mutations of passing centuries. As for Delilah's bra, a photograph was found in a musty volume showing a Minoan woman whose dress had a bra-like sweep to the upper portion. It was far less revealing than Delilah's but DeMille felt its lines were such to justify a bare midriff.

Naturally, Mr. DeMille liked to have the historians on his side, and usually they were; it was when history's verdict was contrary that Henry endured the greatest travail—torn between professional honor and the edicts of an employer who claimed he was *making* history. In this respect *The Story of Dr. Wassell* was a bell ringer. Dr. Wassell, hero of the big rescue at Java, assisted as technical advisor and laid out facts often received by DeMille with the rejoinder, "We won't do it that way. The audience will never believe it." The Navy commander later remarked in good humor, "DeMille pushed me around more than the Japs. I had figured out a way to save my men but no way to save myself from DeMille."

DeMille, popping his head out of his office, would let fly as many as a dozen teasers in the course of a day—"Henry, if a man abducts a bond slave, can he be hanged?" "What kind of arrows did the Senecas use and how long were they?" "Which way does the sun shine on the circus midway when it's playing in Washington and Philadelphia?"

There were times when Henry was shut off from the truth by outside forces, as in the instance where DeMille was required by the Breen censorship office to pile heaps of soapsuds around the upper portion of Paulette Goddard as she bathed in a prerevolutionary wooden tub in *Unconquered*. Henry stood shoulder to shoulder with the boss in the claim that this was an era long before Lever Brothers, and there were no such things as soapsuds! The boss was properly distressed over the anachronism but fortunately it escaped public notice.

During preparations for the circus picture Mr. DeMille sent Henry a note, reading *Get me data on a man bleeding to death.* The script called for a transfusion scene in the melee following the train wreck.

Henry replied with a 3-page report.

The boss said it was too long. "Boil it down to a few sentences."

Henry complied, listing merely the four types of blood.

"I see you've just got four types here," said DeMille.

"Yes, the Moss classification of blood types probably is the most widely used," Henry pointed out. "It divides human blood into four main types or groups."

"I want a fifth type, something rare," DeMille said.

Henry returned to the books, came up with a learned paper on the RH factor, placating the boss by explaining that with RH and the four types there was little left in the field of blood.

One day, the sage Noerdlinger drew reflectively on his blackened pipe. His mind ran to the ebb and flow of history within the bungalow. The impulse of the moment inspired him to a memorable paraphrase of a classic remark: "Between Mr. DeMille's purpose in time and God's purpose in eternity there is an infinite qualitative difference."

It was Henry's duty to keep an ear open for Mr. DeMille's sometimes overly enthusiastic comments that happened to pertain to matters of record. Once, when telling about his trip to Russia, he observed that "Mrs. DeMille and I went 3,000 miles down the Volga River." Naturally this concerned all of us, lest a newspaperman check up and find that the boss had added some 700 miles to the Volga's official length. Henry told DeMille by discreet memo that the river had a length listing of 2,300 miles. DeMille ignored the trifling difference. In time he began referring to their "4,000-mile trip down the Volga."

In his chats with visitors and the press the cost of research on a picture might rise from $10,000 to as high as $100,000 in a period of a few weeks. This drove Henry to worried calcula-

tions as to just how such a sum was being spent in view of
the fact that a single man, Noerdlinger himself, comprised the
entire research effort within the bungalow.

When Gloria Grahame agreed to allow an elephant to poise
a foot within inches of her face in the circus picture, DeMille
was enchanted, and began beating the drums publicly in tribute to her courage. "That was no child's play," he would tell
the press. "That was a 10-ton elephant hanging his foot over
Gloria's face." Ten tons struck us at the time as a lot of elephant, even for a DeMille production. Henry checked the books
and found that it was certainly not of conventional size.
P. T. Barnum's great circus giant, Jumbo, weighed 6 tons, considerably under the weight of Mr. DeMille's imaginary beast.
Henry made reference to the point, and DeMille did reduce
the poundage to seven tons on most occasions but was always
well over the legal elephantine limit.

Another time DeMille was looking for a spirited, but not
jazzy, musical number to use in a sound sequence. Several were
tried and rejected. He then ordered the musicians to try "Dixie."

"Sorry, Mr. DeMille, we don't own the rights to the song,"
said an assistant.

A lengthy discussion over proprietary rights ensued, with
the boss finding every legal avenue closed to him, until finally
he exploded, "Play 'The Star-Spangled Banner' and wire the
President!"

These were natural exuberances with which even his severest
critics could find no real fault. One New York newspaper critic
editorially summarized this part of his character as a "mag-
nified prestige, in its engineering one of the greatest promo-
tional feats of all time. It was the selling of a cult, as well as
a culture." Typical of this strong facet was the occasion we
had suggested that a picture, then in rough form, should not
be shown to the press until it was completely edited. It was a
needless caution, but DeMille pounced on it to voice one of his
little saws of showmanship. "Never in your life say a DeMille

picture is anything but perfect. We refer to every DeMille picture at all times as great." It was as if to say a DeMille production was born full-blown, in all its grandeur.

DeMille was frequently called upon by correspondents to name "the ten best pictures of all time," a chore promptly passed on to staff members and one we always approached a little nervously. The problem was to figure out how many or how few DeMille films to include on such a list. Back in 1923 he had picked "the six best of all time," naming *Birth of a Nation, Cabiria, Intolerance* and *Robin Hood,* and included two of his own, *Joan the Woman* and *Male and Female,* in second and fourth place respectively.

In 1951, he was asked to select the ten best for an art and film festival in Brussels, and obliged with the following:

> Cabiria
> Birth of a Nation
> Ben Hur
> *The Ten Commandments*
> *The King of Kings*
> The Big Parade
> *The Sign of the Cross*
> Gone With the Wind
> Going My Way
> *Samson and Delilah*

Of the ten, the four in italics were DeMille productions. However, a year before he had included only one, *Samson and Delilah,* on a ten-best list requested by the United Press; but that request was made near the release date of the picture and promotionally it was deemed wise to focus attention on a single film, displaying once again his shrewd sense of publicity values. By a translation in the meaning or juggling of events he would add a new glow to an ordinary occurrence. A case in point took place during preparations for *The Greatest Show on Earth.* DeMille was having trouble with the Music Department over an original song for Betty Hutton to sing in the picture. He wanted something light and catchy, but the Department kept coming up with what DeMille considered slow and heavy.

One night the Department head, Louie Lipstone, thoroughly fed up with DeMille's ragging, went out to the home of Victor Young, one of the composers working on the DeMille project, to discuss what could be done about the situation. An evening of canasta was in progress at the Young home and one of the players was a chap named Ned Washington, a top musical hand who had written a number of famous Disney songs, including "When You Wish Upon a Star," winner of an Academy Award. Washington heard Young and Lipstone discussing the DeMille project and offered to try his hand at the lyrics. Since Young had already composed much of the music for the circus picture, the two joined forces and produced a song which they called "The Greatest Show on Earth." DeMille received it enthusiastically but was a little fidgety about the price the upper-bracket composer might charge. Washington reassured him that the price would be high but not anything beyond what DeMille should be willing to pay, being happy to get a credit on a DeMille picture.

At luncheon one day DeMille, anticipating a hit song, told his publicity man to prepare a story on how it all came about, to wit:

"I was up in the Music Department giving Louie Lipstone plenty of hell when some young fellow who was over there playing canasta came over to me and said, 'Mr. DeMille, I'd give anything to get a credit on your picture. I'll do the song for nothing if you'll give me a screen credit.' So he goes away and comes back with this great song. It's going to be a terrific hit. This boy Ned Washington has written a lot of Disney songs but he was just over there playing canasta and he was willing to do the song for nothing just to get a DeMille credit."

Part II

AVARICE AMONG THE AVOCADOS

1.

THE first of the migratory DeMilles, of sturdy Dutch stock, left his native Haarlem for America in 1765, choosing to settle in a section of New York where land was plentiful and cheap. He acquired a parcel of semi-marshland that is now a part of lower Wall Street.

The family's early roots were put down in North Carolina by a vigorous Episcopalian, William Edward DeMille, Cecil's grandfather. In a little place called Pingotown, he studied law, gained admission to the bar, later gave up his practice to open a general store in nearby Washington, North Carolina.

He became the town's mayor and at the start of the Civil War received orders from General Martin to operate a commissary for a southern contingent recruited largely from his own area. He had been away a short time when word reached him that his family had fled to Greenville before advancing Federal troops. He hurried to Greenville to ascertain their safety and to be on hand for his wife's thirtieth birthday. In the midst of muted festivities William Edward was taken prisoner by a cavalry detachment that had just entered Greenville. After a tearful farewell, there was a hurried bolting of the doors. At that moment, Henry Churchill DeMille, father of the future Cecil, was having his own troubles. The youth, having encountered a Federal trooper who had taken freely of Confederate whisky, was sprinting to the nearest haven, his grandmother's home, with the trooper not far behind, drunkenly brandishing his pistol. Henry's diary recounts what happened next:

> I tried to take refuge in the house but grandma wouldn't let me in, knowing that she could not then do what she had been trying for some time to do, namely, keep the trooper out of the house. I trusted then to those two old reliables which many a time stood me in good stead—my legs, and before the trooper came up with me I was safely concealed in an adjoining cornfield. Had the trooper's pistol not become entangled in some way in his effort to draw it quickly, I might not be here now to tell this tale.

Nor would he have married Beatrice Samuels, as he did in July of 1876, and there would not have been born to them two sons, William Churchill DeMille on July 25, 1878, and Cecil Blount DeMille on August 12, 1881.

On his deathbed William Edward called for young Henry and the others, gave them his blessing and issued final instructions, being both a religious and practical man. He told Henry to measure the space behind the vault to determine whether there was room both for him and mother, too. He told him how deep the grave was to be dug, that cement, not mortar, was to be used, instructing him where to buy the cement and how much to pay for it. Also he was to purchase flagstones in preference to bricks, which he did not like, and these were to form a simple tombstone. He chided them for their grief as they stood there, silently, tears rolling down their faces.

Henry DeMille, a dreamy lad given to books and hobbies, wanted to be an actor but took a path trod by other DeMilles, to the Episcopal vestry. One day he asked his mother, "What would you say to my becoming an actor?" She replied, "It would break my heart." His marriage, at twenty-three, to Mathilda Beatrice Samuels was a fusion of two radically different temperaments. She was a go-getter, afire with ambitions for their future and that of their two sons.

Dutifully, Bill was born in the old family home in Washington. Three years later Cecil appeared, prematurely and in Yankee country! The bawling nonconformist ignored the date set for him by the doctor, arriving at Ashfield, Massachusetts, where his father was engaged for the summer in private tutoring in an effort to help along the family's meager purse.

Bill was clearly his father's son, cut from the same cloth—thoughtful, sensitive, creative. Cecil, on the other hand, was obviously a young man in a hurry. He flashed spirit and daring. His daydreams had vigor and more often than not a fearsome adversary. A friend who had seen them making pictures together in the early days of Hollywood touched upon the differences between the two. "When Cecil wanted camels in a picture he would buy a thousand with golden harness and parade them before the camera. Bill would buy one camel and have it psychoanalyzed."

Cecil was Mother's boy, from large, strong features to his remarkable durability. At one point the family rented a house in Echo Lake, New Jersey, for something like $50 a year because it supposedly was haunted. Shortly, they left for a brief spell and returned to learn that neighbors had heard crashing sounds in the place every night. While a curbstone conference was in progress, Mrs. DeMille marched past her neighbors into the darkened home. In a few minutes she had flushed out a tramp, chasing him into the night, brandishing her long black umbrella. The vagrant had been enjoying Mrs. DeMille's choice preserves, hurling the empty jars at a marble clock which he had set up as a target.

DeMille has recalled a little shakily the time his mother followed him out to Hollywood, around 1914. "She bought the biggest, fastest, shiniest Packard and drove it like hell around town. Once she almost ran me down."

There was also the occasion, a few years after her husband's sudden and early death, that Mrs. DeMille decided to enroll Cecil in a military school in Chester, Pennsylvania. Cecil was about fifteen.

The distance from the home in Pompton, New Jersey, to Chester was ninety miles, a good day's ride by coach. This Mrs. DeMille rejected.

Instead, she and Cecil climbed on their bicycles and took off down the coach road, arriving late that day. Enrollment over, the petite, spirited young widow said good-by to her son and pedaled off in the dusk down the dusty road toward Pompton.

The DeMille boys got their first taste of drama early in life. Through Dan Frohman, Henry DeMille teamed up with David Belasco, a struggling young Barnum soon to be crowned the Rialto's first great showman. Belasco sparked with ideas and Henry DeMille reduced them to writing. Each day they would call in Mrs. DeMille and read to her what had been put down on paper.

The two young men worked in a small first-floor room in the DeMille home and evenings were quite often devoted to play conferences, with the family usually being called in for the readings. It was sometimes difficult to get Cecil to sit still that long. The future spectacle-maker was not inspired by what his father and Belasco were dreaming up—intimate social exercises such as *The Wife, The Charity Ball, Lord Chumley* and *Men and Women.* Despite little Cecil's marked disinterest, the plays helped start a new era for playgoers of that day, for the domestic drama was something new to American audiences. During one of these family gatherings DeMille's attention wandered to a cat that had, quite miraculously it seemed to him, strolled down the side of a barn. The boy who was one day to stage such cinematic miracles as the siege of Acre and the Exodus uttered a squeal of delight and for this outcry his father banished him from the scene. On another occasion Cecil, having slipped away from a conference, attacked a stand of Jerusalem artichokes which his mother was grooming in the backyard. Cecil was a fair knight, his stick was a sword, and the artichokes were the enemy. The affable malfeasance may be charitably interpreted as Cecil's zeal for his life's work, a consideration which, were she mindful of it, did not temper the sticking he got from his mother.

Belasco was the son of immigrant Jews. He wore the attire of a clergyman, collar and all. It caused considerable comment as well as confusion. Some credited the display to showmanship. Belasco, however, traced it to an old Jesuit priest named McGuire who befriended him in San Francisco. Father McGuire, impressed by the intense young man, arranged for his enrollment at the Jesuit college there when he learned the boy was too poor to attend. Belasco finished the four years creditably, and vowed always to wear a Roman collar in appreciation of the kindness.

The Wife, the first play written at Echo Lake by the collaborators, gave a twist to an old formula. A husband discovers his wife is unfaithful. Instead of handing her the deed to the house and making arrangements for the children, he takes her tenderly into his arms and comforts her with offers of help.

With this bold offering, Dan Frohman launched a permanent stock company at the Lyceum Theatre.

Attendance was poor and grew steadily worse. Each day the anxious authors stalked Frohman in his office with fresh entreaties to keep the play open for a few more days. They felt it was improving.

Frohman countered with a ledger of mounting debts. After the second week he promised to keep it open one more week, continuing it from that point only if it made expenses.

The two writers began pruning and tightening the dialogue and action. Attendance picked up, but not enough to satisfy Frohman.

One day he sent word to the authors that *The Wife* was in

its final week. An hour later they rushed into his office. They begged and pleaded. Frohman sat at his desk, silent, cold-eyed. Suddenly Belasco seized the producer by the throat.

The sight of the priestlike figure dragging Frohman from his chair and pinning him down on the floor filled the mild-mannered DeMille with terror.

Egged on by his partner, DeMille grabbed a ruler and the two of them threatened to kill Frohman if he didn't keep the play going.

The play, greatly improved by the cutting, went on to post 218 consecutive performances, yielding a nice profit for the management after liquidating a $50,000 debt. Belasco remembered the collaboration with real pride. "We were successful because our way of thought was similar. We were frank in our criticism of each other. Henry excelled in narrative and had a quick wit. I acted while he took down my speeches. When a play was finished it was impossible to say where his work left off and mine began."

Belasco became the family hero. Bill and Cecil stood as sentries in the quiet fields around Echo Lake to herald the approach of the man in the Roman collar, the shrill dispatches occasioning much bustling about the house.

He brought the boys gifts, important ones at Christmas. One year Belasco penned a note to Cecil: *This year a small gift, but next year a pony.* DeMille kept the note, reminder of a boyhood tragedy. "I waited for 365 days, dreaming dreams about the pony. I arose that cold Christmas morning almost before daybreak. I was sure the pony would be in the barn. It wasn't there. Belasco had forgotten all about it. I was stunned. I couldn't believe it. I told no one, just suffered in silence for days. It taught me a lesson I've tried to remember all through life—keep your promise to a child."

Cecil was nine when his father died, at thirty-nine, and once more the family was faced with the same realities. The future had looked unusually bright, for his father's work with Belasco had just begun to impress itself on the critics. Now creditors, not critics, overnight became important in their lives. They found a worthy adversary in Mrs. DeMille. The aggressive little lady converted the Pompton home into a culture school for fashionable young women. Understandably, young actresses were among the first to enroll, increasing in such numbers in a year or two that the mother pressed both Cecil and Bill into service. One of the early pupils, Evelyn Nesbit, remembered that Cecil, young though he was, solemnly tackled the mysteries of drawing-room posture and decorum. He taught the young ladies how to walk, sit and sip tea, and even offered advice in the selection of clothes.

"He had an artistic flair all right," Miss Nesbit said, "because he could demonstrate how a young lady could show disdain in one gesture by winding her wrap about her hips in a regal manner," a scene difficult to associate with the man whose thunderous roars have reduced thousands to craven silence. It provided an answer to one unusual DeMille trait. He took full charge of the original designs of all important costumes in his productions, even down to a leather thrum on an Indian loincloth. No designer dared proceed without first getting DeMille's initials on the sketch of the costume, male or female.

"Few of the celebrated girls of New York's musical hits lost the opportunity of having a season of social training at this Pompton Lake establishment, so far had the reputation of the two young men reached into sophisticated Broadway's gossip channels," according to one observer. "A raw product could be turned out a lady, a show girl could be taught to carry herself like an aristocrat, to dine like one, and with much more grueling training, she might eventually be taught to speak as one."

Belasco detected a strain of real creativeness in the DeMilles and with Henry's passing he beckoned encouragingly to son Bill, in whom he had observed a flair for dramatic situation. Bill was doing some work on his own in that quiet way and before long he delighted his father's old friend with some creditable ideas.

Within a few years, Mrs. DeMille made a logical move. She opened an office in New York to handle Bill's plays and hold herself forth as a mother confessor to young aspirants to the stage and advisor to struggling playwrights. Cecil was worked into the new life, too, with roles in this and that, but mostly in productions that passed through the DeMille Play Agency. Cecil had shed the curse of all boys of the era, Lord Fauntleroy suit and long curls, but he was not entirely free of the horrible tyranny. For some reason, the casting directors tabbed the future strong man of the movies as a pretty-boy-in-lace type. In perfumed attire and decanting lyrical prose, Cecil pranced about the stage in the lead of plays like *The Prince Chap* and *Lord Chumley*.

Cecil tried his hand at playwriting and came up with *The Return of Peter Grimm,* or possibly the idea. The authorship of that once reigning favorite may never be determined. DeMille said Belasco paid him $5,000 for it. Belasco claimed he bought an idea only, that he himself constructed the play, developed the characters, and wrote the dialogue.

The dispute got into the papers. Belasco demanded retraction of a statement crediting DeMille as *part* author. "In view of the fact that my play has not yet been presented in New York—and may possibly prove a failure there—I think it is only fair that I should be held exclusively responsible for my own work."

Neither position tallied with Neil McCarthy's memory of the matter. McCarthy, for years DeMille's attorney and investment associate, said DeMille took the first draft of *Grimm* to Belasco's office. "Then he would come in once every week or ten days and read each new part to Belasco. When he had finished it Belasco wanted to produce it but he told DeMille he couldn't pay him much because he had practically the same story sent him from an author in Germany. There were curtains in

Belasco's office and while DeMille was reading his play a stenographer was behind the curtains taking down every word. Belasco wasn't going to put DeMille's name on the program as author until DeMille threatened to sue, and then it showed up in very fine print."

In a New York *Tribune* interview in 1935, David Warfield was coaxed into breaking his silence over the *Grimm* puzzle. "Well, Belasco was looking for a play to do when he ran across one Cecil DeMille had sent him. DeMille was hard up at that time and needed money, so he had taken an old story called 'Old Lady Mary,' published in *Blackwood's Magazine* way back in 1875, and made a play out of it. Belasco saw possibilities for it and offered to buy it. DeMille agreed, and Belasco bought it outright for a small amount. He mulled over his new property for a while, fixed it over a little and produced it. That's the story of *Peter Grimm*. We opened in Baltimore in 1911, then went to Chicago and finally came to New York with it, afterward going on tour. But it didn't draw very well—people didn't seem to take to it. In 1921 I became ambitious, fiddled with the thing for a time and was determined to try it again. So I did, and the revival was remarkable—it went like wildfire."

With the collaborator still Belasco, Bill DeMille added some luster to the family name by writing plays like *The Warrens of Virginia*, and *The Genius*. It remained for his brilliant daughter Agnes, after much struggle, to have the joy of a personal conquest of Broadway some thirty years later. The ballets conceived by Agnes DeMille for *Oklahoma!*, *One Touch of Venus*, *Carousel* and others were gay, dazzling—and new. Her choreography introduced an art form in the period of the musical comedy's greatest vigor, and quite a number of her admirers today happily salute her as the most sensitively creative of all the DeMilles.

Cecil was nineteen when Dan Frohman gave him $20 a week and eight lines in his new play *Hearts Were Trumps*, a little that yielded much. His eye was drawn to a member of the troupe, a pretty miss, genteel and even as a girl with a composure that placed soothing reins on his restlessness. Over coffee and doughnuts the acquaintance grew into romance. They toured the towns, endured the one-night stops with Sothern and Marlowe. Two years later, on August 12, 1902, Cecil and Constance Adams, daughter of Judge Frederic Adams of Orange, New Jersey, were married in New York.

Hollywood was a decade away, and the years in between were to be filled with hardship and job-seeking. DeMille kept a reminder of those days—"a badge of poverty," he called it. A trolley token! "I'd walk from 14th Street, New York's theatrical district then, to 125th Street to save a nickel carfare."

2.

THE founding fathers were seasoned warriors. They bore the scars of war fought behind closed Hollywood doors. Left on carpeted battlefields were the bodies of competitors pierced, Brutus-like, by the daggers of power merger, power finance and power manipulations.

Historians have yet to set a serious hand to this free-wheeling era. They have been content to leap from peak to peak like polite mountain goats, deriving their notion of what actually occurred from studio statistics and publicists paid to overpower historical fact like roustabouts pegging down a tent flap.

Others, a quite sizable group, have written their chronicles from the recollections of the warriors themselves, who were apt to be the kind of historians that warriors usually are, shaping history from their own bias.

For this reason as much as any, Hollywood can boast of something the scientific mind usually rejects—a multiple birth. Apparently it entered this life on different dates and in different places. If its origin was not multiple, it was at least polygamous. No infant has had more fathers, each stoutly claiming sole paternity. By casual count this plurality of proud papas totals at least a half-dozen. "Mr. A" dates the birth of the industry in 1914, in an orange grove in Hollywood. "Mr. B" recollected it was in New York in 1912. "Mr. C" goes back to the turn of the century, in Flatbush. All, at one time or another, have nodded politely to such titles as "dean of the industry," "the father of motion pictures," "Mr. Hollywood," "Mr. Motion Pictures." And each, at one point or another, has issued his version of film history containing only passing reference, if any, to any other "founder."

In the DeMille bungalow we had our own version of how it all began at a luncheon in the old Claridge Hotel in New York. Supposedly, there were three people there, although occasionally a fourth entered these historic proceedings on that summer day in 1913, a young lawyer by the name of Arthur Friend. Friend, it appears, had a tongue for oratory, though his powers of persuasion were being tested that day. He sat at a table ringed with pessimism. Friend talked spiritedly about something called "flickers." The others, however, just were not listening.

One was chesty, prematurely bald Cecil DeMille, bit actor and fledgling playwright in his early thirties. Up to then his ambitions had been rudely jostled on Broadway.

Another, somewhat less dejected, was Jesse Lasky, ex-cornet player and a moderately successful producer of small-time vaudeville. Lasky had just put a lot of money into an American cabaret version of the famous *Folies Bergère*. The unprofitable results gave him conclusive evidence that the era was poor in critical judgment. Most dispirited was Lasky's brother-in-law, Sam Goldfish, later permitted by a Federal court to rechristian himself Sam Goldwyn. He was a glove salesman and was reflecting darkly on an act of Congress that removed the tariff on gloves, virtually killing his business.

Flickers, said Friend, were developing some real muscle. His companions looked up wearily. Moving pictures were a fad, and who wanted to waste time on a fad?

"Fad!" cried Friend. "Look at that Italian picture, *Ciberia*. The Astor is charging $1 a head and they're turning 'em away."

The air around the table began to improve. Friend pressed on. Was it not true that Adolph Zukor bought *Queen Elizabeth*, starring Sarah Bernhardt, and organized his own company, Famous Players, to produce movies of important stage plays? "And see what he's done with *The Prisoner of Zenda*." Bernhardt, Hackett, Frohman—magic names on the Rialto!

The four left the hotel and entered a nickelodeon down the street. Twenty minutes later they came out. Friend wore a complacent smile; he observed his friends in a close circle, silent, nostrils dilating as if they sensed a boom.

"All those people jammed in there," Lasky murmured. "If they'll buy something like that . . ."

The others nodded.

"If we can't do better we ought to go back to selling gloves," said DeMille, giving Goldfish a friendly pat.

The Jesse L. Lasky Feature Play Company came into existence on paper. They would capitalize at $20,000 if that sum could be dredged up.

Cecil went to his brother Bill. He asked for $5,000, one-fourth interest in the firm!

Bill fixed on his brother a look of mortal disappointment.

"Think of the family pride," said Bill, pointing out that the DeMille roots were deep in the legitimate theater and "you're going to use it in some scheme to drag nickels from little children."

Not only was ancestral honor in jeopardy, but young Cecil was asking for money from a DeMille to hasten its destruction! "I've bailed you out of every one of your other schemes,"

Brother Bill said, truthfully. "I'll just save my money and pay your fare home," he added, therewith rationalizing himself out of an investment which in a few years would have been worth two million dollars.

The others had better luck; still short by several thousands, the organizers decided their first picture would be a stage hit of that day, Edwin Milton Royle's *The Squaw Man*. They agreed to $5,000 for the rights, with a down payment of $1,000.

Next they went to Dustin Farnum, a Broadway star, and offered a share of the company if he would play the lead.

Farnum hesitated; theater people were blacklisting anyone who got mixed up with flickers. One thing was certain: he did not want company stock, but would do it for $1,000 a week—the first week's salary in advance. Also, he did not want his name to appear in connection with the picture. They heatedly argued him out of that demand, but agreed to pay the salary.

With his first male star in tow, DeMille boarded a train for the Far West, excited over the reports circulating on Broadway about a place called Hollywood. There, if a person kept his wits about him, moving pictures could be completed entirely outdoors, summer or winter, under a warm lazy sun. Moving out to Hollywood had another singular attraction for the partners—escape from the powerful trust that was centered in the General Film Company. Distance meant safety; under the peaceful pepper trees struggling producers would find it easy to ignore the trust's many patents that shackled movie making in the East.

In Hollywood, the spirit was militant; an odd assortment prowled its orange groves—fugitives from the trust, promoters, young men with energy and a sensitive eye for plagiarism. "Idea" rustling was the order of the day. With movies being filmed against crude backdrops in the open air, it was considered wise to erect high fences. Stories were short and extraordinarily simple. A fairly alert passer-by who watched the shooting for a half-hour could get a pretty good idea of the plot. It was not uncommon for a producer to enter a theater and unexpectedly see a story he was preparing to release.

Wasted opportunities were few. In 1919 a fire destroyed a good part of the Lasky studio, attracting more than spectators. The shooting crews of two rival firms appeared on the scene with actors who began indulging in slapstick antics, using the blaze as background, while the miserable owners watched the destruction.

The high fences hobbled the efforts of agents of the hated trust, on the prowl for illegal use of unlicensed camera equipment. Thomas E. Edison, one of the more patent-heavy members of the trust, sent a full corps of detectives out in the field to check on these creative scamps with a limited respect for vested interests. At the approach of an investigator, the producer would spirit his camera into a hiding place, then summon his staff into a story conference, as visible proof that the company was not in production. In well-policed areas, a producer might call as many as five story conferences in a day, each materializing suddenly and at the most unusual times. The record must contain a sad annotation on those sleuths who accepted the offer of a bit part in a movie as the price of their loyalty to employers, bribery and larceny being natural handmaidens.

The Jesse L. Lasky Feature Play Company arrived in Hollywood in the winter of 1913. DeMille, ever the showman, was director-general; back in New York, Goldwyn was treasurer-business manager, and Lasky general executive head. There was yet one glaring flaw in the setup. They didn't know the first thing about writing or directing a motion picture. They sent for a producer in New York, Oscar Apfel, who brought his cameraman with him.

By this time movies were big business in the East. One of the industry's fathers, Albert E. Smith, was budgeting million-dollar pictures at his Vitagraph studio. Adolph Zukor was paying stars like Mary Pickford as much as $10,000 a week. The public's desire for flickers was already whetted when the Lasky company moved into the citrus groves of the sleepy little village.

Goldwyn instructed DeMille on expenditures. "No long-term commitments." DeMille obeyed to the letter, renting half of a barn from a Jacob Stern for $25 a month on a month-to-month basis. It sat in the heart of a lemon grove near the present intersection of Hollywood and Vine. The protection of the lemon trees was comforting and on one occasion profitable. Losing heavily on a picture, the crew was ordered out to harvest the lemon crop and recouped its losses. The sewer in Stern's barn was on the firm's side, causing the office workers to retreat to chairs and high ground when Stern was watering down his horses. Two former horse stalls, draped with black cambric, were dressing rooms for Farnum and Winifred Kingston, a glamorous star of the stage who had come out from New York to play the feminine lead. "She was a fine enough trouper. She didn't ask what performer last used the dressing room," DeMille once recalled.

The Squaw Man was filmed in three weeks at a cost of $15,000, most of its scenes taking place on a set consisting of a wooden platform and two walls of canvas with a large cotton umbrella serving as a light diffuser. Early that January 1914, DeMille and his assistants gathered in the barn to screen the picture for the first time in edited form.

Puzzled, angry cries greeted the picture as it began to unreel, showing scratches and dark blotches. Obviously the film had been gouged, probably with a knife or icepick, and the scratches might have been made by someone pulling the film between heel and floor. The sabotage was complete; every foot of the 5,000 feet of film was useless.

In business less than two months, the young firm had its first taste of the film wars. Refilming would require another $15,000 and back in New York Lasky and Goldwyn were impatient for the picture, for its buyers were waiting.

There appears to be some divergence in the accounts of the episode. Bill DeMille in his admirable account of the early days, *Hollywood Saga*, relates that Goldwyn, Lasky and Friend went out and drummed up another $15,000 and DeMille shot the picture a second time.

DeMille, however, rejected this version. "One day shortly before we began shooting I saw a worker touch his cigarette to a small piece of waste film. It burst into flames, and the thought struck me that in a few weeks we would have a fortune tied up in a few lengths of highly inflammable film. . . . We decided to shoot every scene twice to have a spare negative, and each night I took home an extra can of film, and Mrs. DeMille placed it in the attic."

Then, when the picture was screened for the first time and they saw what had been done to it, "panic seized us. I remembered the other negative. Suppose it, too, was ruined or stolen! I phoned Mrs. DeMille to look quickly into the attic and not say a word to anyone.

"The second negative was safe. I took it to New York, cut and edited the film on the train. No sleep for five days but I had to finish it."

Upon his return to the wild and woolly West, DeMille strapped on a gun and holster, and when he drove placed the weapon on the seat beside him. In the following weeks he twice heard sharp sounds near the studio that closely resembled pistol shots, leading to a subsequent biographical note that he was fired upon twice.

Even with its production cost doubled, *The Squaw Man*

netted the partners several thousand dollars. Their next effort, *The Virginian,* was made at a cost of $17,000 and returned $111,000. Then, and largely since, policy was noted for its flexibility. One success started a cycle. The public, having indicated a preference for a certain picture, was deluged with more of the same by producers willing to sacrifice art for certain profit.

In a single year, 1915, DeMille directed fifteen pictures for the Lasky company and wrote the script for five of them. By modern standards they were simple little exercises but at the same time comprised a greater volume of work than one man could consistently manage. He began looking about for a writing assistant.

One day a young woman, dark-eyed, no doubt still in her late teens, entered the office-barn. She was, DeMille later recalled, "a funny little tornado with a nose that turned up, and hair that curled up, and a disposition that turned up, too." She said her name was Jeanie Macpherson, told him at once that she would be willing to work for him and named a price—considerably more than the director would dream of paying. She said she was an actress, a very good one, and that he would be wise to engage her before she left his office.

DeMille glanced up, looked her over for a minute, and then went on with his writing. The youngster began to shift position nervously and at the end of about ten minutes she let out an explosive "Well!" and stormed out, slamming the door violently. DeMille laughed and went on with his writing.

Two days later she returned. "Would you apologize to me for your rudeness the other day?" adding she had written him a letter telling what a frightful person he was.

Something about the girl's personality fascinated DeMille

and when she returned the second time he offered to pay her twenty-five dollars a week to take dictation in long hand. "A blow in the face would have been more of a compliment. She raged and stormed and said she would never think of accepting such a thing, and finally I said, 'Well, if you want to act, I will give you just one day's work.'"

She performed well in a small but important part, and at the end of the day was handed ten dollars—double the usual rate being paid then by the Lasky company. Once more she stormed into DeMille's office, threw the money on his desk and reminded him that she had been paid $100 a day working for D. W. Griffith. That, or nothing, was her price, she said, whereupon DeMille obligingly pocketed the money, smiling serenely as the young woman angrily departed for the third time.

Later DeMille called her in for a long talk, and after telling her that she did not have the right kind of a face for the screen, persuaded her—for twenty-five dollars a week—to try her hand at script writing. He dictated four manuscripts to her and after the fourth told her to go home and write the script of his fifth picture. "The first thing she had to do was make me a brief outline of it. When she brought it in, it was full of mistakes, and I hauled her over the coals for each of them. I told her that she wrote like a plumber. I am sure I was frightfully insulting to her, but that kid took it and plugged along, and I think she rewrote the whole thing six times. Jeanie had no physical strength but she was like a tarantula—when she got her fangs into anything you could not shake her loose. During the rewriting of that fifth play, I fired her regularly, but it did no good, for she would always come back with another version of the script. We worked half the night, night after night, and I used to keep her at the plant through all that, and she would drop from physical exhaustion. One night, after we had worked until one or two o'clock and were about ready to go home, I missed her, and looked everywhere for her. Finally, I saw a foot sticking out from the back of a pile of shingles. I investigated and found that it belonged to Jeanie. I brought her to the office, got a doctor out of bed to revive her, and finally delivered her home to her mother done up like a bundle. I did that time after time. But she would not give up the work. She became my blue-ribbon writer, and I would say that most of my plays were written by her, and some were the best original stories of her generation.

Jeanie appeared to have caught considerable of the DeMille spirit.

When it was decided in 1921 to film Alice Duer Miller's novel *Manslaughter*, she left Hollywood and, by means of a petty "theft," had herself committed to the Detroit House of Correction under the name of Angie Brown.

The firsthand experiences were to help her write a better script from the Miller work, but the escapade was almost spoiled by a fatherly Irish policeman escorting her to the institution; he offered to pay her bond personally.

The first night in the House of Correction was enough for the self-ordained larcenist. "I was awakened by a peculiar crawling sensation that meant but one thing—vermin! I prayed for daylight. I wanted to scream and beat my head against the stone walls of the cell, anything to push them away. I was on the verge of panic."

She told friends later that she made an attempt at escape, was caught and returned to her cell for two more days and nights.

Manslaughter, released in 1922, was a smashing success, costing $380,000 and grossing $1,200,000. It was a story of fast living, woven around a female hot-rodder (Leatrice Joy) sentenced to prison for two years after prosecution by her lover, the district attorney, who performs the unmanly deed to save the girl from herself. It gave Mr. DeMille an opportunity to compare the jazzy decadence of the 1920's with Roman times. He dramatized Rome's golden era in a flashback showing, as one critic put it, "men and women half-stupid with drink in an orgy of pure sense-satisfying pleasure, dancing girls, satyrs springing from the walls to join in the revel, and a rider upon a black charger who was dressed in skin and followed by a swarm of hideous barbarians more like animals than men." The rider was Thomas Meighan on his way with a battery of vandals to perform the historic sacking of Rome.

In this early period DeMille began to entertain a notion that the studio was rejecting manuscripts that would have made excellent pictures, largely because story readers were young or untrained and lacked story sense. He had had a few quarrels with the front office over this general problem. One day, to test his theory, he asked a secretary to write out in longhand a lengthy synopsis of one of Jeanie's scenarios, *Male and Female,* which he was filming at the time on a nearby sound stage. The synopsis was turned over to a relative, who in turn mailed it to the studio, stating in her letter that she hoped the story was good enough for the studio to purchase. The manuscript was returned to the sender marked, NOT SUITABLE AS MOTION PICTURE MATERIAL.

"Can you believe it?" DeMille chortled. "And we were making *Male and Female* not fifty yards away from the very office that turned it down." With high satisfaction he harangued the studio for months, pointing to the incident as an example of the sort of thing a director has to put up with from studio executives.

Though the record is considerably to the contrary, DeMille would admit publicly that he had only one disaster in choosing his stories. This was an item called *Four Frightened People,* filmed in Hawaii back in 1933 with Claudette Colbert and Herbert Marshall. The picture cost $500,000 and had to gross one million dollars in order to break even. A studio executive wired DeMille after seeing an opening showing: JUST SAW FOUR FRIGHTENED PEOPLE. SUGGEST WE CALL IT FIVE FRIGHTENED PEOPLE. Loss on the picture was around $750,000.

Reviewing her lengthy association with DeMille, having

written probably half of his seventy pictures alone or in collaboration, Jeanie looked upon DeMille's blunt and cold attitude as an armor for "an extremely sensitive nature." She said he wanted to make friends but didn't quite know how to go about it. "Actors didn't like him, and I have seen them tremble before his sarcasm and often cry with humiliation. But they unfailingly blamed themselves. He would forgive anyone anything if a person would only admit his error. But try to tell him that the other fellow was to blame, or insinuate another department was responsible for your blunder, and you were in serious trouble with him."

She died on the eve of her thirty-first year with DeMille, during the filming of *Unconquered* in 1946. He had kept her on part time salary through the later years, allowing her to sit with writers occasionally during the early conferences on a story. The industry had surged beyond her era, production was complex, and it was no longer possible or economic for a director and a single writer to team up on a series of pictures.

There is reason to believe tastes of film patrons have materially changed since Jeanie MacPherson's era. The stories of the 1900's reaped undeniably handsome rewards, but no doubt would send present-day audiences fleeing from the theater. *Don't Change Your Husband*, made in 1918 and praised by the critics for its "finished workmanship," was a story of marital discontent enlivened by Elliott Dexter, Gloria Swanson, Lew Cody, Theodore Roberts and Sylvia Ashton. This $17,000 epic, written by DeMille and Jeane Macpherson, grossed more than $200,000. Its plot is typical of the type that shaped careers and seeded huge fortunes in that era:

> Leila is married to James Porter, a glue king. James has lost his waistline. He flips ashes on the rugs, eats onions and

generally offends Leila in just about everything he does.
So, she discards James and marries Schuyler van Sutphen,
who is wealthy, too.

Schuyler is a fashion plate and dances divinely. But he has
eyes for women other than Leila. And as he philanders he
drinks. Now, Leila has to put up with the smell of liquor
instead of onion, and her life is no longer happy.

One day James reappears. Lo and behold he is not the old
James; he is slim around the waist, he smokes cigars with
a holder, his mustache is gone. A very attractive chap, indeed, and still with money, too. So Leila takes him back,
fashioned splendidly to her tastes.

This proved out so profitably that DeMille did a switch. In
Why Change Your Wife?, the *wife* is the bore and the husband
finds diversion in a pleasure-loving flapper whom he ultimately
marries, then sheds upon discovery that she is a worse house-
hold drudge than the original missus.

There was a tug at the public heartstrings in the plight of a
poor seamstress in *Forbidden Fruit,* an original DeMille melodrama. A distracted hostess finds she is one person short at her
fancy dinner party, and presses the seamstress into service as
a substitute guest. The little Cinderella turns into a radiant
charmer, and is energetically courted by her handsome and
wealthy dinner partner. The chap doesn't know the girl is married. She is, though, and to a grisly brute who "openly trades
her for money," as the subtitle discreetly puts it. The seamstress
suffers real torment—shall she follow the finer life or shall she
return to that husband?—in the following interplay of triangular
love, murder and robbery.

The receipts from *The Virginian* shone like a caliph's jewels.
The studio had big plans for original stories, but these were
jettisoned, and the struggle for stage plays was on. Zukor's
company with its motto, *Famous players in famous plays,* was
profiting from its tie-in with Dan Frohman, and was at the
moment trying to make a similar arrangement with David

Belasco. For a movie company, there was power and unlimited profit in the supply of plays controlled by either of these two giants of Broadway. Goldwyn wrangled an appointment with Belasco through the latter's secretary, afterward describing his meeting with the fiery impresario: "His entrance was a dramatic as that of a hero in one of his own plays. The majestic head with its mop of white hair sunk a trifle forward, the one hand carried inside his coat, as slowly without a word he descended the stairs to greet me." The deal was made, a triumph for Goldwyn and his firm. For a $25,000 advance against 50 per cent of the profits, Belasco surrendered the rights to his plays. The Lasky company now preened itself with such sensations as the Belasco hits *The Girl of the Golden West* and *Rose of the Rancho,* turning quickly to other "legitimate" successes: *The Man from Home, The Warrens of Virginia, Kindling, Carmen.*

Public desire for pictures in this period was insatiable, a situation made vastly more attractive to producers by the fact that the required skill did not go much beyond setting a camera and aiming it at an established stage play.

In his first year in pictures DeMille produced seven films, profits from one being applied to the next. The seven cost $106,793 and yielded $510,724, thus stimulating the Lasky firm's appetite for increased production.

The Girl of the Golden West was filmed in eight days for $15,109. Theodore Roberts played Jack Vance, and Mabel Van Buren the girl, in a manner pleasing enough to draw $102,224 from the patrons, a kingly profit.

The following year the studio struck out in earnest. New directors were hired, and Director-General DeMille gave the first hint of what power was stored in that sturdy frame. With something approaching Jovian fervor he wrote, produced and directed, on several occasions performing all three tasks for the same picture, completing a picture a month. By the end of the year, thirteen DeMille productions had rolled out of the barn. When complications developed on *The Golden Chance* with Edna Goodrich and a $100-a-week unknown named Wally Reid, DeMille took it over, too, working on his own picture *The Cheat* in the daytime and shifting to the other at night.

He was not unduly taxed by the experience. *The Cheat* cost $17,000 and grossed $137,000, the firm's highest single picture gain to that date. Also, it introduced to a now rabidly star-conscious public two new favorites, Fanny Ward and Sesue Hayakawa, the Japanese pantomimist.

The company, no longer struggling, was bulging with confidence inspired by large profits. In Hollywood there has been nothing quite as effective as profit in transforming businessmen into self-acknowledged artists overnight.

Fanny Ward was a Goldwyn "find," one of his first efforts at scouting creative talent. He sent her out to DeMille, who was not impressed with the newcomer and wired Goldwyn to that effect. Miss Ward stormed back to New York and showered some plain talk down on Mr. Goldwyn's head, which now had a set to it. He replied by offering her the leading role in *The Cheat*, and sent her back to the Coast. The air on the set was extravagantly cool, nor was it improved much by an accident in the course of the filming. Miss Ward, outfitted in costly ermine and a Parisian gown and hat, was padding lightly over a footbridge when it collapsed, chucking the graceful star into three feet of water. Miss Ward continued her stardom under other auspices; successful though it was, *The Cheat* was her only picture under the DeMille banner.

Though it was difficult, if not impossible, for a properly marketed picture to lose money in those days, DeMille was not one to take his responsibilities lightly. Even then he cast his stories only after much study of the demands of each part, a policy that conflicted horribly with the free-wheeling methods of the day. Players hired in the East were fired in the West. Eastern executives were denounced by western producers. Goldwyn was in the heart of a rich player market, New York itself, and was taking advantage of it. He sent out Marguerite Clark and Blanche Sweet, later Edna Goodrich and Thomas Meighan. Marguerite Clark starred in *The Goose Girl* and was in almost constant discord with her director, Fred Thompson. When Goldwyn wired DeMille to find out how the picture was faring he received the reply: DON'T KNOW MUCH ABOUT THE PLAY BUT THE GEESE LOOK GREAT. In the case of Meighan, DeMille took one look at the actor's first performance before the cameras and telephoned the verdict: "Tommy no good." Goldwyn was in San Francisco when he received this startling word and entrained for Los Angeles immediately to see that nothing happened to the actor's contract.

The tug-of-war between creative intellects in the West and business intellects in the East took curious turns. Taking a cue from D. W. Griffith's experiments with "effect lighting," DeMille borrowed a large lamp from the old Mason Opera House and directed it in such a manner that only one-half of the hero's face was visible, leaving the other half effectively in shadow. Excited over the dramatic effect, DeMille sent the picture to Goldwyn. A few days later came a frantic wire: CECIL, YOU'VE RUINED US. YOU'VE LIGHTED ONE-HALF THE ACTOR'S FACE AND THE EXHIBITORS WILL PAY ONLY HALF PRICE. DeMille, suffering the normal pangs of trail blazers, fumed over the predicament for hours, then suddenly was struck with an inspired reply to the Goldwyn complaint: IF YOU AND THE EXHIBITORS DON'T KNOW REMBRANDT LIGHTING IT IS NO FAULT OF MINE. And shortly a wire from Goldwyn: CECIL, YOU ARE WONDERFUL, REMBRANDT LIGHTING. THE EXHIBITORS WILL PAY DOUBLE.

3.

AN idea had been lurking in the mind of Cecil Blount DeMille for a long time. A "western" with Israelites instead of cowboys! Pioneers trekking westward was Hollywood's richest plot vein, and it did not matter much what the variations were—sheepherders plaguing cattlemen, Indians plaguing new settlements, bad white men plaguing good white men, the hard life vs. determined heroine fresh from big city, the countryside vs. "the dirty railroaders," and on, on and on.

If Brigham Young went West, DeMille reasoned, why not Moses? The people of Israel yearned for a land of hope, too, but on top of that escaped from the degrading cruelties of the Egyptians. Moses would provide *two* big dips of melodrama.

It was spring, 1923. The public was clamoring for spectacle on the screen. James Cruze had released *The Covered Wagon,* a biggie costing $800,000. In its sensational wake *Wagon* left behind one inescapable truth for DeMille—the world was ready for the brand of spectacle he long had dreamed of making. And now he had the format, an epic version of Moses and the flight from Egypt. Its title, *The Ten Commandments.* A different "western" and a spectacle in the same exciting package!

He tested the idea on a few minor officials. They were understandably startled.

It meant a Bible story of major proportions cast loose amid the risky shoals of the bubbling 1920's, an era of whims and high revelry.

It did not seem quite the time for a deeply religious theme.

DeMille was aware that Paramount had not invested in the Testaments Old or New, not on this scale, anyway. He went directly to Adoph Zukor, the mighty mite of Paramount, shrewd, tough-willed, 110 pounds of business agility. DeMille set forth his idea gently so as not to roil the little prexy.

For a moment it appeared a reaction might be stirred up second only to Bikini.

"The story of Moses! The Exodus!" Zukor flushed and slumped into his chair, an action capable of causing a man of his size to disappear from view. From the leathery depths came a moan of disbelief. "Old men wearing tablecloths and beards! Cecil, a picture like this would ruin us."

DeMille essayed the hope the studio would advance a budget in keeping with a project of this dimension.

"How much?", asked Zukor, stiffening.

"A million dollars," said DeMille.

If mere mention of the nature of the project had engulfed the executive, the new demand left him speechless.

Before Zukor could recover, DeMille was spewing arguments like an uncorked Vesuvius: Egypt . . . the glory of the Pharaohs . . . the children of Israel in bondage . . . thousands toiling in the desert under the grinding heel of slavery . . . Moses pleading for their liberation . . . Moses leading them forth . . . a nation on the march . . . men, women, children, animals . . . Pharaoh's war chariots in pursuit . . . the Israelites standing at the Red Sea . . . death in the waters or capture. . . .

His eyes were shining. "Think of it," he cried, "We'll be the first studio in history to open and close the Red Sea!"

Sunk in morose silence, Zukor came to life at this dreamy ejaculation. "Or maybe," he said, "the first director to open and close Paramount."

DeMille did not have in mind a religious picture in the usual sense. *The Ten Commandments* would be a story of sin and there would perforce be scenes showing plenty of sinning. This would give it "mass appeal," an elusive ingredient which somehow makes that which is artistic also profitable.

The orgy before the Golden Calf was planned as the key

scene. In preparing for it DeMille thumbtacked on his walls vivid sketches of dancing girls with undraped bosoms. Visitors learned that the costume designs were authentic Biblical art taken right out of the old masters. These samples of classical exposure may have eased front-office tension a little, but Paramount had its fingers stoutly crossed: a religious argosy in times of sex and bootleg booze had a suicidal ring about it.

DeMille ordered 3,000 costumes of ancient design and $18,000 worth of harness for the horses which would draw three hundred war chariots of the Pharaoh. This, according to DeMille publicists, was "the largest order for chariots in 1,700 years." For the Pharaoh, who would drive the lead chariot in the big pursuit scene, DeMille required something more than ordinary horseflesh. He paid $5,000 for a pair of black thoroughbreds found in Kansas City after a considerable search.

A hundred dancing girls went to work at the studio on routines for the Calf of Gold revel. Meanwhile, a vivacious globe-trotter named Florence Meehan was dispatched to the Middle East with authority to buy up jewelry and costumes of the correct vintage. Miss Meehan's shipments filled a studio storage room—silks, swords, tiger skins, tapestries, earrings, embossed plates, rubies from the famous mine at Magot, Burma, and a 1,000-year-old suit of Persian armor, and numberless geegaws for dressing the sets.

DeMille called in a casting director and told him he wanted 225 orthodox Jewish persons. "I don't want them to be able to speak a word of English."

The man looked a little uncertain; where would he get them?

"I don't care, that's your problem," said DeMille. "Palestine, Turkey, Russia. I want 'em to chant like their ancestors, like in Moses' time."

Advertisements with these specifications appeared in the daily press, and a booth was set up in a vacant lot at the edge of downtown Los Angeles. The harried casting director got his quota after much wrangling with swarms of applicants, and daily needling from policemen for tying up traffic in the area. Included in the haul were several Yemenites from one of the most primitive branches of Hebraic stock. They were visitors in the city and agreed to prolong their stay indefinitely for a chance to appear in a story about Moses.

It was in the midst of these preparations that DeMille was struck by the necessity of a $25,000 organ for his ranch, Paradise. The porch skirted two sides of the house, at two points dipping around the trunks of huge oaks rising unmolested through holes in the floor. The thought of organ music floating out to guests dining under the oaken boughs sent him on the trail of the organ. *The Ten Commandments* made the whole idea plausible; he contracted with the studio for its use in composing the music for the picture. The proceeds from this arrangement enabled him to defray a good part of the cost, apart from providing the composers with a haven far removed from the vulgar lay atmosphere of Hollywood.

As a location for filming the Biblical half of the story (the other half has a modern setting in San Francisco), DeMille chose barren sand dunes near Guadalupe, some 200 miles from Los Angeles, a rolling waste swept by strong winds from the nearby Pacific. Much deliberation at the scene took place before Guadalupe was chosen. DeMille and his staff paced the length of the dunes to determine whether they were long enough for the proposed line of escape of the Israelites. Once he shouted to an assistant, startling sun bathers, "We'll bring Moses and his followers down to this spot and head 'em into the ocean here."

In May 1923, he led 3,500 people and 6,000 animals to Guadalupe. The throng cast its eyes on a strange sight. Before them, standing with grotesque complacence on the desert wasteland, was a replica of a segment of the ancient temple of Rameses II. The great entrance was approached by an avenue of twenty-four sphinxes, each weighing four tons. Off to the right lay the encampment, row on row of pup tents. The tent city would house, feed and entertain the players during those off-the-set moments when the Israelites were not praying plagues down on the heads of their oppressors. The nerve center was the DeMille tent, sitting Monticello-like atop a knoll, furnished in grand Egyptian style with oriental rugs and a huge bed with snake-head posters. As one of the star actresses in the cast, Julia Faye, recalled, "He was up there all by himself. We were all living in the city down below. I guess it did give him a feeling of everything."

The camp was run on a strict military basis. Reveille was sounded at 4:30. Players dressed and put on their make-up before breakfast at 6 A.M. The population was broken into companies and platoons, with a captain and lieutenant in charge of each. The chain of command went from these minor functionaries to a score of assistant directors, and ended with DeMille. He was not so much the final arbiter as the only one. Important players like Theodore Roberts, Charles de Roche, Estelle Taylor and Julia Faye went directly to him with their problems, though entree to DeMille's tent was not easily achieved, even by the stars. On one occasion Roberts in flowing robes of the patriarchal Moses, and James Neill, garbed as Aaron, cooled their heels outside the tent for more than an hour. Finally the patience of the bearded patriarch broke. Rising to his full imposing height, Neill collared a perspiring slave about to enter the producer's tent and bellowed, "Tell God that Moses and Aaron are waiting without!"

In the matter of expenditures, DeMille had gotten up a fine head of steam; bills poured into the studio. Thrice daily, the producer was feeding nearly 10,000 mouths—3,500 human, 6,000 animal. Among the latter were some healthy appetites, including 900 horses and 200 burros, as well as a Noah's Ark assortment of small farm animals and fowl which could not be expected to scratch much nourishment from the sand dunes. With this picture, as with others, DeMille rarely took time off to placate the studio brass. "God save me from the tyranny of the executive mind" was, in variable form, a pet motto.

Generally, what information the executives were able to eke out resulted from informal spying or quizzing a DeMille subordinate. They watched the requisitions flow into the studio from the sand dunes. One was especially irksome; it set forth food requirements for a *single day:* 750 pounds of sugar, 50 pounds of coffee and tea, 4,000 eggs, 900 pounds of butter, 1,500 pounds of meat, 150 gallons of canned fruit. . . .

The $5,000 paid out for the span of black stallions for the Pharaoh's chariot was almost the final indignity.

An angry executive waved the invoice in DeMille's face.

"Are you trying to ruin us? You have spent a million dollars and the picture is only half finished!"

At this time Zukor, Jesse Lasky and DeMille each were drawing $3,500 weekly from the firm, Famous Players-Lasky. Zukor and Lasky shared also in the firm's profits, an exclusion that nettled DeMille.

DeMille's attorney, Neil McCarthy, went to see Zukor, who greeted the visitor with something less than a faint smile.

"Cecil is trying to break us," said Zukor, adding bitterly, "Religious pictures! Long dresses on men!"

"Will you sell the picture?" McCarthy asked.

Zukor was not unprepared for this shift. "My god, can you get me the money? I'll sell it at cost, one million dollars."

Both knew there was nothing binding at that point. McCarthy was interested in knowing just how wrought up Zukor was over the venture, and Zukor was intent on finding out just what would prompt a man to pay one million dollars for a half-finished picture.

DeMille now faced the task of raising a million dollars. He sent McCarthy to see Joe Schenck, the 20th Century-Fox board chairman. Schenck put up $250,000. DeMille visited a short time with the raw-film magnate, Jules Brulatour, and emerged with another $250,000 pledge. So far, so good, but the last half-million is always the toughest.

There was good reason to believe that they might get an attentive ear in at least one quarter—the most powerful banking interest in America, ruled over by the legendary Giannini family.

Indeed, DeMille boasted a close relationship with Papa Giannini, the famed "A.P."

It dated back several years when DeMille undertook what turned out to be a ticklish part-time job—running a bank's movie-loan department! Putting a film producer in the position of making loans to other film producers might appear to be the act of a deranged mind, but it was in truth a shrewd move—when one considered the fiber of a man like DeMille.

Moreover, the banks at the time, 1915-20, put "the movie crowd" in a bracket not far removed from counterfeiters. Loan officers had a standing order, "Watch out for those movie producers." In some banks, a request for a movie loan caused a stir comparable to a hold-up alarm.

The turning point in this attitude came quickly enough; word got about that some of the studios were handling two or three million dollars quarterly. It struck financiers as a lot of money to be circulating without the customary 6 per cent participation on their part.

The Commercial National Bank set up a motion picture branch at the corner of Cherokee and Hollywood. They placed DeMille in charge of loans, the first such arrangement in Hollywood banking circles. It fixed on the youthful producer the awesome responsibility of deciding which film maker was "good for a loan," a position not likely to widen his circle of producer friends. They gave him a brass plate bearing his name, and authorized him also to sign $10 bills, U. S. currency, a privilege which he always regarded as one of the most delightful of his life. "It gave me a wonderful Comptroller of the Currency feeling," he said, adding, "In time it gave rise to a nasty rumor that DeMille has the first dollar he ever signed."

Eventually, the Commercial National was taken over by the Bank of America, then the Bank of Italy, which was owned by the Gianninis. Papa Giannini had begun to build his chain-bank empire, based on the premise that at every intersection where there were two filling stations there should be one bank.

Analyzing the Commercial National's movie-loan policies, the Gianninis shuddered. They were almost savagely opposed to loans without collateral; money on a house or motorcar—something that the bank could reach out and touch—that was one thing, but handing out money on intangibles like movie scenarios or a producer's reputation!

The rules tightened. Giannini told DeMille that all *unreasonable* movie loans would be his, DeMille's, personal liability, and he, Giannini, would decide what constituted an unreasonable loan.

Those who were not able to get money out of the Commercial National agreed the situation had worsened, but not much. DeMille continued to dole out loans sparingly. The Gianninis soon saw his judgment was a good thing to have around a bank. DeMille had an admirable respect for other people's money, plus a sixth sense for sizing up an applicant. DeMille's lawyer once remarked that Cecil "could tell by the lines in a man's face if his credit was any good."

During his relatively brief banking career, none of his decisions backfired. And only one threw him into serious combat with the explosive, hard-fisted A.P. It arose out of a $200,000 loan to Sam Goldwyn, made some time after Goldwyn had resigned from the Lasky firm.

A.P. had turned down Goldwyn's application for a loan.

DeMille knew this but okayed it anyway.

In a few days he received a summons to appear in A.P.'s executive offices in San Francisco. DeMille by now was achieving something of a reputation of his own as a combatant in the film wars, capable of rendering worthy opponents *hors de combat*. Nevertheless, he was aware he was entering the den of a seasoned warrior. For a moment A.P.'s manner was unctuous.

"You knew I refused that loan."

"Yes," said DeMille.

"Then why did you give it?" roared A.P.

"Sam is a great producer, that's why." Then yelling back, "Now just a minute. If I'm just window dressing for your bank in Los Angeles I'm going to resign. If I stay I'm going to make a noise like a bank official!"

A.P. told him to calm down. "You're no figurehead," he said, obviously relishing DeMille's boldness.

Goldwyn got the $200,000, promptly paid the loan and the interest.

Even with this past relationship, DeMille could not be sure he had the right to expect the Bank of America to advance him a half-million dollars in his present situation. He would be asking Giannini to pledge this sum of money in circumstances riddled with controversy, on a picture—as *The Ten Commandments* was—badly crippled and only partly finished.

Also, he was aware of Giannini's ever vigilant sense of economy, as well as his cautious attitude toward film people.

There was one mildly favorable factor: McCarthy had known Giannini before his banking days, having acted as counsel for him when the family was in the vegetable business. McCarthy also helped A.P. buy banks.

It was decided that McCarthy would stalk the financial wizard.

The lawyer decided his approach would be quick and blunt.

"I want a half million dollars," McCarthy said, girding himself for a Giannini thunderclap.

"Have you prepared a statement?" asked the banker, eyes cold as marble.

"I haven't got time. It would take a month."

"Is the company good for it?"

"It's DeMille," said McCarthy, playing his trump card.

Giannini's manner relaxed instantly.

"You can have twice as much as any statement will justify. I know DeMille."

This accomplished, McCarthy sent a wire to Zukor in New York: MILLION DOLLARS IS IN BANK OF AMERICA, 7TH AND OLIVE. PLEASE SEND BILL OF SALE AT ONCE.

Twenty-four hours passed, and no word from Zukor. Whereupon DeMille went to Lasky. Frank Garbutt, a Paramount board member, was with him. DeMille removed a check from an envelope and placed it on Lasky's desk.

"There's your money," said DeMille. "One million dollars. Take it and the picture is mine."

DeMille's recollections of the occasion were always accompanied by a big owlish grin. "Lasky couldn't believe we had raised the money. He called up Zukor in New York, and pretty soon there was quite a conversation going on. Garbutt was sitting there saying nothing. Lasky looked at him, expecting him to say something and pretty soon Garbutt did. He said, 'Jesse, have you seen any of the film Cecil has shot?' Lasky said no, and Garbutt said, 'Jesse, never sell anything you haven't seen.' Lasky repeated this remark to Zukor on the phone and it was all over. They wouldn't sell."

Zukor made one more move, attesting to a high financial acumen that has distinguished his long career in motion pictures. He had McCarthy's telegram, which expressed one million dollars' worth of confidence in a Paramount picture, and an unfinished one at that. He went to the bankers who had been shying away of late from granting the studio any loans for new products. Zukor twitted them for their lack of faith in his firm, then flourished the telegram. The bankers were impressed; Zukor got his loan.

DeMille was up to something else that worried the partners —his flying around in airplanes. In the early 20's a nonmilitary flight was considered as silly and dangerous as a lunar flight today. DeMille had learned flying from the best stunt man of the day, Al Wilson. Wilson owned an old discarded Curtiss biplane, unusable by anyone except the extraordinarily brave.

On the day DeMille showed up for his first lesson Wilson was working frantically trying to get the rickety crate aloft, sensing a fare. After several hours, Wilson pleaded with the young man to return tomorrow. DeMille did return, but the Curtiss wouldn't start that day either.

Wilson heard about a Jenny that had crashed in Canada, killing its owner. He contacted the widow, who asked $5,000.

Wilson went to DeMille with a proposition. "Tell you what. You put up the money and I'll fix the plane. We'll go into the aviation business. I'll carry passengers and do exhibition work, and we'll split fifty-fifty. And you'll have a good plane to learn to fly in."

DeMille never missed a lesson. He took time off from his movie work to buzz around the field, now part of Wilshire Boulevard's present Miracle Mile section.

Soon Wilson was taking Hollywoodians up at $10 a trip, $25 if the passenger wanted a tailspin or nose dive. The charge for a full course was $500. The partners took in as much as $750 a week.

A few months later, DeMille and Wilson formed the Mercury Aviation Company which, according to its owners, was the first airline in America to carry passengers for hire between Los Angeles and San Diego, about 1920.

In a lead editorial that year, Hearst's L.A. *Examiner* praised DeMille "for his enterprise in bringing to this city a fleet of all-metal aeroplanes." It urged Los Angeles to take note of this new industry and "quickly prepare to get into the game."

When DeMille began flying for pleasure, his nonflying associates, Adolph Zukor and Jesse Lasky, came frequently out to the grounds. Glumly they stood side by side, their heads tracing a slow circle as they watched the course of the frail plane.

Lasky and Zukor reflected on what would happen to their picture investment should one of the wings snap off.

"One hundred thousand dollars flying around up there without a parachute," moaned Lasky. Jouncing to a stop, DeMille tried to taunt his partners into taking a ride but received only horrified looks. The studio was greatly relieved when the aviation company, feeling growing competition at a time when it was getting less and less of DeMille's attention, gave up to its creditors holding claims totaling $300,000.

4.

THE studio couldn't have picked a worse time to badger DeMille over costs. The producer was working his own miracles in directing, mothering and policing the biggest location in the industry's experience. Riding personal herd on his many charges, DeMille had troubles enough without the studio sniping from the rear. DeMille's willingness to pay a fortune for the picture sharply overhauled executive attitudes, and the entire venture took on a much rosier hue.

For everyone, that is, except DeMille.

With every Biblical picture, he faced unusual risks. Not the least was scandal. One breath would cripple his venture at the very start. It was a daily specter, what with columnists conning the grounds for little morsels. "Aaron and Pharaoh's wife were seen in an arm-in-arm stroll along the beach," one gossip columnist quipped.

Guadalupe was cursed with biting offshore winds and sand that stung and annoyed the players. Many wore veils to protect make-up. The netting cramped Theodore Roberts' cigar smoking, so he cut a hole in the veil and moved contentedly among his people, a magnificent figure in flowing robes trailed by an acrid plume of black smoke. One day a clipping reached DeMille with a headline, MOSES SMOKES BLACK CIGARS, and a story chiding Roberts for adding something new to the Inspired Word. DeMille thrust the clipping into the hands of an assistant and dispatched him to Roberts' tent with the stern imprecation, "Tell Moses to cut out that goddamn nicotine in public!" It was the custom on DeMille's set to refer to players by their cast names to help to instill the feeling that they were not *playing* the character, they *were* the character.

DeMille took every practical step to prevent any naughty behavior at Guadalupe that might reach the newspapers and harm his costly sally into austere Old Testament times. He let the cast know that if there was any sinning he wanted it done in front of the camera, not behind it.

The tent city was laid out in streets with a sort of plaza in the middle. The men were quartered on one side and the women on the other. Thirty men were deputized by DeMille into what came to be known as the Sex Squad, with instructions to report any mischief, however innocent it might appear. No man and woman were permitted to be seen together after 7 P.M., except at the recreation tent.

This social center was known as "Pop's Place." There, every night, tent flaps shuddered and tent poles trembled under the non-Hebraic blasts of a four-piece jazz band. Held at bay all day, the players cut loose at night, shifting from ancient wails to modern ditties. Only serious illness was warrant for a man to cross the line into the women's part of the town. When Theodore Roberts fell ill, Mrs. Roberts was summoned by telegraph. "She wasn't allowed at first to visit me," Roberts recalled, "until they thought I might die of pneumonia, and then I was removed to a hospital."

Aware of the appeal of the moon on the Pacific, DeMille's deputies patrolled the beach area for questionable behavior not called for in the script. It did not appear that any sandy sybarites were taken into custody, but several raids were made on necking bouts of very high amperage. No distinctions were made, young swains honorably bent on a salt-sprayed romance were ordered to break it up.

All problems, however small, claimed DeMille's attention. His tirelessness was readily seen in his reluctance to transfer the right of final approval to other shoulders. It was a rare moment during production when a queue of nervous servitors did not trail off from his office door, dutifully lined up for the moment of inquisition.

This deep wellspring of energy was pressed to somewhere near capacity during the desert bivouac of *The Ten Commandments.* The toughest scene in the picture from a director's standpoint was the pursuit by Pharaoh's war chariots. It required mass movement, in addition to speed and turbulence, an episode combining the more vigorous moments of Ben Hur and the charge of the Valkyries. There were some 300 drivers in the scene, the opening shot calling for a plunge by six chariots over a 200-foot embankment. The helmeted Egyptians (actually cowboys from San Jose) were going about the affair in a prudent manner. They took the precipitous slope at a speed that would meet traffic safety standards anywhere, but not DeMille's. He went into a bitter and choleric rage with each rehearsal. "Don't you people understand? The Egyptians were making a death drive here." The phrase sank deeper than DeMille had intended. The cowboys shook their heads. Too risky.

DeMille's eye caught his daughter, twelve-year-old Cecelia, who had been charging across the desert on her young roan. "Show them how you do it, sweetie," said DeMille. The pretty redhead rode briskly to the top of the grading, turned and urged her mount down the hill at a full gallop. The crowd cheered as the sand flew from dangerous furrows. The cow hands skulking at the fringes returned gingerly to their chariots.

Best loved among the camp's apostles was an elongated Negro lad named Sam. He played the role of one of Pharaoh's Nubian slaves. His reverence for DeMille took on almost operatic proportions. Each morning Sam greeted DeMille outside the latter's tent with a low bow. To all inquiries regarding his part in the picture he replied, "Workin' for Mistah DeMille." Once he was pressed as to the exact nature of the part. "Ah don't know but my name is Nubian," he said.

When the time came DeMille personally coached Sam for his big scene.

"You see, Sam, you're tired. It's very quiet and you're lying here dozing." Sam grinned approvingly.

"And then," DeMille continued, "a lion comes up and licks the soles of your feet."

Sam sat upright. For the first time his eyes lost that glaze of ritualistic affection for the producer.

"All right, let's try it," said DeMille brusquely.

But Sam was no longer in the vicinity, last observed shuffling across the sand dunes toward Los Angeles, loincloth and all. Stung by the defection, DeMille delayed the scene until a braver, even though less affectionate, substitute could be found.

Among the Yemenites was one who repeatedly approached DeMille on matters of canonical propriety. He would object to certain rituals, saying they were in conflict with the Torah. And each time the solemn Yemenite indicated he was willing to straighten out the script on these points. Lacking time for academic discussion, DeMille made him a technical advisor, thus adding to his rate of pay. A studio interpreter was assigned to the man and was told to make the same reply, no matter what the complaint: "Mr. DeMille understands and thanks you. He will give your proposal serious study." Under this courteous treatment the Yemenite enjoyed himself immensely the remainder of the time.

DeMille suffered less from calculated risks than from minor oversights, despite the fact he mounted his productions on a tremendous framework. The script called for a scene showing Israelites walking along a stretch of beach. This would appear in the picture as the path over which they escaped through the Red Sea. It had to be shot exactly at high noon in order that there would be no shadows on the ground. A few minutes before noon someone made a startling discovery, the beach was dry! If the waters had parted for the fugitives, the river bed would be wet. Faced with a day's delay DeMille charged up and down yelling, "I'll give any one a hundred dollars who can tell me how to get water on this beach!" From the crowd a voice called, "Kelp!" The cry of "kelp" filled the air and several hands made toward the water. The Israelites abandoned their animals and children, rushed into the Pacific, groping under the water for the tangled weed. Long skeins of kelp were strewn over the beach and the Israelites, bedraggled and now exhausted, re-formed their line in front of their camera. "A double triumph," beamed DeMille. "For the first time they look like refugees."

Three hundred soldiers of the 11th U. S. Cavalry had been borrowed from the camp at Monterey to man the chariots in the big pursuit scene, brightly garbed in short-skirted yellow tunics and gilded helmets. To inspire martial fervor, an orchestra composed largely of women was on hand, stationed on a platform near the line of march and protected from the flying sand by a thin wall propped up by boards. Having briefed the soldiers on the necessity of charging "like hell after the Israelites," DeMille signaled for action. The column was mov-

ing swiftly when an accident occurred among the front chari-
oteers, telescoping the charge into a wild melee of rearing
horses and overturned chariots. Horses tugged frantically at
their harness, inflicting painful kicks on several drivers. Some
of the animals, goaded by their injuries, broke for the desert,
their ripped flanks flapping in the breeze like red bandanas.
The pair of $5,000 black stallions were lamed. Two chariots
locked in unexpected combat careened into the wall protecting
the musicians, and sent the terror-stricken girls screaming from
the platform.

To DeMille, who might be forgiven an artist's delight in the
occasion, it was a scene of admirable fury. He sympathized
with, and congratulated, the injured, offering as a solatium
the prospect that the scene would make them heroes overnight.
The episode was used in the picture to dramatize the fate of the
Egyptians when stopped from further advance by a pillar of
flame. Nasty rumors were heard. One was published in a daily
to the effect that the accident was planned, on the basis of a
report that someone saw axles that were partly sawed, but these
stories were blandly ignored by the producer.

The studio fussed a good deal over an approach to publicize
the picture. It feared the public might shy away from it under
the impression it was deeply religious, whereas in truth under
DeMille's hand it roared with action. DeMille had not yet
achieved fame as a muezzin on the stucco parapets of Hollywood. "Let the Old Testament speak for itself," he advised,
and then went out and told the press, "The Ten Commandments are strong meat and I am going to present them as strong
meat."

He had hewed closely to the Bible and felt he had little to
fear from the censors, although he was convinced no one was
ever safe from censors. A ban on *The Ten Commandments*
would amount to an attack on the Book of Exodus; however,
he was taking no chances. In a wire-service story he made it

plain he was ready for the opposition. "The censors may disagree with me. If they do they will have to disagree with
Scripture. . . . I shall be curious to see which of the Ten Commandments will be tagged as unfit by them. . . . You know the
original revel around the Golden Calf was no censorship party."

He had filmed a robust story, perhaps even patriarchal. Certain happenings during production puzzled him. Could they
be construed as signs of approval from on high? If this was
true, the Divine Will could thereby be substituted for the
censors' will, and thus place the censors in the unenviable
position of attacking *both* DeMille and Divine Providence.

After telling reporters in San Francisco he had approached
his task "with great reverence," he said he was hard put to
explain some things that occurred during the making of *The
Ten Commandments;* they did not seem to belong to the earthly
realm.

"When Theodore Roberts was in the middle of the scene
opening the Red Sea, a sudden shaft of light broke through the
clouds and illuminated him like a halo. The multitude saw
this. They were lifted to great heights, and gave me a performance that no ordinary situation could have ever produced."

Then there was the time when his cameras were focused on
the faces of a crowd of sightseers outside a church. "We wanted
to get an expression of reverence on their faces, but were having no luck. Then suddenly a bell tolled in a distance, announcing a funeral. Hats came off. Silence settled on all. Many crossed
themselves and we got an absolutely perfect scene."

He pointed out he was not given to religious hysteria, adding
soberly, "At Guadalupe we finished in two weeks what we
did not think it possible to do in less than a month."

The mystic revelations prompted scores of letters. The more
deeply religious chided DeMille for not coming out and calling
the unusual incidents by their right names, that is, miracles.
The letters were placed in a special file and casually produced
at later interviews, without comment, leaving the guests to de-

cide to what extent, if any, he had had the benefit of divine guidance.

His measure as a showman revealed itself; every incident at Guadalupe reached the desks of film editors over the country. He instructed his publicists to do something with the fact he was the first to re-enact the celebrated escape from the Egyptian hordes. Ward Marsh of the Cleveland *Plain Dealer,* the elder statesman of film critics, went along with the boast, adding, "DeMille was not only the first man to divide the Red Sea in films, he was the first to do it singlehanded: Moses had outside help."

The Ten Commandments was a Christmas offering on Broadway, opening December 21, 1923. It ran for sixty-two weeks, exceeding the fifty-nine weeks played there by Cruze's *The Covered Wagon* and the forty-four weeks of D. W. Griffith's *The Birth of a Nation.*

A miracle perhaps more noteworthy than any presumed at Guadalupe now occurred. The picture received a favorable review from Robert E. Sherwood, then film critic for the old humor magazine, *Life* (absorbed by *Time* in 1936). Apologetically, Sherwood wrote he had long realized that sooner or later the day would come when he would have to utter praise for a Cecil B. DeMille picture. "Even though DeMille has mutilated the works of many writers—from James Matthew Barrie to Alice Duer Miller," Sherwood felt that this time the producer displayed "commendable originality." Some of DeMille's biggest money-makers were unmercifully riddled by the critics, so at word of this astonishing development DeMille pursed his lips: "This means one thing, *The Ten Commandments* could be a failure!"

Will Rogers saw the picture with a friend, who commented enthusiastically on the Biblical episodes, touching off one of Will's better remembered ripostes: "It's easy to see where God left off and Cecil DeMille began."

The final cost of the production was $1,475,836. In 1930, after seven years of playing, its world gross receipts totaled $4,154,318. That meant, spectacularly, a profit close to two million dollars.

5.

DESPITE the virtually assured success of *The Ten Commandments*, there was a severe rupture in the relationship between DeMille and his associates, Zukor and Lasky. Rumors of an impending break spread through Hollywood; the studio countered with statements about complete harmony, that De-Mille had signed "a lifelong contract" pledging the remainder of his professional days to Paramount.

The flag-waving was barely over when DeMille stepped out of Paramount, taking his brother Bill with him.

He had never made a picture for any other company, and now faced the painful task of shaking off sentimental ties that had formed in those ten years. Fights with executives did not lessen his affection for the studio, which owed to him something of its start in life and much of its growth.

On an occasion I asked DeMille about his breakup with Para-mount; there had been many conflicting stories. As always, when in deep contemplation, he fell to touching a tooth with the tip of each finger, in quick succession; he was silent for some time. "I was fired in the middle of *The Ten Command-ments*. My contract was ended right there and then. When they decided against selling the picture to me, I finished it without a contract. They saw the picture in its final form and they knew it was going to be a big hit. Then we got to talking about terms of my contract. Well, it was a little different then. I was in a somewhat better bargaining position. I can remember standing there in the front office and I had told the gentleman behind the desk what terms I would have to have on *The Ten Commandments*. He looked at me, his eyes were sharp as steel. I can still remember what he said as I left the office: 'Cecil, you have never been one of us. If you do this I will break you.' And his two fists came apart sharply like a man breaking a stick."

DeMille did not budge from his demands. When he walked out of Paramount he held a lucrative interest in the picture, about the only thing he could claim as his own out of a world organization which he had watched grow from a barn in a lemon grove.

The Ten Commandments had opened brilliantly, but it would be a long time before the studio would realize anything on its investment. DeMille's final three pictures before leaving Paramount, *Triumph* ($265,012), *Feet of Clay* ($315,636) and *The Golden Bed* ($437,900), returned the studio a mere pittance as major productions went. And they had featured some of the studio's most important stars: Vera Reynolds, Leatrice Joy, Rod LaRocque, Lillian Rich.

The secession of DeMille caused little apparent sorrow within the officialdom of Famous Players-Lasky. A wicked swipe was made at the departed producer at a luncheon for exhibitors on a Monday in April 1926. An 11-reel trailer was shown the guests. What was contained in the trailer provoked *Harrison's Reports*, a film trade publication, into an indignant headline: LET THEM HIDE THEIR FACES IN SHAME. The trade paper went on to say:

> At the end of the trailer there was a little playlet; it consisted of the showing of a dinner table, with vacant chairs arranged around it. On each chair appeared the name of a Paramount director.

In the skit, Ford Sterling represented the Famous Players-Lasky Company. At each chair the actor paused and made brief comments to a companion, Marshall Neilan, in the role of a prodigal son returning to the Paramount fold.

> The last chair bore the name of Mr. Cecil B. DeMille. In addition, however, it had a wreath with red leaves, such as are being used on coffins. . . . The prodigal son asked where DeMille was. "Ah, he went down to the road of yesterday." *. . . Al Harston, an exhibitor, could not stand it; he yelled: "That's lousy! It is too dirty! Take it out!"

In the merger between the Lasky Company and Zukor's Famous Players, DeMille had felt insecure in his position as Director-General, and he had resented attempts by fellow executives and money backers to restrict his choice of stories. As early as 1918 he was talking with various persons about forming his own organization to produce pictures independently, and reap the profits undivided.

Adoph Zukor was busy too. He widened the power of Famous Players-Lasky, soon would change its name to Paramount. He had set the partnership on an equal-division-of-profit basis, among himself as president, Goldwyn as chairman of the board, DeMille as director-general, and Lasky as vice-president.

Zukor, a very short, spare man, kept the closest kind of watch on company affairs. His size was not a measure of his power, nor of the deference accorded that power. He was at his huge desk in his plush Paramount Building offices in New York one afternoon when an irate woman confronted him. "Mr. Zukor, when I enter an office I am accustomed to having the gentleman stand up." Whereupon the diminutive prexy replied, "But, madam, I *am* standing."

Zukor was not happy with Goldwyn's methods from the start.

---

* DeMille's first picture following his departure from Paramount was *The Road to Yesterday*.

He couldn't understand why Sam refused to behave as he felt a team man should. "Every hour on the hour, and sometimes the half-hour, Sam Goldwyn sent a shock through the organization," Zukor relates, "and kept things whirling in what amounted to a frenzy."

Goldwyn's forceful approach continued to grate on Zukor, convinced that Sam disagreed with him many times "only for the sake of argument."

Zukor made up his mind that if Goldwyn did not go, he would. "One of us was out of water in Famous Players-Lasky," he put it recently.

It was not easy to broach the matter to Lasky, who was Sam's brother-in-law. Zukor called DeMille to New York, told both Lasky and DeMille they would have to choose between himself and Sam, one or the other. They chose Zukor. Goldwyn left with a substantial settlement for his quarter interest in the company—a little under a million dollars, according to Zukor— after four years in the business. Even with DeMille and Lasky still in the picture, little remained of Lasky company policies.

The feeling between Zukor and DeMille was considerably more mutual—*neither* could understand the other's thinking. Soon DeMille would leave, and eventually Lasky.

Zukor, little Napoleon of the conference table, was gobbling up some titans.

DeMille took an initial step in August 1920. He formed, at first as a partnership, Cecil B. DeMille Productions, Inc., with himself, Mrs. DeMille, his attorney Neil McCarthy, and a relative of Mrs. DeMille as partners. The corporation agreed to pay Cecil $1,500 a week to retain his services as a director. Then, it would "sell" Cecil as a director to producing companies under agreements which entitled it to guarantees, plus a percentage of profits from pictures directed by DeMille.

It was, roughly, the kind of contract favored by the DeMille company for many years.

The aim of the four partners was to accumulate a fund of $4 million with which some day to finance their own pictures.

The break with Zukor was bitter, and surprising to Hollywood, long accustomed to rumors of feuding between the old associates.

DeMille knew it might be costly; Paramount controlled a lot of theaters around the country and consequences would be disastrous should Zukor decide to bar the theaters to future DeMille pictures.

In the spring of 1925, DeMille went into business for himself. He contracted an alliance with powerful New York interests and set up production facilities at the old Thomas H. Ince lot in Culver City, an aggressive little community between Los Angeles and the ocean. The town greeted him with a band and dancing in the streets. A holiday was declared on the day of the studio's formal opening. Under the banner Producers Distributing Corporation, DeMille was both artist and executive, a new role for him. He hired directors and doled out stories for them to film, and gathered a stable of important stars.

Part III

MATTHEW, MARK, LUKE, JOHN—
AND CECIL

1.

IN the move to his own studio, fate assigned DeMille a unique mission. He came under the influence of Jeremiah Milbank.

Milbank's distaste for publicity went as deep as DeMille's reliance upon it. The New York financier was extremely spiritual, a curiosity in a land of revelry.

From this association came the shining jewel of DeMille's career, *The King of Kings.*

Though universally acclaimed as Cecil B. DeMille's *King of Kings,* a proper enough designation, the picture owed an enormous debt to the quiet fervor of Milbank. Because Milbank somehow managed to keep out of the Hollywood columns, it was known by few that his money was behind the venture. Today the narrative of the Christ life is still his property, handled by the Milbank-owned Cinema Corporation of Paterson, New Jersey, a firm whose chief function is to guide this remarkable film in its admission-free odyssey over the world.

The stage was set. DeMille had displayed marvelous prescience. *The Ten Commandments,* he had been told, would probably destroy the studio. It did not; on the contrary it made an outstanding profit. Having quelled the suicidal cries of his associates, his judgment in matters Biblical now took the shape of something to be revered and sought after. He had made costume drama pay off at a time when few producers would risk their money even on "safer" pictures of later vintage. He had injected into a Biblical picture a very elusive quality called "popular appeal"—an evanescent term used on every Hollywood level. Many a producer has said to the front office, and many a front office has said to a producer, "This is a great picture. This the people will love," and often the people have not loved it. It therefore became a mysterious casualty, a great picture that somehow was rejected by the public.

Popular response to *The Ten Commandments* established DeMille's reputation as a combination soothsayer and miracle man. He had played equal amounts of sex, religion and spectacle against a Biblical background, a "western" set to Old Testament. The formula was to be with him always—the fate of a nation or a way of life hanging on the outcome of a conflict between powerful individuals, one good, the other bad.

The story of the Christ would not fit into DeMille's plot formula of sexual sound and historical fury. That was pretty plain to all hands from the very start and it was only a matter of time until one would surrender, the New Testament or DeMille. He told his scenarist, the late Jeanie Macpherson, that he wanted "a story of Christ with popular appeal," indicating the Gospels of Matthew, Mark, Luke and John lacked "boxoffice." This deficiency could not be charged against the authors, it must be charitably acknowledged, inasmuch as they were not writing with Hollywood in mind.

It was shaping up as quite a battle, DeMille vs. the Inspired Word. Maybe there could be a compromise, namely, retain the original and at the same time weave in Hollywood's concept of popular appeal, which it was now decided the Gospels lacked. At first DeMille thought of dividing *The King of Kings* into two parts (as in *The Ten Commandments*): the first part would be the Christ story, the second would be strictly modern, thus permitting a byplay of sin and razzmatazz. The sin and razzmatazz would deliver a shattering sermon to those who ignored the Savior's admonitions, as set forth in the first part of the story.

On this basis, then, the story conferences went forward. As they talked, wrote, and talked some more, the Savior half of the story got stronger, the modern part weaker. Finally, as if the Christ had broken from their grasp, the decision was made to devote the entire screenplay to the Gospels. The modern epilogue was abandoned.

This decision was received jubilantly by the St. Louis Jesuit, Dan Lord, who had been consulting with the producer from the start. Still, the battle was not yet entirely won. While the Scripture had a strong hold on DeMille, it had not yet pinned him down.

Something quite fascinating occurred to DeMille. The character of Mary Magdalene! She had the same old weakness, part and parcel of the DeMille formula, and here it was right in the Scriptures waiting for him to utilize it in the most effective way possible. Yes, the sinner of Magdala should be made use of *before* her repentance set in.

Here, DeMille turned his attention to Judas, the Christ betrayer. Wait! Is it not true the Bible is silent on Judas' love life? He must have had one; a chap who would betray the Savior of Mankind for thirty pieces of silver no doubt had other interesting vices.

DeMille eagerly supplied a few details.

First, why did Judas betray Christ? For money! Well, perhaps, but it was a trifling amount for so heinous a deed! No, there had to be something else—a woman's love! Unquestionably, a woman's love.

The woman? None other than Mary Magdalene, of virtue both easy and ruthless! The she-devil who lured men to her palace in Magdala, city of pleasure, where, no doubt, she played sweet music and anesthetized her clients with the wines of Chios and Lesbos.

The rest of this part of the story was easy. One day Mary Magdalene meets Judas, and he has nothing but eyes for this luscious dame. He wants her but she's an expensive item, and he must have money. He sees in Christ a chance to improve upon his personal fortunes. But before he realizes it, Magdalene accepts Christ, and her character begins to change as she turns away from Judas.

Judas resents this. He grows to hate "the simple carpenter" and one day soon he would play his trump card—betray Christ for a fee.

"My heart sank at the possibilities of this plot," Dan Lord recalled in his memoirs years later.

DeMille had turned to Mary Magdalene with joyful fury. He converted her into a perfumed and silken seductress, "gorgeously dressed by four slave girls." A velvet cape swirled piquantly over her bare white shoulders, hiding none too successfully a jewel-studded bra, as she rides off in a chariot drawn by six zebras to follow the lowly carpenter of Nazareth.

Hollywood watched the struggle between DeMille and the Evangelists with lively interest. He had no intention of getting in hot water over a matter as delicate as this; if Magdalene was evil it was because the Bible made her so. He was simply adding a few trimmings, a little zip, as he did for Poppaea, the first classical graduate of his school of glamour.

At the first rumblings from a religious group, he let it be known he was approaching his subject with "reverence marked by a deep sense of responsibility." He said *The King of Kings* would not be filmed without the guidance of the clergy, and asked churches to pick their representatives.

The Federated Churches of America sent Dr. George Reid Andrews, and the National Catholic Welfare Council selected Father Lord.

Dr. Alkow, a rabbi, took up residence at the studio as an expert on Jewish customs, along with Bruce Barton, son of a prominent minister.

DeMille did not confer with them as a group but worked out objections with each separately, preferring not to let the

Protestants know what was disturbing the Catholics, and vice versa.

DeMille liked Father Lord immensely, found him understanding, patient, receptive to ideas that would send hard-shelled clergymen screaming into the Biblical underbrush. The priest was comparatively young then; he confessed to the producer he had had for years an intense interest in the film medium. DeMille, pondering this, may have concluded the youthful priest wanted to make a change, for he asked him one day, "Do you like your life and work?"

"Enormously."

"You seem interested in Hollywood, and I believe you are alert to the possibilities of motion pictures."

"Yes, very much so."

"Would you consider coming out here, learning pictures from the ground up, working with me on production, and becoming a director and producer?"

It was apparent Lord would never qualify as a DeMille yes man. "Not for anything in the world," the young priest replied. "I love my life. I am completely content with it."

DeMille, complete stranger to contentment, smiled. "You are a lucky man."

About twenty years later a priest did join the DeMille staff, during a sabbatical of several years, and when his official leave was over he advised the producer he was returning to his sacerdotal duties. DeMille did not take kindly to the coming separation, but did manage to maintain a rigid silence. There were delays in his leaving. DeMille told us he believed the clergyman, a man of intellect, had changed his mind. He felt the priest could do greater good through the far-reaching cinema medium than from the pulpit—echoing once more his mother's logic of a half-century ago.

The priest eventually left, and when he had reached his destination DeMille, without our customary aid in letter writing, penned him a long note which left little doubt that his return to the priesthood was a shortsighted act, of much lesser benefit to mankind. At luncheon that day DeMille reviewed the matter, concluding, "He has gone to serve a greater master."

2.

DeMILLE took Father Lord aboard his yacht, sketched out the plan of the story and the motives behind it. Lord had agreed with Will Hays, the code chief, that Hollywood was entering upon the most important religious work of a generation. At that time eighteen million persons attended movies every day; in a week the number equaled the country's population. To millions of these, Christ was less real than Napoleon or Babe Ruth. Hopefully all this would soon change.

Filming started August 24, 1926. The clergy prayed for blessing—a Protestant bishop, a rabbi, a Catholic priest, a Salvation Army commanding officer, a Mohammedan teacher and a Buddhist swami.

A ten-stop organ played "Onward, Christian Soldiers!" each morning as DeMille entered the sound stage and all stood by solemnly. Spiritual mood music was piped in, strains from Handel's "Largo," Dykes' "Holy, Holy, Holy" and Strainer's "The Crucifixion."

Bibles were distributed to the principal players, who were asked to acquaint themselves with the four Gospels, and answer to their Biblical names—"Tell Caiaphas to get his make-up on," "We're ready for Jesus," "Peter's wig is slipping, someone fix it." Once an impatient director, demanding to know "where in the hell is Judas?" drew a stinging rebuke from the producer.

Players in robes and sandals moved about quietly, talking

in hushed tones, in odd contrast to the usual on-the-set banter. One day a newspaper photographer snapped a shot of H. B. Warner as Christ, in full Biblical robes, lounging in a chair and —the old specter!—smoking a cigarette and scanning the sports pages. It alerted DeMille to the dangerous possibilities of the wrong kind of publicity.

Not long after, DeMille realized how right he was. He got word that a certain woman would soon become a mother, that she was unwed and that, moreover, the father of the unborn infant was H. B. Warner! The paternity suit threatened to wreck the most careful shepherding on DeMille's part. He had got Warner through most of the picture in impeccable taste, temporal and ecclesiastical. Investigators were sent off in several directions. They learned the woman had spent time at Tehachapi, that she was not pregnant, that she had never met Warner, much less had the pleasure of his company. The whole incident was cloaked in the utmost secrecy, to the point that Warner himself never learned of it until years later.

There was talk that DeMille had paid the woman $10,000 for her silence but such was not the case. She was cowed by a threat of prosecution for attempted fraud, though even that action would have done the picture considerable harm.

In clear, strong language DeMille told his press agents that the fate of the picture rested on how well they were able to keep frivolous remarks out of the papers. "They'll print anything to get a laugh. I want to get through this picture without someone writing that she saw Caiaphas drunk at Ciro's last night, or Mary Magdalene sparking in a rumble seat on Mulholland Drive."

At DeMille's request, Warner confined all his secular activities to the privacy of his dressing room. There he ate his meals alone and spent his time when not before the camera. When he left his dressing room to go outdoors he put on a hood concealing his face.

DeMille himself found it difficult to observe these stringent rules in the heat of directing a large picture. Once, displeased with a scene, he subjected Warner to a flow of sarcasm, whereupon the actor startled DeMille and the company with the indignant retort: "Mr. DeMille, do you realize to whom you are speaking?"

An order banned wisecracks under the penalty of immediate dismissal. The studio announced that both Warner and Dorothy Cumming, playing the Virgin Mary, had signed a 5-year contract stipulating they would not accept any film role which might lessen the dignity of their parts in *The King of Kings*. DeMille urged Warner and Miss Cumming to remain away from night clubs, and at least until the production was finished to avoid riding in convertibles, swimming, card playing, attending ball games.

Other featured players signed a special agreement by which they promised to behave "in a chaste and becoming manner" during the period of the filming. It caused a lot of waggish comment. A person favorably disposed toward improper venery now might hesitate—breaking the moral code was one thing, but violating a DeMille contract was quite another.

In the circumstances, one might guess that Warner's magnificent portrayal of the Christ would have made his career secure. Hollywood condemned players to types. Once having appeared in the role of the Savior of Mankind, Warner found there was little else available. He played the Head Lama in *Lost Horizon,* but other than that, Warner told friends, his film career ended with *The King of Kings*. Ironically, he died a few days before Christmas, 1958; the services in a Hollywood chapel were attended by fourteen persons.

DeMille spent a good deal of time with Jacqueline Logan, a bubbly, vivacious redhead, going over the part of Mary Magdalene. He sought to impress upon her that it was a tremendous role. He said she would be called upon to give two performances—a beautiful and voluptuous creature in the early

sequences, then changing to a saddened woman whose beauty
had become spiritual. She was urged to "act all the deadly sins
as they leave your body—lust, greed, pride, envy, gluttony,
anger, sloth." Two days later Miss Logan finished the scenes
in which she cast out the seven deadly sins. The next day she
was guilty of sloth. She overslept, appearing on the set an hour
late, one of the more deadly sins on a DeMille set. The cast
and crew, tense at the expectance of a DeMille explosion, saw
him greet the contrite actress with a fatherly smile. This rare
behavior left no explanation except to conclude the showman
was affected by the pious atmosphere.

When Father Dan Lord arrived at the filming, the story of
Mary and Judas was possibly one-third of the whole plot. But,
little by little, an astonishing thing was happening. The priest
recalled, "Whenever Christ appeared on the screen, all the
other characters simply became background. If Jesus walked
into the scene, Magdalene or Judas or both at once became
absolutely subordinate characters. His story became so absorb-
ing that the fictionary story which had been built up to satisfy
modern audiences seemed cheap, unimportant and trivial in
comparison. It was becoming the story of Christ alone, and
any other story treated as equally important seemed an im-
pertinence. By the time I left I had seen the story of Judas and
Magdalene cease to be the main or even the secondary story
and become a trifling incident, left as a sop to the groundlings."

Father Lord related that they were watching rushes one evening when Mr. DeMille leaned over and touched his hand.

"He *is* great, isn't he?" he said.

The priest pretended not to understand. "Warner?"

"Jesus," DeMille replied. "He's great." Then after a long
pause, "I doubt that we shall need the story of Mary Magdalene
and Judas."

The clergy were busy with questions that would have strained
a scholar's Scriptural knowledge. "Why do not Catholics say,

'For thine is the power and the glory' at the end of the Lord's Prayer?" "How was St. Peter likely to have held the portion of the bread at the Last Supper?" "Is there any ancient authority who maintains that Judas was moved by thwarted ambition rather than by greed to betray Christ?" "If Peter were fishing for a single fish, would he be likely to use a pole, reel or net?"

The board of editors consisted of Father Lord, Dr. Andrews, Clifford Howard, DeMille and Miss Macpherson. They gathered in DeMille's private office in the morning and continued until 7 P.M., returning after dinner. They wrote and rewrote titles, cut and recut, thumbed their Bibles to put events and reasons into subtitles of 25 words or less. They realized how perfectly the Evangelists had written the Christ story when they tried to match wording against theirs.

Meanwhile DeMille publicized a questionnaire to find out what people knew about the Scriptures. Thousands of persons replied. Among the answers was this gem: *The elders are a sort of bush from which you get berries to make wine.*

3.

DeMILLE and Sid Grauman, another showman of local repute, joined hands in unveiling *The King of Kings.* Grauman's new theater on Hollywood Boulevard, dubbed by the late showman "Sid Grauman's Chinese Cinema Temple," had just been completed. It was equal to the title. Its rococo towers, rising like battlements of some ancient oriental fortress, were visible for miles in any direction in that smog-free period.

On the evening of the première of the film story of the simple Nazarene, a gigantic fountain in the forecourt shot tongues of water some 100 feet into the air. The effect was further enhanced by orchestra music which, it was explained, blended with "the moods of the water." Instead of the usual drop-curtain, Grauman planned a junior-miss size Niagara Falls illuminated by colored lights. He wrote a personal note to Calvin Coolidge asking the President to push a button in Washington to signal the start of the waterfall curtain. An aide regretfully declined. A corps of damsels was imported from San Francisco's Chinatown to act as usherettes, lending an attractive, though sharply un-Biblical, flavor to the proceedings.

One of DeMille's cardinal rules was an early start at a première to insure a fresh, bright-eyed audience. As a showman he considered it a basic precept—no picture should be called upon to fight off the blight of boredom brought on by lengthy preliminaries.

As it developed, he spent one of the unhappiest nights of his life at Grauman's première of *The King of Kings*. Speaker after speaker felt it proper to shower much rosy prose on DeMille's dauntless spirit, to a point where DeMille was sure he was going to be stoned out of the theater. He sensed that the patience of the elite $11-a-seat assemblage was growing thinner by the moment. With each pleonasm of praise for DeMille's rare fortitude in undertaking such a speculative venture, the perspiring object of this mass affection became more desperate.

It was near 11 P.M. when *The King of Kings* main title flashed on the screen. That DeMille's feelings were justified was indicated by comments in the New York *Mirror* review:

Their faces looked muscle-slacked. Many eyes were sleep-laden, as though rudely aroused from slumber. No enthusiasm. Loquacious disappointment, spiced with such startling comments as "H. B. Warner's beard seemed moth-eaten.". . . and from one facetious soul: "No love interest."

At a later opening in another town, there was one speaker, DeMille himself. He said, "Ladies and Gentlemen, if you will look at this picture and see with eyes that see and understanding that understands, my life's work will be complete," and sat down.

Hollywood as a place for DeMille's premières was done for. Neither hell nor high water and no power, Biblical or lay, could persuade him to stage another opening in the film capital. His resentment grew geographically, spreading from Hollywood to the entire coastal region, where, he raged, "not people live, only smart alecks." He was especially chary of Pasadena, which in grandiose moments he tagged as a community of "tired rich who turned up their noses at simple human drama," adding, "The only thing that will go in Pasadena is a psychological plot by two youths trying to decide whether they should poison their rich aunt or hang her by her toes from the rafters." He felt kindly toward inland cities, in time developing a fiery affection for the Middle West: "The heart of the nation pumping blood to both coasts." He staged his "sneak previews" in Denver, Salt Lake City, Chicago, Omaha. In Kansas City he lashed out against unseen critics who condemn the Middle West as "corny." "Be proud of corn," he told citizens and reporters. "Corn is soul, corn is that which makes you cry and laugh. Corn is all humanity. Yes, my pictures have corn and I am proud of it."

The King of Kings cost $2,265,283. Its profit record was poor, but this was by design. The Cinema Corporation for many years has loaned it to civic, religious and charitable groups, asking only a nominal fee to help replace worn prints. Apart from an occasional percentage check to the DeMille organization, no profit of any size has been made on the 32-year-old silent movie. Distribution has been extraordinary—it is said no week passes without *The King of Kings* playing in some corner of the world.

When it opened in New York City in 1927, the late Alexander Woollcott wrote: "It is my guess *The King of Kings* will girdle the globe, and the multitude will still be flocking to see it in 1947." Woollcott was right. It is estimated 800,000,000 persons have seen the film, at one period shown some 1,500 times yearly in the United States alone. Scores of 16 mm. prints were sent to missionaries throughout the world.

In remote regions Paulist Fathers have shown the movie to audiences who have seen no other pictures. Missionaries in India replace their old prints every three years; others have taken it in canoes up the Ganges and Congo. It was the first film ever seen by Eskimos at Point Barrow, Alaska. One missionary reports having shown the film to 125,000 persons. The picture's titles have been translated into twenty-three languages, including Chinese, Turkish, Arabic and Hindustani.

The King of Kings was shortened to fit a new policy after general release. Most of Ernest Torrance's portrayal of Peter was cut out. This grieved DeMille, as he considered it almost superior to Warner's handling of the Christ role. His feelings were close to shock when the Cinema people lopped off virtually all of the opening episode containing the affair between Mary Magdalene and Judas. After this, neither Magdalene nor Judas made much sense to him as characters. He viewed it as unlikely that a man would betray a King for "a lousy thirty pieces of silver." "There must have been a dame in the background," he told us in a tone of finality.

Letters poured into the DeMille office from many lands, urging the producer to "carry on your new ministry" and hailing the rise of a "power for good in sin-laden Hollywood." A number were critical, indignant or outraged, and were placed in a file in a secret vault. The others were bound into three thick volumes. For years they remained within easy reach in De-

Mille's office, to the considerable discomfiture of correspondents and others who had taken a cynical view of the entire project. (John Steinbeck's comment: "Saw the picture, loved the book.")

A woman wrote she was renouncing "a life of sin for the way of Christ." A burglar, self-styled, vowed a return to the path of goodness after seeing the picture. A boy in the Bronx, New York, wrote: *Gee, I am going to give back that nickel's worth of candy I swiped from Nick last night.* A Los Angeles Superior Court judge felt "it is worth a thousand sermons." A woman in Yankton, S. D., stated she had been cynical about religion, "but you answered the question for me in such a manner that a great light came into my soul." The late George M. Cohan wired: IT IS THE MOST INTERESTING, MOST IMPRESSIVE MOTION PICTURE I HAVE EVER SEEN.

There arrived one singularly moving letter which DeMille rarely failed to mention in any serious discussion of the picture. The writer, a woman, said she was suffering from an incurable disease and did not have long to live. *Seeing your picture has changed what must happen in a short time from a terror to a glorious anticipation.*

DeMille remembered fondly Will Rogers' summary: *There will never be a greater picture because there is no greater subject.* DeMille felt it was a supreme tribute, although he pondered its nuances, once suggesting to a staff member, "There is no greater subject, true, but it could suffer from poor treatment."

DeMille's own attitude toward his stature as a film maker changed drastically. He was emerging as a Biblical chanticleer of no mean proportions. His voice was reaching far and wide, accomplishing in a single stroke what might conceivably require the efforts of a thousand missionaries. Even the usual adverse criticism of the DeMille technique collapsed when it came to *The King of Kings*. He developed, as time went on, a repertoire of phrases to dramatize the film's influence. "Thousands of half-clad savages sitting on the banks of the Congo watching this story of Jesus of Nazareth," he declaimed to visitors. "No one can imagine what this picture has done in the recent strife in the Holy Land. They asked for prints because this is the sort of thing they need to quell riot, bloodshed and larceny."

4.

WITH the establishment of his own production setup, DeMille had warned that he would fight Paramount with the same weapons which that studio had employed so successfully. He would build theaters in every key city if Paramount made an attempt to freeze him out by not playing his pictures in Paramount's theaters around the country.

He had entered into a complex financial alignment with New York capital. It provided ready money and lessened the possibility of a "freeze-out" by Paramount. Then came his next major move—an arrangement with the Keith-Albee and Orpheum circuits, putting at his disposal a coast-to-coast network of 1,400 theaters.

Even with four corporations involved in the elaborate studio-theater structure, DeMille controlled all matters pertaining to stories, scenarios and artists.

Trouble began almost immediately. Initial funds from the New York concerns were not promptly advanced, another failed to pay picture expenses, and on several occasions DeMille's own company had to guarantee the weekly studio payroll. Friction was almost continuous.

On the other hand, the backers were not encouraged by the returns from the first picture under the new setup, *The Road to Yesterday*, released in August 1925. Beulah Marie Dix and Jeanie Macpherson had collaborated on the scenario, with Joseph Schildkraut, Jetta Goudal, William Boyd and Vera Reynolds as the stars. It had cost $447,479 and was to gross a meager $552,663. The next film, *The Volga Boatman*, released the same year, performed somewhat better, returning a million and a quarter on a half-million-dollar budget—a fair profit.

The King of Kings cost well over two million dollars and would one day return that much, but it was *The Godless Girl* —the fourth and last picture under DeMille's personal banner— that destroyed the remnants of confidence in the new venture. Máde in 1928 at a cost of $722,000, the film grossed $486,000— failing to pay much of its basic expenses.

In 1929, DeMille moved over to Metro-Goldwyn-Mayer studio. Under a contract entered into by his own firm, DeMille Productions, Inc., he was given complete authority as to pictures, stories and cast. The DeMille company was to receive a guarantee of from $150,000 to $175,000 per picture in addition to a percentage of the income from each.

Disputes arose with the very first picture. In April 1931, the parties agreed to terminate the contract.

Once again the arguments were over DeMille's choice of stories and types of production. He made three pictures at Metro:

Dynamite cost about $700,000 and yielded a million and a quarter.

Madam Satan cost $980,000 and brought in only $742,000.

A remake of *The Squaw Man* cost $742,000, yielding only $356,000.

Both for Metro—and DeMille at this stage of his career— the showing was disastrous.

Financially, however, he had not fared badly. Nor had DeMille Productions, thanks to the guarantees in the contract with Metro. In the prior seven years the company had been active in real estate and securities. It acquired a number of business properties, which it let. It bought a theater or two, purchased several ranch properties, and took interests in varied enterprises—Arizona cotton lands, oil development, a construction company, and others—some successful, some not.

It had made no pictures except under contract, and into the production of such pictures it put no money of its own, the funds being supplied by other parties to the contracts. Most of the picture profits were from productions personally directed by DeMille.

From 1924 to 1929 the company had built up a surplus of well over a million and a half dollars, and in that time DeMille had received in salary a total of $366,000; Mrs. DeMille, $229,000.

Now the world seemed to close in on him. He had been stifled in efforts to produce his own pictures, and the specter of executive interference in creative matters continued to bedevil him.

"If Edison had a supervisor we would not have electric lamps, and nothing of any real worth in a creative way has ever been done if the creator has been hampered and utterly restricted," he fumed at the industry in a statement to *Variety*. "Raphael would never have painted the Sistine Chapel if his patrons had told him just what and how many cherubs he could paint in. . . . And individual contribution is just what the present picture system hampers and almost totally destroys."

Then he announced he was going to Russia and could not think of any place offering more drama at the moment. He described it as a great prehistoric beast shaking off its shackles and stepping into civilization. He saw the capitalistic system as a failure. There was no integrity in it, and he believed that the fundamental integrity of the American people would revolt against it.

He was quoted in *Variety* on June 23, 1931:

> I am not a radical, but now things are a question of right and
> wrong. The public has been milked and are growing tired of it.
> It is not speculation alone. There is something rotten at the core
> of our system. We have to get back to the simple, true principles
> that our government was founded on. Even legitimate stock-
> holders now have been turned from partners in a business into
> goats and they will get sick of it.
>
> There is something all wrong somewhere when a man can't
> invest his carefully accumulated money in the big industries of
> a country without having them manipulated by those at the top,
> with the result that his life savings and the protection for his
> family are wiped out.

DeMille spent a month in Russia with special permission
from the Government to move about almost at will. The con-
trasts of Soviet life in the year 1931 sat gently, and comfortably,
upon his conscience. His notes of the trip indicate that perhaps
there was not so much awry with capitalistic America:

> In Moscow . . . five divorces and three mariages in the half-hour
> we watched. About 55 per cent of divorces to marriages. . . .
>
> At the prison . . . 600 convicts . . . all cheerful. Receive thirty-
> five rubles a month for their work. . . . Young man who killed a
> friend got two years. Greek priest for counterrevolution, ten
> years.
>
> Little boys gathering about us. . . . Wanted to see gold. When
> shown a $20-gold piece one boy said he hoped I didn't intend to
> use it to make money. . . .
>
> Old man said he couldn't understand why America didn't
> recognize Russia, that we had loaned money to every nation in
> Europe who had gone bankrupt except the USSR, which was
> a success.
>
> Story of the engineer and Bolshevist as to who is greater.
> Engineer said he brings order out of chaos and Bolshevist said,
> "Well, who made the chaos?"
>
> Professor has no concept of American government. Believes
> lynching of Negroes is government inspired or at least condoned.
> Believes shooting of political prisoners is okay but is shocked at

America having capital punishment for murder, calls it revenge. Believes Lincoln was a capitalist President and freed the slaves to help capital. . . .

Gravest danger between the two countries is lack of understanding of each other's true condition and purpose . . . children begging . . . gangs of women laborers working beside railroad tracks. . . . Everywhere the feeling prevails, "Why does America hate Russia?"

Passed through a town that has had no new building in 200 years. . . . Film stars unknown. . . . Asked a man whether he liked Greta Garbo and he said he had never tasted it. . . .

Russia is a land of no liberty, much paper money, vast slum areas, some ideals and much determination. . . . It is a land of two million bureaucrats regimenting 150 million slaves living in hopeless poverty. . . .

DeMille had made *The Godless Girl* in 1928, labeling it "a triumph of Christianity over atheism." While touring Russia DeMille was warmly complimented by Soviet officials on one of his early pictures. The film's title had been changed by the Russians; there was no clue as to which one had so engaged the Marxist mind. In Tiflis, a Russian of previous acquaintance gave the answer. It was *Godless Girl.* In the story Christianity does not triumph over atheism until the last reel. The Russians had eliminated that reel. Now it appeared atheism was approved in American schools.

Part IV

THE SIGN OF THE BOSS

1.

TWO framed cartoons hung for a time in the office of a staff assistant in the DeMille bungalow, one showing the crisis that occurred when, according to the caption, *An assistant says* NO *to Cecil DeMille*. Actors appear to tremble like aspen leaves, secretaries are fainting and crewmen leap from high towers as if preferring suicide to the director's wrath. The other cartoon depicts a fleecy scene in heaven, with the celebrated showman wearing an outsize pair of wings, of the sort properly reserved for epic-makers. He is chestily facing up to a shaft of light, presumably emanating from the Creator, and delivering an edict promptly upon arrival: *"One of us has got to go!"* Rival producers would not be apt to regard the symbolism as even a trifle overdrawn. Having observed what DeMille had accomplished on earth almost singlehandedly, they would be willing, however irreverently, to classify this exasperating man as a potential dark horse on the celestial scene; at least they would expect him to give the Incumbent a good stiff battle.

As might be expected, DeMille often found himself in fetters to the tight little world within the bungalow, which frequently trembled under his mastery. He considered himself hobbled by mediocre minds incapable of rising to heights reached by his own imagination. He felt his trouble was with people who kept him from moving steadily toward his objectives.

He appeared clad for battle, first with field boots and breeches, then adding whatever equipment or people he deemed necessary as the years went on. The microphone, which came into wide use in the 20's, DeMille found a real boon; now he could be heard above Acre, Fort Pitt, the Crusades, and other campaigns of similar scope that roared from the DeMille barracks.

In time, he hired a chair boy, microphone boy, small-equipment boy (ready with pencil, pad and such), yielding a sort of key to his stage character. The corps of specialists soon became a favorite target of the press. Their humorous jibes left little impression on the epic-maker. His stature considered, the chair and microphone boys made sense to him, though for public consumption he was careful to justify the contributions of these minor functionaries.

"What the gentlemen of the press don't understand," DeMille would grieve, "is that my sets cost me anywhere from fifty to a hundred thousand dollars a day. I move around pretty fast and even a minute's delay waiting for a microphone can be pretty expensive."

During production he was as busy as a general launching a major offensive. Appointments were next to impossible. On one occasion a critic from an important paper asked for "only twenty minutes of Mr. DeMille's time." "Twenty minutes," the boss ejaculated. "I haven't given Mrs. DeMille that much time in ten years." He was irritated when the staff felt compelled to take time off during filming of a picture; news of the illness of this or that member left the boss cold as basalt. In production, he was interested only in maximum effort. Anything less than that was traitorous, or at least an unspeakable defection. One aide's father died while the DeMille party was en route by train to Philadelphia to join the Ringling circus. Word of the death was communicated to the man en route, and he left the train at that point to return home.

He had been away from the DeMille party two days when DeMille inquired as to his whereabouts.

"You remember, Mr. DeMille, his father just died."

The boss glared at his informant, "His is not the only father who ever died. We'll all pray for the good man but there's nothing he can do for him now, and there is something he can do for ten million dollars' worth of motion picture. Please convey that message to him."

The message was so conveyed, and the assistant caught the next train for Philadelphia, with the dedication of a martyr serving a secular cause.

The cluster of DeMille aides widened—a field secretary, a script girl and one or two first-assistant directors who shuttled between him and numerous "field" assistants. They added to the difficulty of reaching the ear of the producer at a critical moment. The microphone boy probably suffered most from this press. No signals were given; he had to be not only alert but intuitive, poising the microphone in front of the producer's face at just the precise moment of utterance. A long microphone cord trailed this harassed functionary. At times it tangled with chairs or stools, often when the producer was bellowing like a wounded lion for the mike.

But it was the chair boy who caught the popular eye. Some wagers were made on the expectancy of his failure to place the chair under DeMille when the latter took an unannounced notion to sit down. It was the late DeWolf Hopper who expressed a longing in the breasts of many a friend and adversary:

> In five years this gentleman has sat whenever the spirit moved him and never looked behind nor hesitated, secure in the knowledge that the menial was there with a chair in position. I have lived these five years in the impious hope that this shadow might some day be visited with a momentary lapse and the famous director sit unexpectedly and violently upon the floor.

Hopper's unmanly wish never came to pass. Whatever it was, fear or divine guidance, DeMille's chair boys never once were remiss in their duty.

DeMille's dual personality—the gracious, well-turned-out, soft-spoken gentleman vs. the ferocious director—was often confusing to observers. There were instances when Citizen DeMille denied the existence of Director DeMille. A number of years ago he had undertaken a violent scene in which an actor-cowboy was to be tumbled from his horse by a rifle shot. Sound had just come in and he was not on easy terms with the new medium. The picture was a remake and he was especially anxious for it to be a good one. Besides, it was a dangerous scene and he was not convinced the cameraman would hold up under the strain.

"No matter what happens," DeMille told him, "I want you to keep grinding. Understand? Don't stop for anything!"

The scene went perfectly. It was so realistic, in fact, that a substitute studio doctor, on a movie set for the first time, himself came unglued. When the cowboy toppled from the horse, as the script directed, the doctor assumed it was an emergency. He therefore sprinted out to administer first aid.

At first DeMille was startled. Then he was enraged. With a bellow, he dug out after the doctor. The doctor, catching a glimpse of the furious director over his shoulder, picked up speed and wisely kept going, past the forgotten cowboy and off the set entirely. Winded, but still shaking his fist, DeMille gave up the chase and returned to his chair. Meanwhile, the cameraman had been faithfully grinding away.

The next morning, DeMille was in the projection room looking at the rushes of the previous day's shooting. Suddenly, the bewildered doctor fled across the screen. In close pursuit was a bald-headed man in boots, screaming abuse at him.

"Who in the world is that?" DeMille asked in genuine surprise.

"That's the substitute studio doctor," an assistant said.

"I know that," DeMille said impatiently. "I mean the man using the frightful language."

"That, sir, is you," the assistant said.

"Young man," DeMille answered, after a painful silence, "that may *appear* to be me, but I assure you it is not. I never used language like that in my life!"

A large segment of the film colony, however, will testify that there was nothing complex about DeMille's nature. In fifty years a considerable number had a chance to watch him in action. Quite a few felt the sting of his lash at one time or another, either as bit player or extra on one of his densely populated sets. They are willing to vow that he was nothing more or less complicated than "a cruel and evil old man." This concept, if gained from DeMille's behavior during filming of crowd scenes, is not without some merit.

On epic sets seething with extras, the boss was a convulsive force. The memory of one case in point caused the staff to shudder for months—the siege of Fort Pitt scene in *Unconquered*. If they but knew it, the extras had more to fear from DeMille than from the Indian braves who were storming the walls and lobbing real fireballs into the fort.

In the course of that day's shooting, we watched the boss driven to new heights of wrath. Time after time, the extras failed to give him the kind of reaction he wanted.

"You're about to be scalped alive," he shouted at them through a microphone as he rode high on a camera boom. "Then suddenly you hear bugles and drums in the distance and you know you're going to be saved. Do you understand? You're going to be saved! You and your kids and your loved ones. So WHAT DO YOU DO? YOU JUMP UP AND DOWN, YOU CHEER, YOU GRAB SOMEONE AND DANCE, YOU GO CRAZY WITH JOY. Have you given me that kind of reaction? From the way you're acting I merely assumed you have just read the market reports and your favorite stock has gone up a couple of points. Now, I WANT YOU TO GO CRAZY WITH JOY FOR ME. GODDAMN IT, I'M GIVING YOU THE CHANCE OF A LIFETIME TO ACT IN A DeMILLE PICTURE. I WANT EVERYTHING YOU'VE GOT!"

DeMille took real pleasure in, as he put it, "picking the brains of my staff," making it clear to us that he was forever mystified how his operation managed to sustain itself on so little food. In the course of a day's shooting, under pressure of time and expensive sets, DeMille might be successively teacher, preacher, tyrant, imperious master, or soft-voiced ridiculer. His attack was octopuslike, and it was hard to tell when or how a tentacle would reach out for an unsuspecting victim. Seeing two assistant directors idly chatting on an important set one day, he intoned into the microphone in the matter-of-fact voice of a general briefing subordinates: "I'm running a set costing $50,000 a day, and you gentlemen seem to have found time to play at marbles. If you are not quite up to this whole thing, may I suggest that you find yourself another picture, perhaps one with a kindergarten hour. Think what fun it will be not having to put up with the bad temper of an evil director."

A newcomer learned quickly the difference between a "hot" and "cold" DeMille set. The distinction was enormously important to his future as a DeMille man. On "cold" DeMille sets all was usually well with the world—the actresses knew their lines, the cameraman was lighting up the scenes quickly, the assistant directors marshaled their extras before the cameras with the greatest effectiveness—in a word, everything on the set was working smoothly, and DeMille was happy.

On a "hot" DeMille set, DeMille was not happy. Many things or just one thing might be wrong. One could tell by his manner that his temperature was near the bursting point. It was very quiet. Some of the older staff members, seeing the telltale crimson flush creep up the back of his neck, headed for the storm cellars. On that day, the staff would find reason to be occupied elsewhere.

It might not have occurred to the newcomer that a set was sometimes something else. Least of all could he anticipate that he would be staked out for slaughter in order that a totally unrelated result might be achieved.

It was DeMille's policy never to criticize a star once the picture had started. All sorts of psychology, yes, but never open ragging. It wasn't sensible to unnerve a star who held the fate of the picture in his hand, once the camera started to grind and the costs began to pile up, as they did very quickly on a DeMille epic. But there must be some way to discipline a performer who was, say, frivolous on the sets or failed to memorize lines, or rejected little niceties in make-up. The sources of irritation to a mind as intense as the boss's were numberless.

Though he may have wished it, he could not confront the offending actress with a large-caliber revolver and invite her to use it—on herself. He took another tact—peering behind and around for someone engaged at the moment in some frivolity which might be regarded as improper. This was not easy on a DeMille set, where discipline and behavior were usually quite exemplary.

Should he find a casual offender, maybe guilty of nothing more heinous than popping his chewing gum, a roar like the collapse of burning towers would come over the microphone, rocking the company back on its heels. All, including the playful actress, were cowed into reverential silence, and discipline was restored. It was on just such an occasion that DeMille chose a new recruit to be the sacrificial lamb, though it must be said in full truth that DeMille had no idea who the lamb was going to be, until the moment he brightly turned up at his side to reveal what ordinarily might have been a very cheering piece of news—namely, that a magazine had accepted an article which could do the picture immense good. The publicist had hardly touched on the more important aspects of his triumph when the microphones thundered DeMille's pent-up wrath to every corner of the sound stage. The *bel canto* outburst went on endlessly against "the crime of interrupting a $50,000-a-day set to chatter about some idiotic magazine article...." Obliquely, DeMille had let the errant performer know that he was in no mood for tomfoolery, while the startled rookie stood by too shocked to move.

All that remained for Mr. DeMille to do was to repair the shattered spirit of the shorn lamb. This he always undertook personally, favoring him with pleasant remarks but never mentioning the episode directly. DeMille went to the newcomer's office to which he had repaired, dazed and wounded, less than an hour after the ordeal. The boss sat down, exhibiting the greatest charm and affability. "I know you understand how DeMille works," he murmured. "I'm afraid it's a kind of martyrdom for a great cause, and we all must give a little bit of ourselves."

Soon the recruit begin to see a great deal of logic in the way DeMille represented it: a sacrifice to expiate for the sins of others! A high form of charity, was it not, and he considered it so until he had witnessed a succession of these disciplinary attacks and found himself struggling to keep the faith. At times they were awesome, even to us, but more so to visitors on the sets who of course could not understand why a trifling misdemeanor should evoke such wrath and went away feeling sorry for the staff.

One of the granddaddies of these outbursts occurred at Sarasota at the Ringling Brothers circus grounds, where we were filming *The Greatest Show on Earth.*

One of the scenes required a bit of doing because it involved a full circus train departing from winter quarters with tardy performers boarding it helter-skelter. The "traffic"—movement of the players in a scene—was very difficult and the more De-Mille shouted instructions the more confused each "take" became. It was apparent the actors were having more fun than the script called for. Some eight or ten assistants, trying to synchronize the movements, finally were ordered to stop everything. DeMille stood at the microphone until a complete silence fell on the outdoor set, by this time ringed with hundreds of tourists and townfolks.

We knew the assistants were marked for slaughter the minute DeMille called a halt, and so did the older ones among them.

He ordered them to line up, and they did, like prisoners at the bar, as DeMille began his remarks. "Ladies and gentlemen, the men you see before me are assistants. It is their job to assist. Assist means to help. We are here on an important picture and this is an important scene. It takes a lot of time and money to bring people and equipment all the way from Hollywood. Maybe these gentlemen don't realize this. Now, unless I can do this scene we will have no picture. These gentlemen know this but they either don't have the ability or they don't care. In either case they are useless to me. I should encourage them to pack up their bags and return to Hollywood, as a favor to me, to the cast and the cameramen. Errors in judgment I can forgive, stupidity never. If you can't do the job please have the courage to tell me, so I can get someone else. . . ."

There was murmuring among the spectators, and puzzled glances, and that night Sarasota buzzed with gossip about that man who was directing a motion picture out on the circus grounds!

The feeling was not appreciably lessened by the report brought back the following day by witnesses to a shorter but more spirited cannonade against a minor subordinate, who just happened into a line of fire: "I hate to put this strain on you," bellowed the voice through the microphone. "I know these are trying times. Indeed a troubled era. This world is upside down. Perhaps I should not be asking you to help this scene out by bringing a sandwich to one of our players, especially in times of grave national emergency. What I am asking for is A SANDWICH! ONE, PLAIN, SIMPLE, UNCOMPLICATED SANDWICH!"

No matter how his operatic explosions appeared to others, DeMille insisted that they did not arise from impulse. "My ferocity is always studied ferocity. When something really makes me angry, I get extremely quiet. Anger is no time for words. I use a careful lash. Something of the sort is necessary in order to steady a company before a big scene."

The punishment, rarely fitting the crime, did not cause wholesale resignations, as one might expect, nor anything resembling it. No matter how taut the set, these skilled craftsmen stayed on, appeared with DeMille in one production after another. Some risked his spleen because they admired him, others because of the prestige of a DeMille picture, and still others because they loved a stout heart. And "the old man" had the stoutest in the business. They returned—chief electrician, "boom" man, special effects—for picture after picture. Their skins were thick enough to emerge smiling from a crushing assault because, in the historic phrase around the DeMille unit, "they know how to work with C.B." Set decorator, art director, sound recorders, they were the all-Americans on the Paramount lot. They measured up to DeMille's perfectionist methods. A good deal of affection developed between these veterans and the producer, and if they were to know the truth, DeMille would not have started a picture without them, though it was unlikely he would ever tell them so.

The boss's burdens were not eased by the fact that after years on the sound stages veteran actors find most roles wearisome. Particularly was this true of players wrestling with a DeMille plot, which had a quality usually associated with the birth of an earthquake and did not leave much room for triumphs of acting, much less any sort of personal *tour de force*. They were actors who approached a DeMille assignment with something short of boundless enthusiasm. DeMille kept an alert eye for such blackguards, sizing up their attitude by the way they spent their idle moments on the sets. Those who stood at a discreet distance in the background, intently observing DeMille's management of a scene, were apt to be rewarded with a wave of the hand or an affable comment from the boss—a sort of gentle recognition of their sense for values. On one occasion he had promised a young actress a chance in pictures, and possibly a contract, if she proved as capable as her several boosters claimed. On the day she appeared on the set Mr. DeMille was directing a difficult scene. While waiting her turn before the camera, the young woman chatted with a visitor. Noting her indifference, DeMille turned to an aide: "Tell that young woman to take the rest of the day off. We'll call her the moment we are ready for her." It developed that the moment never came.

While he could not always control the doings of his players between scenes, there was nothing to prevent him from maintaining order in the house. He was rabidly sensitive to background noise.

"That goddamn murmuring behind my back is a hideous conspiracy," he would moan amid a rising babel.

A half dozen times in the course of a production he would seize the microphone and deliver a passionate tirade on the evils of idle chatter. For the superlative discourtesy he had a pet comment: "WHAT I WANT IS QUIET! QUIET BEHIND THE CAMERA AND INTELLIGENCE IN FRONT OF IT. I KNOW I CAN'T HAVE BOTH AT THE SAME TIME BUT LET'S SEE IF I CAN GET ONE OR THE OTHER!"

We had watched him work tirelessly twelve to fifteen hours almost every day during the Samson shooting. At the start of the episode in which the strong man slays a thousand Philistines, the platoon of actors playing the role of the doomed soldiers were supposed to give forth with a low rumble of hate.

The armored soldiers tried. DeMille didn't like it; the rumble didn't have enough body.

The men tried again.

"I must have the right murmur from you men," said DeMille, not satisfied.

For a moment he brightened.

"You know the kind I mean. The same murmur I've been getting behind my back day after day and year after year."

He turned and pointed to crewmen and actors behind him.

"Listen to it!" he cried, and at that moment the chatter broke off. Complete silence.

"I guess the DeMille era is over," he said, mopping his brow despairingly. "Now I can't even get them to prattle behind my back."

An occasional extreme measure was taken to stem the flow of his vitriol on the sets. One veteran assistant tried a daring feat of sound-stage buccaneering, first enlisting the aid of a wardrobe worker. When the unconventional abuse was hitting thick and fast, two extras dressed as nuns were spirited onto the sets, as if visiting. The subterfuge worked a couple of times but was called off when DeMille acknowledged the presence of the good sisters, apologized, and resumed the usual fire and brimstone.

DeMille has been described as "the gentle tyrant who has left strewn behind him the broken bodies of underlings and assistants, though an astonishing number of people profess to have told DeMille at one time or another to go jump into a lake." It is possible that one per cent of these have actually mustered the necessary courage. DeMille, on the other hand, has frequently offered to supply the gun if the object of his disaffection would go out and shoot himself.

Some incidents indicate that a degree of retaliatory courage has stirred the souls of a few spirited workers.

At a costume preview one day DeMille asked an assistant for an opinion on a Delilah outfit to be worn by Hedy Lamarr. He said he liked it.

"Well, I don't like it." DeMille said and, turning to the expert, added, "I am not sure I can trust your judgment in these matters."

The assistant made no reply.

A few minutes later DeMille asked him to express himself on another outfit, and the man said, "If you feel you can't trust my judgment I see no point in expressing it," and walked from the room, a few minutes later notifying the front office of his resignation.

Many of course have left DeMille for more serene pastures, giving rise to a remark popular with the staff during World War II—"Anyone who leaves DeMille for the service is a slacker."

There was one occasion at the bungalow that was looked upon with feelings both of pleasure and dread. The first showing of any picture, in its roughly edited form, before select members of the staff who regarded it as their day of judgment, followed months, even years, of effort. Weeks in advance writers, secretaries and aides would begin to feel the tension of the first unreeling; on that day they would witness for the first time a continuity of visual proof as to their skill—or lack of it. Their work passes in review on immutable film that, at this stage, allows for no major retreat or apology. For good or ill, what has been done is done.

There was no need, then, for words of caution among members of the staff. The writers naturally would be careful to refrain from anything except laudatory comment about the set decorator's work; and in equal vein the decorator, should he speak of anything outside of his own interest, will have pleasant things to say about the writing.

It was no occasion for boldness. One might feel inspired in the way of criticism of the picture to make minor suggestions toward corrections that were both possible and economical, but criticism of a sort that looked to major revisions would be sheer folly. It would be too late for major changes and no staff member would be so unrealistic as to suggest any.

The usual tensions were felt on the day we gathered for the first rough showing of *Unconquered.* Two writers, a film editor, researcher, and script girl were among the small group led into the studio projection room by Mr. DeMille. They knew that they would be called upon by the boss to give their estimate of the total effort—an effort that required three years of work and five million dollars!

They would watch the picture as intently as possible, at the same time their minds would be busy thinking up pear-shaped adjectives with which to shower the picture and the boss. Pushed well to the rear would be any impulse to "level with the boss," even should they happen to detect serious defects that might call for major revision, itself a remote possibility. At this point, it seemed, it was too late for the truth.

The veterans of the staff never varied this principle; but this time there was a newcomer in their midst.

The picture ended, and Mr. DeMille began pacing back and forth on the center cross-aisle, shooting little glances at the staff people. The newcomer sat to the rear of the room. Ordinarily he might be justified in feeling quite relaxed because, being new to the bungalow, there was little in the picture that could be traced to his department.

DeMille stopped, looked in his direction.

"I'd like to have you tell me what you think of the picture," and with the question all eyes turned toward the young man.

He began on a proper note.

"It's a very great picture," he said. If he had stopped then, all might have been well.

His next comment drained the blood from every person in the room, with the possible exception of DeMille.

"But there is one thing, Mr. DeMille. I don't like the ending. I think it's all wrong. It makes a fool out of the villain."

DeMille nodded, without expression.

The newcomer continued.

"There's Gary Cooper with his gun drawn, pointed at the villain's back. Now the villain is a pretty shrewd guy. He's a powerful villain all through the picture, but what he does next makes him look like a fool, maybe even an idiot. He tries to grab his gun out of the holster on the horse saddle, swing around and try to shoot down a man who's already got the draw on him. It doesn't make sense."

The awful truth was that it *didn't* make sense. Why it had not been detected in the script or before shooting will remain a mystery. Gary Cooper had gone away, his contract finished; the crew was dispersed, the sets dismantled—it was too late now to make a point of the ending. . . .

There was not a sound when the new man finished. Mr. DeMille continued to pace to and fro, his eyes cast to the floor. Then he turned and glared at the writers.

"If what this man says is true we might just as well throw this picture into the ashcan."

The writers promptly disagreed with the newcomer's estimate. Reason after reason poured forth in the next half-hour, in a do-or-die effort to overturn his logic and justify the villain's last desperate act.

The scene was not reshot. It was, however, tightened by the removal of a number of frames from the footage in order to speed up the villain's movements as he reached for his gun.

It had been a terrifying experience, a monumental disregard for one of the bungalow's most sacred rules—*Don't try to out-*

shine a staff member. Remember, there are no promotions in the DeMille bungalow.

Another staff member had a haunting memory of the time he was called upon to write an article for Mr. DeMille's by-line for a weekly publication. Having little time to prepare, he dug into the files and composed the article with data taken almost verbatim from two previously published articles.

This was submitted to the boss, who promptly returned it with his verdict succinctly set forth in several places, in one word—*Baloney.*

Irritated, the assistant apprised his employer that the article was a combination of two articles, setting forth the date and place of publication of each. He added in his memo, *The portions which are marked "baloney" are in exact text from the two articles.* Taking the bull by the horns, he added, *I had assumed that what passed your by-line then would be satisfactory now. In view of this may I suggest that someone else may wish to try his hand at an article on the same or any other subject.*

The boss made no mention of the matter, other than to instruct another staff man to "write a fresh article unless we all have agreed that we are utterly devoid of new ideas."

A key to his progressiveness may be indicated in the incident —perhaps a partial answer to the wonderment of so many as to how he was able to keep pace with a constantly changing industry. The acceptable patterns of yesterday may have lost their value and meaning to a mind constantly probing for today's challenges.

Occasionally a coltish staff member would risk the uncharted seas of repartee, at which the boss himself was no raw hand. One day he stepped out of his office to read aloud a fan letter which ended with the devout hope, "What this country needs is more Cecil B. DeMilles."

With sudden bravado an assistant who was listening blurted out, "Gad! what a frightful prospect."

DeMille broke the stunned silence with a loud guffaw. "Yes, isn't it so. The world can hardly handle the one it's got."

The assistant later confessed to a sudden panic the moment he had uttered the remark. "It could have been curtains if C. B. were having one of his bad days."

On one occasion he was on stage at a local theater, commenting on the picture the audience was about to see. A few of the stars of the film were seated in the front row. Suddenly someone at the rear of the house, apparently fearful that DeMille was not going to call the performers onto the stage, shouted, "We want to see the stars."

DeMille paused, peered into the darkness beyond the lights and with an elfish grin shouted back, "Evidently, my good man, you do not understand the egotism of a director!"

2.

OF all our duties none caused more anguish than the writing of letters for DeMille's signature.

He had a hard and fast rule: prompt replies to all letters. Promptness though was not enough; each letter must be brilliant, a gem of the purest ray serene. We were only too well aware of his vibrant animosity to conventional business phrases.

The boss would not have been caught dead with such humdrum pleasantries as "Thank you for your very kind comment," or "It was courteous of you to trouble to write."

Nor would he permit a letter to begin with the personal "I." That was, he felt, a mark of arrogance, so we usually began his letters with "There was ..." or "It was ..." keeping in mind always that the spirit of a letter must reflect most admirably on the signer.

We struggled with what came to be known as "hog letters."

A "hog letter" was viewed with universal horror by the staff. It meant that draft after draft had been rejected by DeMille, that in all likelihood an unfortunate aide was pacing back and forth in his office, exclaiming to anyone who would listen, "I've got one of those ____ hog letters cooking."

"Hog letters" came into being shortly after the filming of *The Story of Dr. Wassell.* The Navy hero of the story, Dr. Corydon Wassell, an Arkansas country doctor, sent DeMille a razorback hog. It was a royal animal, big and firm, representative of its breed.

Touched by the gesture, DeMille rallied his staff.

A letter to Dr. Wassell must be written that would rank as high in the art of letter writing as this hog ranked among razorbacks. The letter must move Wassell as much as the hog has moved DeMille.

In a brief caucus out of DeMille's hearing, the staff agreed the only way to achieve that effect was to send Wassell a comparable hog or maybe one of DeMille's "epic turkeys." Both being out of the question, they set to the task of trying to fashion a piece of prose that would engulf Wassell with its transcendental beauty.

Sydney Biddell, a literate fellow who was then helping with production affairs, was the first to send in a draft.

It was rejected as "too lofty."

The second was "not lofty enough."

The third, "not warm enough."

By the fourth and fifth submissions, Biddell had vowed a permanent oath against all hogs, with special calumny on the heads of Arkansas razorbacks.

Observing Biddell floundering, DeMille called for drafts from another assistant.

Then another, until two weeks had passed.

Wassell still had not been thanked. Now courtesy was in jeopardy.

DeMille angrily rescinded the order and advised the staff he was writing the reply himself. The next day he wired:

DEAR CORYDON. THANK YOU VERY MUCH FOR THE HOG. SIN- CERELY, CECIL B. DEMILLE.

There was no parallel in memory; the Wassell note was the least ornate ever known to leave the office.

DeMille dispensed the letter-writing chore on an assembly- line basis, assigning letters requiring a light touch to a staffer presumed to have a sense of humor, and weighty ones to him having a way with more portentous phrases.

He might reject an assistant, as he did one, because "that fellow has no soul," the reply in question being one that re- quired a great deal of soul.

Most of our misery developed over letters in the twilight area, neither light nor grave; here we had no clues how to measure up to DeMille's high, and sometimes mysterious, con- cept of what the reply should contain.

We undertook in one letter to describe DeMille's boyhood affection for the late David Belasco, using a phrase, *My awe of him was full and unremitting*. He returned the draft with the marginal comment, *I don't know what unremitting means but it sounds unfortunate*.

On another occasion DeMille had been presented a glowing testimony by a group of Canadian exhibitors who collectively represented four hundred years of experience in their field.

A staff man suggested the reply:

What answer can there be to such praise as you have given, founded on experience reaching back 400 years? Because of what it represents, your wire is a scroll of honor for any man. I can

only accept it with the deepest humility, and thank you for it.
Cecil B. DeMille.

DeMille's one-word judgment on this effort was written across the top: *Nuts.*

Another letter was supposed to tell of the episode in Mr. DeMille's boyhood when he was promised a pony by Belasco. It pictured young DeMille on the point of tears because no pony was in sight; then we had him saying in momentary revolt, "If the pony is in the barn, I won't take it. I'll pass it by." This part DeMille slashed out, commenting on the margin, *I may have been young but not an imbecile.*

We had no desire to return fire with fire; on the contrary, we thought only in terms of defense. Our sole hope was to parry a sudden DeMille thrust in a manner that would not result in too great a loss of dignity; a victory always was farthest from our thoughts. Our little caucuses featured a dominant note: "If he comes up with this objection, I'll tell him this . . ." Whatever the difference of station among the staff members, the common menace bound them into a sympathetic brotherhood. A high-salaried writer in his hour of trial would seek the counsel of a mere hireling, at that moment quite inclined to agree with DeMille's historic remark to a newspaperman: "My assistants think I'm an insane poodle because they never know who I'm going to bite next."

His oft-repeated pronouncement that he would fracture any man who tried to alibi his way out of a situation worked a hardship on those who had valid excuses. It became a matter of shrewd presentation, perhaps prefaced with, "Mr. DeMille, I know how you feel about alibis and I wouldn't think of mentioning this if it wasn't the plain fact of the case. . . ." The staffers agreed DeMille had a faculty for sorting out dishonest alibis. A confession of atrocious guilt might please and soften him. Once an aide, having committed what he felt was a modest error, said, "I've made a stupid mistake beyond all belief," to which DeMille replied, "I've made some pretty bad ones myself."

The salutary result of this confession in open court spread quickly, and as a painful but quick remedy, full admissions of guilt grew in popularity among staff members.

DeMille could take eulogy in stride, but like most men of accomplishment he was sensitive to criticism. His doings inspired a great many letters, a hundred favorable to one unfavorable. Few though they were, the critical letters were apt to slow down the operation, sometimes even bring it to a halt.

In the summer of 1947 Kasper Monahan, the wise, affable drama editor of the Pittsburgh *Press*, visited the bungalow and spent the night with Mr. DeMille at Paradise, later writing a series of three articles under the title, "The Fabulous Mr. DeMille."

One was about Paradise, which the critic described as "a walled-off valley ruled by an absolute monarch . . . a wilderness domain where DeMille reigns as king . . . a Shangri-la echoing to the cry of mountain lions and the pop of champagne bottles."

It turned out that the *Press* articles stirred a soul in Munhall, Pa. This particular reader was moved to criticism by Monahan's crisp references to Paradise, picked up his pen and wrote DeMille that such men as Tom Edison "did not see fit to wall themselves in," adding, *No, Cecil, I am afraid that, stripped down, you are just a forked carrot like the rest of us. . . . You, I fear, are a little man trying to look great. Why don't you try screening a play about a proud, selfish, narrow man with delusions about cheating nature and base it on your own life.*

Mr. DeMille called us into conference on how to handle the situation and dissipate whatever similar public sentiment was aroused by the *Press* articles. We called Monahan, who agreed to print the letter alongside whatever reply Mr. DeMille cared to make. After endless revisions of drafts, a reply was sent to the man in Munhall, and a copy to Monahan.

DeMille's reply pointed to his father's ministry which he said he was now privileged to carry on through motion pictures, the similarity of work between Edison's and his, causing him to retreat to a mountainous wilderness when wrestling with "picture ideas that I believe will bring happiness to millions," just as Edison retreated to the "little dark room in his house in Llewelyn Park." He concluded: *Will you write another letter and tell me in what way I am a "proud, selfish man"?*

Both letters appeared in the *Press* a short time later, providing readers unexpectedly with a candid, softly mordant insight into the workings of the Hollywood producer's mind.

DeMille went to special pains to inject certain touches in his pictures, some merely decorative. His clinical survey of every set kept decorators and researchers in a whirlpool of uncertainty. There were times when they would have sworn he had a telescopic lens attached to each retina, so remarkable was his ability to single out little faults in the most populated scenes.

This sensitivity was put to a severe test many times during production of his Biblical pictures, mostly by extras unfamiliar with religious symbols. At the end of a particularly rough day he spied several "followers of Christ" making the Sign of the Cross improperly, that is, from right to left shoulder. DeMille told his first assistant, the late Edward Salven, to find out what their religious beliefs were. The result was varied, but there was not a Catholic among them. "Fire them. Get me all Catholics and have them here tomorrow," DeMille ordered. Relating the incident later, Salven said he didn't get replacements. "We taught the ones who were fired how to make the Sign of the Cross, and brought them back in, and we got by with it. But you don't take a chance like that often with the old man."

DeMille was almost irrationally allergic to sloppy, half-hearted acting. Even more than an alibi, it caused him immeasurable grief. There is an oft-told episode, typifying his shrewdness underfire, that took place one day when he was deploying an army of civilians for a battle scene, itself a killing job. DeMille had shot take after take. It was then well beyond the luncheon hour. Briefing the players on the meaning of the next scene, his eye fell on a feminine extra talking to someone next to her. He called her up to the microphone, suggested that if what she was saying was that important she should tell it to the entire company. The woman hesitated.

"Go on, dear lady, tell us," urged the producer in a polite tone.

She was a cool-spirited lass, obviously no newcomer to pictures. She bent on him a glare of resentment.

"All right, if you insist. I said, 'Why doesn't the bald-headed old bastard let us go to lunch?'"

DeMille's eyes danced. He loved this kind of spirit. He released a charming smile. "An excellent idea. Company dismissed."

The boss looked upon each scene as a personal challenge. Having spent months in preparation, his mind encompassed every step in the script, first to last. There rarely was need for a caucus on the next move, each sequence laid out ahead of time in bold outline. Delay, therefore, meant only one thing: someone had blundered. Assistants on the sets spent a good deal of time running from cameraman to electrician to "props" to dialogue director, inquiring, "Mr. DeMille wants to know what's holding us up." Once, his patience shattered over the time taken in changing Betty Hutton's trapeze bar, he roared into the microphone: "I opened the Red Sea in less time than this."

Another severe test of his patience took place on the huge "Pennsylvania forest" set for *Unconquered*, spreading across two Paramount sound stages. Midway in the shooting, a sound was heard, like a dove cooing. Someone spied the bird—an Indian dove. That morning it was in splendid voice. DeMille was familiar enough with Allegheny wildlife to know this basso chanticleer had no place in his scene. He ordered it caught and turned over to some humane society. The entire company waited as the pursuit led from one tree to another. Time was ticking away the budget, and a few minutes of such capering was sufficient for the producer. Could it be that the agent of some rival producer was behind the ghastly jest? "Find that little son of a bitch and *shoot* it," he shouted, "and if there's anyone here from a society for the prevention of cruelty to birds I'll be very happy to consult with them in the privacy of my office."

3.

FOR years DeMille would not undertake a picture without Eddie Salven, who became indispensable for his ability to marshal large crowds in scenes involving difficult "traffic."

The tireless, ebullient Salven eased many a tense DeMille set with his lively humor. Crackling rejoinders which press agents often attributed to their famous clients could be traced to Salven. One of the more famous sluiced out during the preliminary work on *Samson and Delilah*. Salven had paused at a writers' discussion of the scene in which Samson slays the Philistines with the jaw of an ass. After a few minutes, Salven raised a hand. "Just a minute," he said. "The jawbone of an ass! Never! This is a DeMille picture and we gotta use the whole ass."

Salven appeared entitled to number himself in the small and brave clique who have undertaken to parry DeMille's thrusts. The claim grew out of one of Salven's most adverse days. DeMille had been roasting him all morning, the abuse growing in volume and variety until Salven could stand it no longer. He confronted the producer, who was sitting in a high chair and pouring vituperation into the microphone held by the perennial "mike boy."

"I'm no mind reader," the harassed director lashed out furiously. "Tell me what you want and I'll do it. Now! What in hell would you like to have?"

Feigning an expression of hurt innocence, DeMille let a few moments elapse as his gaze went slowly from Salven, to crewmen, back to Salven. Then in a low voice, meek, almost cringing, he said, "I'd like to have an assistant director who won't bawl me out in public."

A DeMille favorite of silent days, Thomas Meighan, often testified to the producer's talent for getting results through terror. Meighan apparently was one who came under the boss's hypnotic influence, for he willingly faced the hazards of wild animals and physical upheaval. In *Male and Female*, he agreed to play a love scene with a chloroformed leopard flung over his shoulders. A hero making love while wearing a 250-pound neckpiece was viewed not only as unique but the last word in implacable gallantry. Midway in the love scene with Gloria Swanson, Meighan thought he felt movement in the soft underbelly that lay athwart his neck. He was right; the beast was regaining consciousness because of insufficient dosage. Now, in silent films a little movement does not matter, and sounds of course do not matter at all. DeMille was eager to finish the scene and gestured wildly toward a "safety man" with a high-powered rifle.

"You're doing great, Tommy! That cat's just dreaming! We can't stop now!" he yelled from behind the camera.

Meighan wasn't too sure the cat was only dreaming, for now there were definite tremors and guttural groans; but he kept going, and finished not a second too soon. With a lurch the leopard broke Meighan's hold and flopped crazily to the ground as crewmen with ropes moved in, and actors scattered to safety.

Meighan's recollection of this incident remained vivid for

years. "I took my chances with the leopard. You just don't know what DeMille does to people who spoil scenes."

On the other hand, the producer was filled with dark perplexity over Victor Mature's refusal to engage in controlled combat with a lion in *Samson and Delilah*. He was not expecting more of Mature than was called for by the Book of Judges. There was no gainsaying the fact that the actor was portraying an Old Testament hero who not only crushed beasts with bare hands but is Scripturally acknowledged to have carried away the huge city gates of Gaza. DeMille decided not to meet the problem head-on, thinking Mature might be converted over to the idea if it simmered for a while. He went into the actor's dressing room one day. Mature had not yet given an answer. DeMille broadly hinted at the importance of the Samson-slays-lion scene.

"I never use stuffed animals in my pictures if it can be helped," he said. "And I'll tell you why; they always look stuffed."

The fun-loving actor grinned. "Look, C.B., there's only one Mature and I would hate to see him go this way."

The producer asked him to consider the disposition of the beast they were to use. "I am not going to press the matter, but I can assure you it will be perfectly safe. This lion was trained as a cub and fed on milk."

When DeMille had departed, Mature mused to a friend, "I was raised on milk, too, but I eat meat now."

As a last-ditch measure, DeMille discussed the problem with Hedy Lamarr, who volunteered to parade the aging beast past Mature's dressing room door. This she did, nervously clutching a chain-leash. Mature poked his head out of the dressing room and applauded. "You're so beautiful, Hedy, I can see how any lion would follow you around." He felt the attitude of the lion might change drastically toward a male, particularly one attempting to apply an unfriendly headlock.

What Mature finally took on in combat was an expertly

stuffed specimen. DeMille was morbidly uncomfortable. He ordered the set closed to all except a skeleton crew, and police-men guarded every entry. Once when a workman let out an amused chuckle at the sight of the perspiring actor squeezing the inert mass, DeMille raged, "If I hear another laugh, I'll clear this goddamn set." The scene was intercut with other shots of a bruising scuffle between a real lion named Jackie and his trainer. It proved to be one the best sequences in the picture. Even so, DeMille's congenital showmanship inwardly recoiled at making any concessions to the stuffed creature publicly. Whenever asked by reporters to explain how he staged the lion fight, he would reply mysteriously, "It is a real fight between a man and a lion. You saw it, tell me what *you* think."

It was not unusual for a visitor to exclaim on what was going on behind the camera, for the boss was able at any moment to put on a more fascinating show than his script writers. The train wreck climax of *The Greatest Show on Earth* was a superb challenge to DeMille—splintered cars, fire and smoke, wild animals prowling in the shambles, great numbers of dead and wounded. It took a week to shoot the hand-made cataclysm in the course of which DeMille unloosed a flow of commentary reflecting how he was able to manage scenes of such size. Typi-cal is the following verbatim excerpt:

> I saw them coming in and around ... the men and poles in and around ... I know it, I know it ... I am looking with my eye. You are looking with the finder ... Hey! What have you done with your hands. There are three men here, and I see only two pairs of hands ... Do you hear me? What have you done with your hands? Damn it! Listen to me, what have you ... There, that's better ... You're right, right. There were only two men when I rehearsed it. ... The elephant was much farther forward. The elephant was much farther forward! Will someone in this vast assem-blage of talented assistants listen to me? We've only been at this three days now. Not a bad record, you know. If we

keep going at this speed we may finish the picture by 1963.... GET THAT ELEPHANT BACK! He keeps edging forward all the time.... [To Miss Hutton, who is urging an elephant to lift wreckage off Charlton Heston] Betty, is it better for you if the elephant starts there? Okay, that's all right with me. All right. Elephant! Action! Hold it! Mel, you take out the kitty. TAKE AWAY THE KITTY! I won't be using her on this line.... Let me see the action from where you drop down.... Are there any legs or anything in there? Get your leg there. No! No! YOUR LEG! Do you want me to show you where your leg is! That's it, that's it, you're doing better already. Now you know where your leg is. You have me to thank for that. You see what you learn working on a DeMille picture.... Are there any legs on the other side? ... Wait a minute. I want to see this spot where he says that. I think ... I think we should give a little bit of play ... I want to get you in while he's saying his line to you.... Do you need a cushion [To Miss Hutton kneeling]. She can have a cushion if she needs it. It doesn't show.... Do that with the entrance once, will you, for me, Betty? ... I would keep John's legs right there, to look like he's still pulling on that pole.... Here's my ... Oh! for God's sake, why don't you turn it? All you have to do is turn it. I don't care whether you focus the mike or not. It takes you longer to do that than it does for me to make a motion picture.... [To sound man] It isn't a lion roaring from the cage. It's hard to get tiger roars but it's easy to get lions. Pick up tigers whenever you can.... Get me a finder.... Wait a minute, wait a minute! We may have to ... STOP! EVERY-BODY STOP! DON'T DO ANYTHING....

DeMille's bold methods on the sets were viewed with envy by most Hollywood producers. Though they considered him foolhardy at times, they secretly admired his skill in getting important stars to take the risks. Producer Leo McCarey, a DeMille booster, looked upon the showman's powers of persuasion as a form of black magic. "No one knows how or why the stars do it," he says. "Not even the stars themselves, but they do."

Implacably, DeMille weighed the dangers. He made a point always of holding one solid trump in reserve. Should an actor show the least inclination to back away from a dangerous assignment, DeMille would stoutly come forward, with studied gravity to alert the company to the imminence of a *tour de force,* then perform the feat himself in the grand manner of a Shakespearean tragedian.

For the Samson picture he had engaged a 6-foot-5, 260-pound wrestler named "Wee Willie" Davis to play a character called the King's Wrestler. In his big scene, Wee Willie was to snare Victor (Samson) Mature with a bullwhip thirty feet long, the end of the whip to wind sharply around Mature's waist. The actor was questioning DeMille closely on the possible effects of this maneuver, it being evident that Mature's confidence in Wee Willie as a handler of the bullwhip was not overwhelming. In reply, DeMille strode out onto the set, and struck a muscular pose twenty feet from the bearded giant. "Okay, Willie, let me have it." Willie brought the whip forward from a long backhand swing, snapping it sharply around DeMille's chest, which was protected only by his shirt. It left a welt as thick as a pencil, but no one that day knew of the injury. DeMille walked loftily back to his high chair. He said it was as simple as that, and suggested they get on with the picture.

Later, in the wedding-brawl scene, DeMille stepped into the breach for Bill Farnum, brother of Dustin. Bill faced the task of being struck by a plaster block hurled from a balustrade by Mature in the midst of the free-for-all, which, as the Bible intimates, reached quite a nasty stage. DeMille went through the movements necessary, he said, to avoid injury when being hit on the chest by seventy pounds of plaster.

"One has to roll with it," he said.

He waved to Mature to hurl the object. Mature, eyes gleaming, raised the chunk over his head and let go with more *élan* than the occasion seemed to warrant. The full force of the blow sent the sixty-eight-year-old producer to the floor with an alarming crash. Dazed, he rose, calmly turned to Farnum. "A little more rolling with the blow will do it," he said.

Physically DeMille was as tough as a steer's horn. He directed the last half of one of his epics from a stretcher, brushing aside the doctor's advice to allow himself a few weeks to recuperate from an operation. He was seventy-three when he marched onto the Egyptian desert in the van of thousands of extras, recruited from nomadic tribes by sheiks acting as his agents, to film the final picture of his life, *The Ten Commandments*. While climbing the volcanic peaks of Mount Sinai he suffered a mild heart attack. This time he obeyed a physician's orders against further effort of the kind, not only out of fear for the now real danger to his own welfare but also of what might happen to his and Paramount's $12-million investment should he be sidelined. The film, released in 1956, was his second version of the Exodus. The upheaval that beset the first version in 1923 was still a piquant memory. Notwithstanding, his indomitable press agents sent dispatches from Egypt to the United States relating how DeMille had carried on against medical advice. The press was enchanted but back at Paramount there were alarmed reactions. The attack forced him to film scenes at Paramount which he had planned to shoot on the African location. The concession to his doctors was a temporary one; back at the studio the boss returned to his old pace, with family members and Paramount executives failing in an effort to slow him down.

Times considerably less lush would have befallen Hollywood doctors had all their movie clientele been blessed with DeMille's sturdiness. His dentist proclaimed him to be dentally perfect except for one small filling. At one period, however, he was afflicted by severe back pains that almost brought him to heel. Unwilling to take the time to see a doctor, he became interested in a powder which a studio executive credited with having almost mystical powers. "It's called Gamma Ray," the friend said. "I put it next to my back once for a few minutes and the aches disappeared." Not a little mystical himself on occasion, DeMille prevailed upon the friend to secure for him some of the Gamma Ray, about $500 worth. The powder was sealed in glass inside a gold case about the size of a five-cent piece. DeMille taped it on, at the small of his back, and later told the staff his aches had disappeared. Although the powder had no therapeutic value in that particular application, the boss put great store by it, even insisted that an assistant experiencing similar aches tape it to his back. The man did, with no results other than several days of anguish which he suffered when he misplaced the precious vial and thought for a time it had been swallowed by his two-year-old daughter. The boss's seeming immunity to run-of-the-mill illnesses from this or that virus evoked many astonished comments, to which he usually replied, "No bug is brave enough or mean enough to live in me."

4.

IN his office one day Mr. DeMille was commenting that he had not had the benefit of a college education. "I have been accused of not being able to read, but no one has ever said that I can't add."

To prove his point he began telling us how in the old days they poured chemicals from the film-developing room down an open gutter that ran to a nearby sewer.

"The chemicals discolored the gutters and we were warned by the City of Los Angeles to dispose of the solutions in some other way. A kindly old soul came along and offered to haul away the hypo for twenty-five cents a tank. I did a little figuring and found he couldn't make expenses that way. While I am a great believer in human kindness, I never heard of anyone doing anything for nothing so I refused his offer and waited to see what would happen. Other studios had signed up with the old guy and a few days later he came back and offered to do it for nothing. Then he said he would *pay* me twenty-five cents a tank. I eventually told him I would not sell the stuff at all but would go fifty-fifty with him if he let me in on his secret."

He paused, opened a drawer of his desk and withdrew a glittering little ingot.

"I've kept it all these years as a reminder to be careful when someone wants to buy something from me. Well, it's solid silver. You see, this man had discovered that the silver in the hypo could be reclaimed. I learned his secret and it paid most of our chemical bills for quite a while."

There was much of the mule trader in DeMille, a trait that ran like a golden thread through the fabric of his business contracts. The native shrewdness was observed by a Federal court in a tax suit against the DeMille corporation in the early 1930's. In the action the Government claimed the company had accumulated a surplus far beyond its corporate purposes, and demanded additional taxes on more than a million dollars.

The Government lost, and DeMille preserved his company's capital-gains advantages. In an *obiter dictum,* the court took time to take a perplexed and admiring glance at DeMille's way of doing business. It commented on the company policy of investing no money of its own in film productions and using the facilities of other studios.

As a bargainer, DeMille had a rule of thumb: "Cut the price in half, then argue like hell." He enjoyed a tactical advantage in the case of actors eager for a DeMille picture "credit" on their record, and was able to press this advantage with considerable effectiveness among up-and-coming stars.

During the casting of *Greatest Show on Earth* James Stewart, the actor, sent word through an agent of his acceptance of the part of the clown. It was good news; DeMille was secretly determined to engage Stewart, at the right price of course, for a role which he felt the popular star was eminently qualified to play. What almost upended the boss was the disclosure that Stewart's charge would be only $50,000—one-fourth the actor's usual price per picture!

Mr. DeMille was edified, and naturally perplexed. Even after Stewart explained his decision, he remained perplexed. Stewart told us that all his life he had dreamed of playing a clown, a burning desire from boyhood, and his elation over the offer was so great that he decided to set a price that DeMille could not refuse.

Noble sentiments always moved the boss, especially in later years when his numerous political and union adversities impressed upon him the value of higher motives. On this occasion, however, he was able to put aside this reverence long enough one day to reflect on the outcome if he had had the foresight to reject Stewart's offer and haggle with him. "After all," he mused, "the role of clown wasn't the biggest in the picture."

During his relatively brief association with Mr. DeMille, Dan Lord observed him to be "a strange and fascinating blend of absolute monarch and charming gentleman, a prince with the instincts of a Barnum, a man with the Midas touch, a film director who made even more money in the banking business, extravagant, *while all the time he never lost sight of a penny or really wasted a single foot of film.*"

The late Roy Burns was DeMille's purchasing agent for forty years. Stocky, humorless, irascible, Burns won some eminence as one of the toughest traders in the movie mart. In time he drove bargains that drew grunts of satisfaction even from the boss. Burns moved in mysterious ways, never revealing the nature or outcome of a mission except in whispered disclosures to the boss. He did a good deal of scurrying back and forth, and had little to say to the staff; he communicated his findings to the boss, mouth-to-ear, in the manner of a man about to disclose the identity of a new ocean.

For the circus picture, Burns grappled with the task of moving hundreds of extras and "bit" players to Sarasota for a six-week stay. But worse, he was not to pay more than $175 weekly in the face of the fact that most, under guild rates, earned $200 to $300. Burns was able to keep the figure at $175 or under by holding up the combined lure of Florida sunshine and DeMille prestige.

Some years before, much secrecy was provided to protect well-known players who had taken minor roles in *The King of Kings.* They were artists whose pay ranged from $350 to $1,000 weekly, some working for as little as $25 a day to tide them over the dull season. Beards and flowing robes concealed their identity, and their names were not mentioned in the cast of characters.

One of DeMille's old hands, Art Rosson, a capable second-unit or "location" director, foraged for years in out-of-the-way places to film unusual backgrounds. His first assignment was back in 1935, on *The Plainsman.* A small man with a world of patience, Rosson's eyes twinkle when he recalls efforts to meet the boss's specifications. "I don't remember a single time when he approved immediately any scene I ever shot," he says, "and of course he would jump up and down over what he felt were wasted dollars." But most of Rosson's work somehow always appeared in the final footage.

During the screening of considerable location footage which Rosson had shot for *Unconquered,* DeMille found more than usual to complain about, at one point severely rapping a particular scene.

"I cannot understand why Mr. Rosson wasted his time," Mr. DeMille growled, addressing, not Rosson, who was sitting nearby, but the assembled technicians. "To put it plainly this has cost us a lot of money, and to make it even plainer, the scene stinks."

He turned and glared at Rosson. After a few moments, Rosson said softly, "I didn't shoot that scene, Mr. DeMille."

"You didn't! Then who did?"

"That was one of yours, sir."

Like a flash, DeMille barked, "I don't care who shot the scene, I say it stinks and it has got to come out!"

In the early days DeMille had a cameraman whose skill was marred by an unfortunate habit. He would forget to remove the cover from the camera lens, the equivalent of shooting without film. When he was engaged, DeMille gave specific instructions as to this failing. "If you discover you have forgotten the cover," DeMille advised, "don't tell anyone. Just leave the studio quietly and don't come back." One day the man did forget; he left the studio without a word and was not heard from again.

The Hollywood climate bred an appetite for wealth that could be attained with speed and, if at all possible, honor. At the height of its most acquisitive era, the colony bristled internally with resourcefulness, sly gambits and display of wits. On the prowl for largess, the untalented chased studio executives with lively vigor, well-dressed mendicants wreathed in smiles. With this much hounding going on night and day, affable and deceptive as it was, dispensers of favors were ever on their guard. Personages like DeMille were often forced into protective retreat, sweeping aside all appeals of favor-seekers and proposition-makers.

It was only a short step to two-fisted cynicism. We took the same attitude in the bungalow: No deal was right unless we got it on *our* terms. DeMille himself had adopted the policy years before. He had a knack for polite, adroit escape from his pursuers.

On the other hand, his own talent for pursuit was not inconsiderable.

In the early 1920's he set out to buy Margaretta Tuttle's

sensational novel, *Feet of Clay*. The post-bellum tale of the hero who lost half of a foot in battle was first published serially, and in book form quickly reached a sixth edition.

Several parties were interested in the movie rights. The gossip indicated that substantial offers had been made, one reportedly as high as $25,000, another $50,000.

DeMille instructed a Paramount spokesman in New York to telephone Mrs. Tuttle and offer $2,500, but not to divulge his name.

The spokesman began by asking Mrs. Tuttle what she would sell the movie rights for.

"What will you give?" asked the author.

"Twenty-five hundred dollars."

Her reply was typically feminine but irrefutable. "Why should I accept $2,500 when I've already been offered $25,000?"

The caller asked who had made such an offer and Mrs. Tuttle replied that she could not say. It was a straight-forward reply; at that point the $25,000 offer had also been made by an agent for an undisclosed principal.

The maneuver revealed two things to DeMille—the highest offer and the possibility a matching offer would buy the movie rights.

The following morning DeMille's agent called again, this time offering $23,000.

Mrs. Tuttle again referred to the $25,000 bid.

The caller said he would contact her again tomorrow.

The third proposal was in combination—$25,000 *and* Cecil B. DeMille. Mrs. Tuttle gleefully accepted, recalling in later years that though she had never seen a DeMille movie up to that time she "did remember he had written the Peter Grimm story, which I admired extravagantly."

Readers were beguiled by Mrs. Tuttle's story—a hero with half a foot, and it was that feature that aroused Hollywood's interest. But DeMille felt there was not enough bounce in a loss of toes by shell blast. His film version, with Rod LaRocque in the male lead, changed this item procedurally to reflect what has often been called "the DeMille touch." A shark bites off the hero's toes!

DeMille's sense of economy seemed to drive him unwillingly to little frugalities. These, when smilingly called to his attention by intimates, embarrassed him, and he would speak of the poverty of his boyhood and early marital years. He ordered his office to use the back of old scripts for scratch paper. He kept score on each razor blade, discarding it only when it had served him a required number of times. During a postwar drive for clothes for the needy of foreign countries Mr. DeMille, moved by their plight, instructed the family to choose an older suit or two, some shirts and socks. He owned a costly array of cashmere suits, some a decade or two old but showing little sign of wear. A few of these older models, with other articles, were laid out on his bed for his approval, prior to shipment abroad. The boss eyed these selections, and returned them to the closet. The following day they were back on his bed, whereupon DeMille returned them again to his closet. The silent contest went on a few more days and finally the family, who had been through this sort of thing before, sent the shipment off without any contributions from the head of the house. When DeMille learned he had been left out he was furious, demanding to know why some of *his* things had not been included.

Great skill was often reflected in his thrift. He had staged a march of British soldiers in his early version of *The Buccaneer*, holding up the episode as an inducement to the wise employment of special effects. "You could see the line of British for five miles," he said. "It was done with eight soldiers and six mirrors." His contract with Paramount usually called for a percentage of a picture after his share of the production cost had been liquidated by income. Therefore, any expense or salary paid by Paramount to DeMille's staff was reflected in his ultimate share of the proceeds. This necessarily caused him to eye Paramount's expenditures rather closely, particularly in areas where such expenditures had no direct or visible effect on the picture itself. He detested "hidden costs," but would authorize any amount whatsoever that could be seen on the screen. Any other expenditure was a waste.

He was faced one day with deciding how much "in-between salary" should be paid a staff member, a veteran of more than forty years of continuous service. It was Paramount's policy to keep DeMille's production assistants on the studio payroll *between* pictures, periods that often ran as long as two years. For this particular assistant Paramount suggested a weekly salary of $150, which would cut the assistant's regular stipend in half. DeMille said he saw no reason for that figure, reduced it to $100. The employee was a woman, an expert in her field, performing a task of which no one else in the DeMille organization was capable. She had devoted her professional life to the boss, yet his bizarre sense of equity, recoiling at anything other than what he deemed a fair consideration, compelled him to take an action that was in painful conflict with his sentiments.

On another occasion, a battle of claims and counterclaims featured a negotiation over a contract between Mr. DeMille and the writer. We had committed ourselves to prepare a series of syndicated newspaper articles to appear weekly under the title, "Cecil DeMille Speaking." It was proposed by Miss Rosson that I should prepare a contract in letter form, setting forth what I felt the agreement should provide.

In the first several drafts, I suggested that we should divide equally whatever proceeds were derived from *my* articles about *his* life. This did not strike him as equitable, proposing instead a 90/10 split. I then offered to perform the service without charge rather than accept so small a share.

He rejected this as unthinkable, and agreed to the fifty-fifty arrangement. At this point, he called in Miss Rosson, whose advice on day-to-day matters guided him almost entirely in later years. She felt that a clause should be added to cover lawsuits that might result from the articles. Acquiescing, the boss penciled in a provision whereby my share of the proceeds would be used to satisfy legal judgments. Miss Rosson was openly critical of this unilateral approach, so finally it was agreed that, if we were sued, all proceeds from the articles would be put into a fund for settlement of court judgments. We left unanswered the question as to who would pay the balance of judgments when the fund was exhausted.

DeMille was indefatigable in his march toward conquest by contract, and would sacrifice a key actor if he felt he was being pushed.

Unhappily, casting brought him into contact with agents. If such an estate were possible, DeMille would have assigned player agents to a category several degrees below the low esteem in which he held newspaper critics. He viewed them as cuckolds misrepresenting their clients for vulgar gain, a subject which the producer could discuss coolly only with difficulty.

At one time he was considering a young English actress, Deborah Kerr, for a leading role in *Unconquered*. Though notably successful in her own country, Miss Kerr was new then to Hollywood, a factor that would seem to have an important bearing on the asking price.

Much maneuvering for position preceded Mr. DeMille's first conference with Miss Kerr's agent.

He suggested with more than an inference that the actress's career in America would be greatly accelerated by her appearance in a DeMille picture, perhaps even to the extent of stardom overnight.

The agent nodded agreement.

"Her name does not mean very much in America now," the boss purred.

"Her price is still $4,000 a week, plus expenses, with a minimum of eighteen weeks," the agent said. "That adds up to a minimum guarantee of $72,000, plus expenses."

"Not worth it," shouted the boss. "She's trying to make money off of DeMille, and DeMille only wants her if he can make money off of her. Good day, sir."

When the agent was gone, the boss recalled he had paid Gloria Swanson only $75 a week "and she was with me for years" and, ever mindful of the infirmity of front-office mentality, added, "Then Paramount took her over for $3,000 a week."

Another time a Ringling circus performer asked $500 for his stint in *Greatest Show on Earth*. We offered $200. This was rejected. We then offered $250, and stood firm. No deal was made. This brief encounter was typical of the outcome of negotiations that, unfortunately, began at a level reasonably near the performer's real worth. Were he alive to the boss's cut-the-price-in-half-and-argue-like-hell philosophy, he would have doubled his original offer, and settled at one half the figure.

Prior to the filming of the Samson script, DeMille ran across an old book called *Judge and Fool*, by a deceased Russian author, that unlocked for us one of the plot puzzles in the Bible story.

DeMille authorized Paramount to offer the widow the sum of $750 for the right to use the story twist. No word of the progress of the negotiation reached the bungalow, so one afternoon the boss called Paramount's New York office, which was handling the matter.

"We bought *Judge and Fool*," the voice announced.

"What did you pay for it?" asked DeMille.

"Five thousand dollars, sir."

Livid with rage, DeMille unleashed a flow of invective, banged the receiver, then, panting like a chased fawn, sat quietly for several minutes until his composure returned, describing this latest executive sortie as the product of a palsied nature. Later, however, he rose to the nobility of the transaction, concluding that anything less than their gesture to the widow would have been gross cruelty.

This sort of bustle and fuss reached out one day to envelop a piece of classic writing by James Fenimore Cooper—an essay about the circus. DeMille wanted to use it in his voice-in-the-background introduction in the opening reel of the *Greatest Show on Earth*.

Representatives of the Cooper estate sent word it would allow use of the material, about two hundred words, upon payment of $500. Mr. DeMille authorized a counter offer of $200, which was refused.

One of the lines in the Cooper essay referred to the circus as "a driving, dogged, almost desperate thing."

Rather than pay $500 for the entire excerpt Mr. DeMille decided he would use only that line. But Paramount attorneys advised that use of the phrase alone would require payment of the full amount.

"We'll change the phrase," declared DeMille, visualizing himself in the throes of economic warfare.

The attorneys agreed that if a word or two was substituted the phrase might be safely used without risking a law suit.

The staff was then set to work thinking up synonyms for "dogged" and "desperate." We came up with quite a few— "tenacious," "unflinching," "frenzied," "indomitable."

The phrase, shorn of Cooper originality, appeared in the script as "a driving, determined, almost frantic thing."

"Now," chortled DeMille, "let them sue on three words!"

5.

MR. DeMILLE would not carry used currency, so secretaries made frequent visits to the bank to exchange wrinkled bills for crisp ones. His bulging wallet contained another item—a small cardboard disc that was GOOD FOR 1 QUART OF MILK. It reminded him of the early days of privation, and those memories influenced his love of good things. His productions were big, colorful, often gaudy. His clothes were not. There was subtle showmanship in his sartorial taste. He leaned toward soft colors, browns and grays, in his suits, hand-tailored to a meticulous fit. He loved the feel of cashmere but fine imported worsteds were also featured in his wardrobe. Even in this respect, he showed his distaste for waste; he did not have row on row of suits, as might be warrantably assumed. They were, however, in considerable number, some quite old but reflecting the great care which the owner lavished upon his personal things.

He was inclined toward color ensembles with custom-made shirts of pastel hue and conservative four-in-hands. A modest display that escaped most observers were his ring-and-tie sets, the color of the tie always matching that of the semiprecious stone in the ring.

For a time, a deaf-mute tended to Mr. DeMille's English-imported shoes. The service was performed in the boss's office and it appeared he found pleasure in chatting with the boy, always paying him handsomely. On one occasion the fee was accompanied by an autographed picture, on which he had written, *The eyes are the windows of the soul.* CECIL B. DE-MILLE.

His on-the-set attire in later years was casual, open-throat shirt and trousers, but considerably more showy in the early days. A local newspaper noted in 1923 that he wore "a green sport shirt with one of the world's five green diamonds to match, set in a ring of green gold."

During the remake of *The Squaw Man* a few years later he passed around gold-tipped cigarettes to reporters visiting the set. On that occasion he was "a symphony in brown—chocolate-brown rough cloth with Norfolk jacket, soft shirt of jonquil yellow, tie of yellow and ruby floral design and cuff links and ring with ruby setting." The outfit alternated with shirt open at the throat, pants and puttees, Louis XV hat, drooping pipe and silver whistle, which gave way to the loudspeaker in 1924.

He was unable to work in unattractive surroundings. The cluttered museumlike look of his office served to accent its air of casual wealth. When he opened his own studio in 1925 he took over Ince's personal suite, which resembled a small cathedral in one room and an old Spanish galleon in another. DeMille tore it all out, designed one large room from two, removing every vestige of Ince's kind of meaningless display. If display had meaning, it was admissible. There was hardly an item in his office that did not tell a story or yield a moral, and visitors were treated to the genealogy of each object as DeMille ceremoniously conducted office tours lasting for hours.

His favorite transportation for years was an aged Locomobile, built for General Pershing. He paid $11,000 for it. His sprightly humor rose to the surface when reminiscing about this possession. "After I bought it I took it to Don Lee, the Cadillac dealer, and told him I wanted another body for the car. He began to jump up and down like a chimpanzee released in its native jungle among a lot of bananas. He drew a sketch of his idea, a long, low car. It was the first chassis that gave him a chance to build a passenger car that was long and low. Immediately the Cadillac people took it up and started to use it. And that changed the whole pattern of cars."

Until recent years, when budgets forced him to keep longer hours, he considered it unthinkable that anyone would not dress for dinner. He traced it to the total decline of culture in America, and the low estate of the spoken language. "The murder of the English language starts in the schools with the terrible abuse of daily speech. We have completely stopped speaking the pure language. Use of a broad English or similar accent is not a sign of culture. It is merely a coating of polish. On my yacht I always dressed for dinner every night, even though I was alone. It gave one a feeling of self-respect, of culture. If we forget all the niceties of life we revert to a lower civilization eventually."

DeMille was frequently interviewed by beauty and fashion editors, who found his observations in these fields extremely printable. He told one editor that his ideal actress was "a blonde with a brunette soul." To another he commented, "A well-cut negligee can make a woman look as stunning as a man does in a polo coat."

He had a nightmarish memory of a conversation with an aspiring actress. "She was the most beautiful woman I had ever met, and when I asked what experience she had as an actress she replied, 'Whatever I have did I have did good.'"

He once told Paulette Goddard, "Never go across the alley even to dump garbage unless you are dressed to the teeth."

A woman's page editor who titled her article "Venus de Mille" quoted him as saying, "To me little signs of personal habits of life are more important than pure physical beauty. If I found that the greatest beauty in the world habitually let her shoes run down at the heel and failed to adjust her petticoat to the proper length on all sides, I would be doubtful about employing her. Because slovenly habits usually betoken slovenly brains."

He was inclined at times to pooh-pooh what he called "ravishing beauty." Some women are "delightful to look upon but, well, don't make very much of an impression. On the other hand we see a girl come along whose nose tips up, whose mouth is too large—and in a moment she is surrounded by admirers. What is the reason? Charm. She has warmth and vibrance of personality. People look at a cool, statuesque beauty much as they would admire the statue of Venus; but they love the girl of vivid interest, sparkling eyes and instant emotional reactions."

He contended that most of the so-called beauties in Hollywood look alike.

"It's mass production. They all have the same hairdress, the same make-up. They don't look alike when they arrive here, but Hollywood pours them into a mold and stamps them like coins."

He saw a beauty-isn't-everything parallel between choosing a wife and casting an actress. "You bring home a round-eyed, vapid little creature, and when the first ecstasy of marital bliss is over you wonder why she doesn't say something. You look for a sign of intelligence and none is forthcoming. You walk into the clear cold night air and you say to yourself, 'What have I gotten myself into? Maybe Mama was right!' Pictures today demand more than a pretty face, but I am afraid too many film-goers choose beauty instead of brains. They choose a rounded figure that can't enunciate a line and reject a flat chest capable of a brilliant performance."

He said he chose leading women who had the ability to create the illusion of beauty. "Sarah Bernhardt and Duse are examples of what I mean by this. Neither was a beauty. Bernhardt, all her life, was scrawny, and her features were anything but classic. But to the day of her death—a poor, crippled old woman with a wooden leg and with her wrinkled face rouged and powdered—she could come on the stage and by the alchemy of her talent and charm produce the illusion of a young and beautiful Camille. This power is far more precious than real beauty. Beauty is one of the cheapest things on the market today. It is so cheap that it has little value. The sidewalks of Hollywood, the classrooms, the restaurants, are full of beautiful girls. My objections to beauties as leading women are briefly summed up. They are too posey, too stilted, too unwilling to reflect emotion and thus ruffle the beautiful calm of their classic features. This may be conscious or unconscious, but it is always there in a really beautiful woman. She inclines to drape herself in classic poses. She moves with lack of fire, she is aloof from emotion. Spoiled by life, she does not feel the urge to improve herself, to be pleasing, to exhibit feeling. There is always someone who tells these beauties in their infancy that worry and emotion destroy the fine fabric of beauty. They never forget this, and this ruins them as actresses."

It was a rather drastic admission for one who had put such store by beauty.

A few years ago, when asked to give his definition of personality, he drew back with feigned alarm, retorted, "Am I supposed to isolate and hold up to view the spark which once in a lifetime kindles and enflames the soul of some mortal?"

One day he related the circumstances that led him to some of his early leading players.

"Bebe Daniels came to my notice in a 2-reel Harold Lloyd comedy and after seeing her fall off a roller coaster in one of them, I decided she was just the person to be introduced to the public as a siren of ancient Babylon in *Male and Female*. Bebe's mother brought her around to see me. The girl had stooped shoulders and walked like a duck. I felt she could act. Acting came natural to her, but I almost lost my mind teaching her to stand up straight. After weeks of working with her I let her remain on the screen for only 150 feet, but upon that brief appearance she built an important career. In the days when Bebe, Gloria Swanson, Wallace Reid and the rest were being placed

before the world with echo-ringing ballyhoo, it seemed that
they were some sort of superhumans, that they had been carefully nurtured in luxury and suckled by art. Not so. Wally Reid
was just what we call a 'young punk' when he was being given
all that fanfare. I had seen him do that fight as the blacksmith
in *The Birth of a Nation* for D. W. Griffith, and had put him
under contract for $75 a week. He was wooden and for many
pictures had to be led around by the hand. A failing studio
asked us to take Agnes Ayres off its hands. We found her
beautiful, but the victim of depressing mannerisms which were
soon eradicated.

"Leatrice Joy was so frightened by the realization that her
chance had come that it was difficult to get any response at all
from her. She was shut right up inside of a shell and could not
let herself go. We had a terrible time, and finally decided that
the only way to handle her was with a club. We knew we had
to smash that reserve, that shell, that tightness with which she
was holding herself; otherwise, she would never get anywhere
on the screen. So I started out on my campaign with her. It
almost killed both of us. I scolded and stormed and did my best
to break down that shell, but she seemed to shrivel up all the
more. We went through two weeks of the most terrible agony
for her and for myself. One night, after we had worked very
late, I brought Leatrice and her brother into my office. Leatrice
was all upset, thinking I was going to discharge her. I realized
that she thought this, so I decided to tell her I was going to fire
her. I told her she had not made good, and that although we
were two weeks on the picture, I could not go on with her.

"She went all to pieces, and wept all over the chair, all over
her brother and all over me. I let her go on. She thought she
was through and she wept her heart out, saying that I had
ruined her life by taking this from her, and that her heart was
broken. Right at the height of this, when she was in the middle
of the floor, broken and crumpled up, I stopped her and asked

her to look at herself, at her position, to note how her hands were clutching, and the position in which her head had fallen, and the condition she had gotten into through letting herself go and breaking through that shell in which she had been living. I told her not to move, but to think, and soon she realized that the fear was gone, and she said, 'I know what you mean.' After that she had an easy road to stardom."

6.

A LARGE population of extra and "bit" players migrated from one DeMille picture to another and we were besieged daily by appeals from actors hungering for a "DeMille credit." Old-timers, particularly, knew from experience that a DeMille part was not something easily come by. The reward often went to the actor with the greatest zeal and ingenuity. Mr. DeMille usually treated petitioners kindly, and on occasion would hire a player for the witty manner in which his attention was courted.

For this reason the older and wiser employed a special approach. They would maintain a luncheon-hour watch at the lot entrance next to the bungalow. At a pre-arranged signal, often from a staff member, they would hurry to DeMille's side as the producer emerged from the bungalow followed by his retinue of assistants. DeMille always walked briskly to the studio café a few yards away, so it behooved the job-seeker to be fleet of foot, speed to DeMille's side and quickly blurt out the supplication, which was always most carefully rehearsed. Probably the most historic of such entreaties was uttered by a middle-aged woman who, with a Paramount guard bearing down upon her, cried, "Mr. DeMille, you probably don't remember me but I was a harlot in your *Golden Bed*." Through the years two and sometimes three generations of the same family appeared in his pictures. One energetic mother hurled her proudest lineal boast, in the effort to get herself and son engaged as extras: "Sir, you killed my four-year-old Bobby in *The Sign of the Cross* and he's a married man now!" Persons thus woven into the past were given preference and their names were added to a roster of "DeMille alumni."

Paulette Goddard proved herself most resourceful while angling for the part of Louvette, a sexy half-breed in *Northwest Mounted Police*."

It was a big part and DeMille was keeping pretty quiet about it.

Paulette tried telephone calls, chatty notes and occasional visits to the DeMille luncheon table, then hit upon something bolder.

She knew about DeMille's weakness for petite feet.

Intimates are quick to proclaim that Miss Goddard's feet are shapely, though perhaps not as small as Gloria Swanson's, whose window-display size 2½ AA was a Paramount boast for years.

One day Paulette appeared in an inner door leading to De-Mille's office, dressed in a sparse costume, her reddish hair falling carelessly over shoulders gleaming with walnut dye— and feet connivingly bare. Altogether she presented a most pleasurable picture, walking into DeMille's office with a slow, primitive gait that proved to be effective, though hardly indigenous to the North country. She struck an artful pose on the couch in front of his desk, and announced, "I am Louvette," then quoted a line from the script: "You lyin' Scotch Indian! Son-uma-gun! I t'ink I keel you!"

DeMille liked what he saw and gave her the part.

Paulette confessed she was fascinated by the complex machinery of a DeMille movie, but even more by what it could do for her career. "Every actress wanted to get into a DeMille picture. Just one could keep your name in front of the public for years."

Paulette played a bond slave in *Unconquered* and brooded all through it. There were virtually no moments of finery or romance such as actresses cherish. Moreover, as the heroine of the piece she was a bit weary of being pushed around by an assortment of frontier roughnecks. White traitors and painted Indians alternated taking her into custody, and with each seizure fresh violence broke out—with Paulette in the center. In the "torture stake" scene DeMille had three Seneca braves lunging at Paulette with heated spears. Always a good trouper, she rehearsed the scene for hours, memorizing the movements of the "braves" as they thrust the (real) smoking spear tips within inches of her face.

DeMille had prepared for the climax, the siege of the Fort, with his usual gusto. Arrows and fireballs were dipped in kerosene, ignited and tossed into the Fort yard by means of makeshift catapults. The crew called them "DeMille cocktails." Before the day was over, several players had suffered burns, the worst by a drummer boy. This lad, apparently inspired by the martial atmosphere, did not flinch when one of the fireballs landed on his hands as he was beating a call to action. DeMille later handed him a Walter Raleigh anniversary half-dollar, his customary token for performances "beyond the call for duty."

There were no rehearsals of the massive episode. The players themselves were unaware of the number or kind of fiery ordnance that was to fly into the enclosure from the outside. DeMille's instructions to the cast were that no matter what happened they were to react as they would in real life. The result was graphic. Two women, their long skirts ignited, screamed and jigged as they brushed the sparks, and there was much dodging of the fiery pellets.

Paulette's place in the scene was at the business end of a bucket brigade composed entirely of women. She was to take a position atop a ladder and pour water on a structure ignited by one of the fireballs. The siege was reaching a high pitch of volume and fury when a discovery of quite serious import was called to DeMille's attention: There was no heroine. Paulette, taking one look at the proceedings, had walked off the picture. From her dressing room she sent word to the effect that, love him though she did, DeMille was carrying his siege too far. The producer, white with indignation, stormed up and down the set and finally ordered a double to take Paulette's place. It meant a long shot instead of a close-up; the double suffered slight hand burns. It was a galling substitution that deprived him of the opportunity to demonstrate to the world once more how in a DeMille picture the stars also take the risks.

Paulette frequently made it known she held no grudge against DeMille for asking her to risk her life. A few years later she began another series of overtures, this time aimed at getting one of the top spots in *The Greatest Show on Earth*. DeMille was preparing for the picture in the spring of 1950 and happened to be at a Ringling circus performance at Madison Square Garden. Paulette was there too, and joined DeMille in his box. A few days later she wrote him:

DEAR C.B.

I'm sorry I missed saying goodbye to you after my thrilling evening with you at the circus.

I *do* hope and pray that I get "The Part" in your coming film. I will be a good, good girl!

In the meantime I shall be working hard in summer stock.

Yours,
PAULETTE

P.S. You can get me from Paramount. I have pretty feet, too.

Love, P.G.

To this, DeMille replied by letter:

Indeed your feet are beautiful. What bothers me is that those same lovely feet might be tempted to walk off the set a second time.

"No one," he commented later, "ever walked off a DeMille set and came back."

Though Paulette failed to land a part in *The Greatest Show on Earth,* others were busy with little stratagems calculated to shatter DeMille's careful defenses. One of the more spirited competitors for a key spot in the circus picture, Betty Hutton sent over an elaborate floral creation—in circus motif, festooned with hundreds of expensive blooms. Its centerpiece was a china doll swinging from a trapeze, the part Betty was after. A note with it read:

> My career is in your hands! I've never been so happy in my life at the thought of working with the greatest of them all— C. B. DeMille.
>
> > Love,
> > BETTY (*can do anything— will travel*) HUTTON

We were set to work devising a reply to all this, and from several samples DeMille selected one with a lighter touch:

> Tournament of Roses was never like this. Definitely favor your directing as well as playing in the picture and urge you to consider me for role of elephant boy. You are marvelous. What other man in the world can tell his grandchildren that Betty Hutton once sent him a bouquet of nineteen orchids, seven hundred fifty Esther Reed daisies, two thousand stock blossoms, two dozen garnet roses and three dozen Lillies of the Nile. My heart belongs to Annie with or without a gun.
>
> > CECIL B. DeMILLE

(*His mention of Annie was in reference to the title role played by Betty in* Annie Get Your Gun.)

DeMille had called in Gloria Grahame to discuss the elephant-girl part. He had to have an understanding with her because the part involved what the Ringling people call a "foot-on-face" act—an elephant lowers a foot close enough to the performer's face to smudge the tip of her nose. A few days later DeMille received a second floral piece, arranged about an elephant with foot resting on the face of a circus figurine. DeMille commented on the ingenuity of the sender and told his publicity man, "Even if I didn't know who sent it I would give her the part."

A similar but smaller gift arrived a few days later. It was from Dorothy Lamour, with the note:

> Dear C.B.:
> Sorry that this "elephant girl" cannot offer a larger floral display to bring herself to your attention. However, I feel sure I can do the part well if you will just give me some consideration! This would make two of my lifetime dreams come true —First to do a picture for "the greatest master on earth"— Secondly, a part that I know I can do well enough to make him proud of me!
> If you agree, even slightly, I will make myself available to tell you in person how easy I can make the entire thing for you.
>   With greatest anticipation and love—
>   Dorothy Lamour

Four days later DeMille sent a noncommittal reply:

> AN ELEPHANT GIRL WITH AS MUCH CHARM AS THE ONE NOW GRACING MY DESK NEEDS NO LARGER FLORAL DISPLAY TO BRING HER TO ANY-ONE'S ATTENTION.

Whereupon the following from Miss Lamour:

> My Dear C.B.—
> Words can never express what your wonderful telegram meant to me. It has given me a "slight ray of hope" that you might be giving me, at least, some small consideration as your "Elephant Girl." I would still love to have that visit with you at your convenience—whether it will be to talk business or just talk.

You see, C.B., I appreciate culture and gentlemen. Your telegram proved to me that you are truly one of the few top gentlemen left in our industry.

Again, thank you, from the bottom of my heart!

Fondly,

DOROTHY

The leads in the picture went to the three actresses, warranting no inference, however, that merely flowers had turned the trick. DeMille had exercised rare judgment in the casting. Both Betty and Gloria performed the risky feats without benefit of doubles, a matter that DeMille had left to their own decision.

One afternoon, Lucille Ball called upon the boss with the hope of getting the role of the Elephant Girl in the circus story, at the time not yet cast. She had never played in one of his films and the occasion was marked by unusual eagerness on her part. Moreover, as it was prior to the redheaded comedienne's rise in television, she concededly was in need of picture work.

Mr. DeMille assured her the part, and the actress figuratively floated out of the office.

A few weeks later she returned, tears in her eyes.

She told DeMille she had to give it up.

They were expecting a child, their first, and the doctor felt that the activities of a circus elephant girl might be too taxing for impending motherhood. Ecstatic over her first-born, Lucille was nevertheless properly tearful in DeMille's presence. She sincerely regretted losing the opportunity.

With this viewpoint DeMille heartily concurred but was nonetheless piqued by the caprice of fate. He said to the staff, "You can have a baby anytime but how often in your life do you get a lead in a DeMille picture?"

Part V

"HIT SEX HARD!"

1.

HE was the custodian of a language of drama cut to his style, and viewed with suspicion those who advised a change. There was little reason for change when his own formula had proved so consistently fruitful. "Never meddle with a success," he counseled his staff. What amazed observers was not that the language was simple as that it was so little understood or imitated. DeMille's drama was not meant for, as he frequently put it, "the *New Yorker* magazine crowd." It did what it was supposed to do; it sold pictures on a mass basis, and in the mass market he found his strength.

He guarded the formula jealously and allowed no writer to veer from it.

He once thought he might develop scenarists with minds attuned to his style. He gathered together a dozen young women writers, mostly from newspapers throughout the country, paid them a small salary as they sat on the sets observing him at work. For months he watched for a creative spark, and for months they sat and whispered to each other. They became known around the studio as the whispering chorus, the mere mention of DeMille's name causing them to exclaim what a grand fellow he was. Eventually he had to let them go. His passion for simplicity of plot was the despair of the staff. Once, during an impasse in the writing of the *Unconquered* story, an aide thought he had an idea on how to move the plot forward.

"Look at it this way," the aide said; "her life can be elevated at this point."

"How?"

"By sublimation. . . ." But he proceeded no further.

"Sublimation! My god, what's that?" DeMille cried. "A cure for pregnant women with falling breasts? Now I go up to a newsboy. You know I rely on newsboys too for the success of my pictures, and I say to him, you ought to see that DeMille picture up the street, it's all about sublimation. Boy, it's great, all about sublimation. Can't you see him dropping his papers and tailing it up the street!"

The chemistry of DeMille plots can be summed up in Hamlet's remark to his old pal Horatio, "Give me that man who is not passion's slave." Time and again disaster visited DeMille's heroes because they were sorely afflicted with this basic urge. Gary Cooper deserted his military post to chase after Paulette Goddard in *Unconquered* and Victor Mature as Samson fell prey to a daughter of his enemies, the sex-laden Delilah of Hedy Lamarr, betraying his own people in the bargain.

Actually, DeMille did not come into his, as his brother Bill once called it, "sex à la mode era" until after World War I. There was a hint of its coming in *The Cheat* in which a wealthy Oriental brands a white girl for refusing to keep her promise to become his mistress. The relationship of male and female became a possessive feature of the DeMille scenario. There was nothing psychological, or complex, or depressing about it, a simple Freudian concept pointing up what DeMille agreed was the big driving force in man's nature. He contended many "otherwise normal people take an unreasonable and irrational attitude on the subject of sex." He recognized this force as something which is "to human beings what a piece of magnetized steel is to isolated pieces of iron." In 1930, in a magazine reply to a critic who asserted sex was through as a subject for films, DeMille counted off the current successful films. Four out of five were sexy. "One thousand years from now the situation will be the same," DeMille wrote. "I recall experiments in which scientists expect to produce babies in test tubes. . . . Perhaps if we had to say 'Mother' to a glass bottle the enjoyment of the world in love stories would pass." In that year he told a Cleveland newspaperman that three things were necessary to a woman's happiness—"art, religion and a man." Though he was unaffected by appeals to art, his pictures embodied the other two requirements, leaving little doubt that most of DeMille's heroines were at least two-thirds content.

Some nifty catchlines were used in this rakish period. Advertisements for DeMille's *Adam's Rib* in 1922 contained such come-ons as *It is easier for a man to say he will stop loving a woman than to stop loving her; The dangerous age for women is from three to seventy; The flapper has a weapon her mother hasn't—Youth. Mother's is experience; A tale of the youngest flapper and the oldest sin.* Wives were urged to see *Don't Change Your Husband* in 1918 to find out how to resist seducers who "promise you chests of smouldering rubies and shimmering silks as soft as your own brown curls."

DeMille visualized his stories in terms of whatever had the greatest appeal to the greatest number. The sex excitant, a still highly marketable commodity, fit both counts of DeMille's formula: it was common to everyone and it was strong.

While others allowed cheapness to creep in, DeMille tried to maintain a balance, enough of allure and not too much of boldness, but not successfully. He did not escape the critics, a great many feeling they knew what DeMille was up to. One day in 1950 he was telling Hedda Hopper how fortunate he was that fate had allowed him to bring so many Biblical pictures to the screen, and thus send the Holy Word to remote corners of the world. "Now, just a minute, C.B.," exclaimed the peppery correspondent, not the least reticent of women. "You're talking to Hedda now. Those Bible pictures of yours had plenty of sex!"

In his review of *Why Change Your Wife*, Burns Mantle

acknowledged the producer's superiority in this field. "The Sennetts and the Sunshine boys may outdo Mr. DeMille as masters of the lower limb display," Mantle wrote, "but he completely outdistances them in the technique of the torso."

DeMille faced a wall of opposition from his own studio associates when he first brought up his idea for an epic story about Samson and Delilah. The project would cost at least three million dollars. Their minds were baffled—"A pretty expensive haircut," they said. Most of the great masters, particularly Doré, painted Delilah as a chubby, matronish female and Samson as a thick, hairy giant of a man in the twilight of fifty.

Probably the executives were thinking of Doré conceptions. DeMille was not.

He set an artist to work painting a sketch, and one day whipped it out before the executives, cackling, "How do you think a movie about two people like that would sell?"

Their eyes fell on a young man with slim hips and the chest of an all-American fullback, with a scantily clad temptress looking saucily over her shoulder at the Biblical strong man.

The wet-lipped executives nodded approvingly at this up-to-the-minute rendition of Samson and Delilah.

DeMille pinned the color sketch on his office walls. On the back was the notation, "This sketch sold Paramount on making *Samson and Delilah.*" He frequently referred visitors to it as an example of how to combat the lack of imagination in Hollywood.

There was exceptional vigor in pictures he conjured up in his own mind. At a luncheon of his staff a few years ago he gave this description of the incident in the Garden of Eden: "There was a man named Adam who looked like Errol Flynn and this Adam was lonely. So he complained and God did something to the man's side. Lo and behold there was a lovely thing lying on a pallet of straw."

Constantly battling what he felt was a paucity of imagination in the contemporary world, he advanced upon James Barrie's *The Admirable Crichton*, turning the old classic of the heiress who gravitated to the butler into a highly successful movie (the first of his pictures to reach a million-dollar gross). It was not done as *The Admirable Crichton*. That title disturbed DeMille; it lacked color and could be confusing. "People might think it's a story about a naval officer." He changed it to *Male and Female*, thus removing every possible inference of anything nautical.

The "sex-à-la-mode" period was set off by such sparkling accessories as vaporish lingerie, luxurious baths and fantastic boudoirs. "He could make a screen version of *Uncle Tom's Cabin* and yet manage to edge in a boudoir and a bath," the New York City *Mirror* chuckled editorially in 1925.

In decking out his actresses suitably, DeMille felt that much was to be said for feminine charm that was not unduly concealed. "Cassocks are for altar boys, who have nothing engaging to exhibit, but not for women." Like the Brothers Minsky, DeMille rarely permitted his heroines to suffer from too much coverage. A favorite outfit was the bra and skirt, often got up with an artistry that made the costume seem appropriate for other than bathing.

DeMille's conscience as a historian may have hurt a little when he suited Hedy Lamarr as Delilah in a bra, then vigorously backing it up as an accepted item of apparel in Old Testament times.

He was not alone among producers of the mid-20's to recognize the power of the barren midriff, a development logically brought on by Mack Sennett's bathing girls, who ably demonstrated its box-office value. Producers vied with one another in out-exposing their heroines; it soon was not enough to show them merely bathing. Claudette Colbert was bathing in a stream in the jungle scenes of *Four Frightened People* when a sportive monkey stole her clothes off a hickory limb, giving DeMille a chance to prove the effectiveness of tropical leaves as clothes in this type of emergency. In the play *The Admirable Crichton* the author, Sir James Barrie, has the butler Crichton (Thomas Meighan) indulging himself wistfully with regard to Lady Mary (Miss Swanson):

> Or ever the knightly years were gone
> With the old world to the grave,
> I was a king in Babylon,
> And you were a Christian slave.

Sir James saw no reason to carry out this wish, but DeMille felt differently. He turned to Babylonian days in a lavish flashback featuring Miss Swanson sparingly clad in leopard skin.

Thus the flashback was a handy device when the story itself did not give producers an opportunity to unfurl the heroine. In *Manslaughter* the district attorney, prosecuting the girl he loves, points to the wild youth of his day and observes that it was just this sort of thing that made Rome fall. And presto! The DeMille plot goes whirling right into the middle of a Roman orgy with Leatrice Joy, temporarily absolved from a charge of manslaughter. She is the hostess at this ancient jazz party, sensuous enough to have hastened Rome's fall by a score of years. In the script itself, notes for the flashback ran for six pages, revealing DeMille's thoroughness in screen revelries of this kind:

> Steps lead up to the throne on which sits a Roman patrician.... This patrician is Lydia (Leatrice Joy) in magnificent Roman costume. Below, her guests are at a long table, feasting. Wine is being passed by black nude slaves. Bacchanalian dancers are circling in front of the table (hung with garlands of roses).... At top of throne, held by a heavy golden chain, is a tiger, guarding the patrician noblewoman.... Part of this wild Bacchanal consists of several

of the men picking up the girls above their heads, and running off with them. . . . Several young nobles (very drunk) grab pretty dancers, pulling them down into their laps, bend them back, giving them wine, etc. One man—a soldier among the rest of the patricians—fills his Roman helmet with wine, and gives it to woman next to him, whom he is caressing. . . . The guests at the feast are leaning forward eagerly watching the Chief Dancer, whose long scarf has almost unwound. The last of it drops from her, as she reaches the throne, entirely nude. (Very beautiful, though very small figure.) Kneeling, she offers winecup to patrician woman, who graciously takes it.

DeMille heroines were not women of half-formed purpose. Their influence was in no way local. If vain, it generally developed that a nation's fate hung on their vanity. DeMille felt he had perfected such a female in Delilah. Few storied sirens exerted such a hold on the showman's imagination as the harlot of Gaza. It appeared Delilah was just about the perfect vamp. She was beautiful and sexy, she knew the power of the combination, and how to use it. That made her dangerous.

With Delilah, DeMille utilized an old maxim, "Every man hurts the thing he loves," but reversed it, and carried it further. In his story, Delilah destroys her lover, himself a lad of some strength. She thus eliminates a Jewish hero who has been a stumbling block to Philistine supremacy, a solution satisfactory to DeMille if not to Bible scholars.

In the climate of a DeMille plot, betrayal played against lust, greed against human flesh. The hardest wallops were delivered by silken ladies with powdered cheeks and ruby lips. When a blushing youth was pitted against a full-blown DeMille female, there could be little doubt which one was in for a fearful shellacking. As individuals, DeMille heroines would hardly be suitable for a Sunday school cantata, but it is easy to see how an organized group of them would add up into quite a striking force. With soft touches (they always appeared eminently feminine) they subdued the toughest male, it being evident such gals were not to be approached on tiptoe.

Moving boldly on the sex front, exposing the feminine calf when the sight of an ankle was considered an orgy, DeMille was drawn to the bathing scene as a reliable piece of glamour. Even though in later years he feigned a horror for the showy exercises, Hollywood wags declared his trademark to be a bathtub and a halo. To a critic who chided him for his espousal of the tub, DeMille replied, "I am proud of it. My mind is not one that grasps the immorality of the bathroom." He began to resent such tags as "the patron saint of plumbers," "the plumber's best friend," and smiled patiently when a plumbing firm displayed a tub with a poster describing its design as EARLY DEMILLE.

As the father of big-time bathing on the screen, DeMille did not, however, hesitate to take credit for popularizing the Saturday-night rite. "I cannot say whether more people have been in DeMille bathtubs than in the Yale Bowl, but at least more celebrated persons have been seen in them under more interesting circumstances." His boudoir *tour de force* was persuading Claudette Colbert to take a bath in a black marble pool filled with asses' milk in *The Sign of the Cross*. His enthusiasm on that occasion cost the studio $10,000.

Back in 1929 he prepared a glass bathtub for *Dynamite*, his first sound movie, but he could not talk the heroine, Kay Johnson, into doing what might have been one of the more provocative sessions of screen bathing in film history. "It would have made any seat in the house a good one," *The New York Times* said, recalling the episode a few years ago.

His bathtub scenes are always surrounded with a lot of secret business. The sets are locked and guarded, and hands become very secretive, pretend to be looking for spies of rival producers seeking to unlock an important trade secret.

DeMille's first important use of the tub was in an unrefined soiree called, *Old Wives for New,* in which he hit upon the idea of having Sylvia Ashton leave hairpins and all sorts of debris around the place, while Florence Vidor's bathroom was as bright and neat as a Tiffany showcase. The moral for American womanhood was clear: a slovenly wife can wreck a marriage.

Then he revealed Gloria Swanson to the public in *Male and Female* in 1919. She was in a sunken bathtub, the Model-T of its day. "We thought that was pretty hot stuff." DeMille smiled reminiscently. "From that I went on to *Saturday Night,* then to *Why Change Your Husband?* and *Don't Change Your Wife.*" These were DeMille's marital-mixup movies, and all had bathing scenes—piquant sauces that caused talk. And talk sold tickets.

He traced his affection for the pretty bath to childhood memories of a dingy boxlike tub into which he was dunked every Saturday night. "The cockroaches used to come out, look at you and say, 'Hi, boy,' and go back." He resolved, should he ever have the chance, to restore bathing to its proper estate. Even fate had a hand in this legend. The DeMilles became engaged in December, 1899. "We were watching the new century come in, sitting on the steps of No. 9 Beacon Street in Boston. It was one of those old houses with colored panes of glass. For sentimental reasons we decided to visit the spot many years later, and what do you think we saw? It was occupied by a plumbing company and in the window was a huge bathtub!"

As a young actress at Paramount, Claudette Colbert played only "sweet young thing" roles. One day DeMille saw her on the studio grounds. He had been searching for someone to portray the wicked and beautiful empress, Poppaea.

He went up to her and without preliminary, said, "To me you are the wickedest woman in the world."

It was unusual even as Hollywood introductions go. Already he envisioned her in the silks, jewels and sultry dalliance of Nero's wife. Drastically transformed, Claudette turned out to be an eyeful as Poppaea, and gave DeMille an opportunity to show how wrong Paramount was in putting a sweetness-and-light label on the actress.

DeMille labored hard on the feminine characters in his plots —"Feminine allure is a ruthless tool that has changed the course of civilizations."

There were times when these predatory females sorely tried him. He once set about to find a symbol of all women, something that would typify female power. He asked around and one day came upon what he felt was the answer: the snake. A woman's allure can be as deadly as a snake, plaguing the male in its glistening coils.

After that, snake symbols were everywhere on DeMille sets. Some were cast in bronze as ornaments, pot holders, cane grips, often placed close to the heroine, on her person, or as part of her furnishings. In speech, too—"forked-tongue adder" was the phrase he used to describe Delilah.

The Cleopatra of history took her own life in a classic fashion, so far as DeMille was concerned. She may not have had the producer in mind when she committed suicide by clasping an asp to her breast, but a knowledge of his philosophy might have made the act a little more pleasant for her.

When he decided to film her story, DeMille mulled for some time over how to persuade Claudette Colbert to do the death scene with a live snake. DeMille was opposed to stuffed substitutes as strongly as most women detest the live ones.

At the first suggestion she might be expected to handle the real article, Miss Colbert shuddered.

"Oh, Mr. DeMille, I couldn't touch a snake."

DeMille had not yet given her the part, but he told her that if she stood firm on that decision he would have to seek another actress.

"Don't say you will or won't," he suggested. "It will be the last scene in the picture, and let's leave the whole problem to that time."

The death scene, ready for the camera, found Claudette, a magnificently gowned Cleopatra, seated on a black onyx throne from which stretched a red marble runner, making the journey to the dais a long and dramatic one. The cameraman had adjusted lens, awaiting the call for action, when the actress saw DeMille approach her from the far end of the marble strip. He was moving, slowly, step by step, and pointing in her direction a huge snake. She blinked, but she was not mistaken—it was a Mexican boa constrictor, eight feet long, its head lying on the palm of DeMille's outstretched hand.

"Mr. DeMille!" screamed the actress.

"Yes," he said, stepping toward the dais.

"Don't! Don't come near me with that thing!"

Quickly DeMille's other hand, up to this point hidden behind him, flashed out at the actress. In it he held a small harmless snake a few inches long, resembling a sand adder.

"How about this one?"

"Oh, that little thing," she said, almost a sigh of relief, and in a few minutes the death scene was filmed.

In 1922 in *Fool's Paradise*, Julia Faye played the Queen of Siam ("I've played five queens for DeMille!") with two black snakes coiled around her arms. "We were working at Balboa at night. I was miserable because of the cold and petrified because of the snakes. I was holding the heads of the snakes in my hands and what part of them wasn't wrapped around me trailed to the ground. They were that long. After a while I felt a pressure. I ran to DeMille screaming, 'They're squeezing me!

They're squeezing me!' With the air of a mother scolding a petulant child he said, 'Look at the way you're holding them. Just relax your grip and they'll be all right.' I did, and they were."

DeMille treated his lady players with an almost fatherly patience, once having impressed upon them a few ground rules. He was extraordinarily indulgent. Those who reported some anxiety over a line of dialogue, perhaps suggesting a change, would receive a grateful hearing, often with a word of advice, such as, "Speak the line which seems the most natural. Writers, you know, don't often realize how people are supposed to talk."

While he obliged with small concessions, no amount of weeping on his shoulder could prevail on him to permit basic changes in a portrayal. He saw to it they were amply forewarned.

If there was one tenacious precept in the DeMille operation it was that no leading player was hired without benefit of a ceremony in the boss's office. DeMille did not cast a part casually, either as to person or price.

Agents were morbidly aware that they always faced the same problem, DeMille prestige vs. player salary. The former, DeMille felt, was great enough to warrant a modification of the latter. To win over one agent he unreeled a long list of players owing their stardom to DeMille pictures.

In the usual procedure, a producer instructs the studio casting head to suggest this or that player for a certain role, and the deal is made. DeMille looked upon this method as slipshod. Poor casting reflected on a man's pride, no less so than poor writing. He worked on his stories, day after day, through each step of the plot, engaging his writers in a continuous round of pungent debate, denunciation and malignant outcries. DeMille, more than any producer, sired his plots and was keen to every little nuance in them, and therefore not just any player was qualified to bring the narrative to life. He made it not a point but a ceremony to tell every player just what a part meant and how it might be portrayed.

It is impossible to say how many among the elite of filmdom, after a casting interview with DeMille, have floated out of his office on a fleecy cloud of dreamy anticipation. These sessions with the producer gained quite a little local repute, and were often the actress's first introduction to DeMille and his world.

It was in his office that the producer rose to full stature as a storyteller, a proficiency which once inspired his private secretary, Florence Cole, to enthuse, "He could make the telephone directory sound dramatic."

Agents were banned from the interviews, arranged after the field of candidates for a particular role was slimmed down to two or three. Each candidate in turn was called in.

With DeMille at his imaginative best, the actual role suffered much in comparison with his expanded conception. He promenaded back and forth across his office, explaining, portraying, always embroidering. The actress would sink back in her chair, awestruck, convinced that DeMille was offering her the most marvelous role of her career.

Such a conclusion, though in error, was understandable, the actor having heard the plot from the standpoint of a single part, thereby greatly inflated.

No matter how lofty her prestige, to DeMille every actress was considerably less than a goddess. He had been set back on his heels too often by their interpretations of what he had labored to put into his scripts. DeMille scripts, short on dialogue and long on action, were susceptible singularly to one translation, and its author felt duty bound to translate it to the world himself. In the hands of mere technicians like actresses DeMille felt the risk could be frightening. "Actresses are pretty things, and nice to look at. But don't turn them loose on your script."

2.

THE sex-for-the-masses policy that influenced his early pictures drew DeMille into many conflicts. Some columnists suggested he was getting rich on nudity, especially where Biblical subjects were involved. "I didn't write the Bible and I didn't create sin," he would reply. What irritated a number of the correspondents who had covered the Hollywood beat for years was their inability to get "the old man to break down just once and confess what he was really up to." They were convinced DeMille *was* playing a game, but it was dangerous to question his sincerity. Try as they might they could not succeed in luring from him an admission that his claims to a unique ministry by way of movies was a brilliant piece of showmanship. Their sly digs drew from DeMille a pet reply—"If you condemn my Bible pictures, you condemn the Bible." To this there appeared no sufficient answer unless they could prove he was playing fast and loose with Biblical text.

On the other hand, he had an incisive faculty for knowing how to "sell" a picture. He set the mood of the promotion and publicity on every one of his pictures; while most producers were happy to rely on the advice of others, DeMille fussed, fretted, probed, experimented, until he came up with an approach. He was jubilant over his analysis of the Samson and Delilah theme—"We'll sell it as a story of faith, a story of the power of prayer. That's for the censors and the women's organizations. For the public it's the hottest love story of all time."

In Samson, he had evolved a striking, climactic tale out of a few episodes from the Book of Judges. He held no doubts about its power, and his confidence in a full public approval was never greater. Rarely had he had so many ideas about one of his movies.

And he got a chance to express a few, though under circumstances he could not have foreseen.

It was in March 1950. Paramount was disturbed over a regulation in the Chicago area that did not permit a picture to run more than two weeks in any downtown theater—to prevent exhausting the picture's market before it reached the residential houses.

A mere two weeks! A DeMille picture was just getting warmed up at that point, and the public, forgetting all the nasty things the critics had said, were discovering for itself the picture's real merits. DeMille felt he could always depend upon the public.

Paramount went into Federal court in Chicago with a request that the regulation be set aside and *Samson and Delilah* be permitted an extended run in the downtown area.

DeMille was the principal witness for the petitioners.

Motives were inquired into quickly. Paramount's attorney asked DeMille whether he was interested in making a profit on the picture.

The witness smiled. It wasn't a question he would have preferred, but a record had to be made on the point.

What had motivated him in choosing this particular Bible story?

"You mean other than money?" asked DeMille.

"Yes, other than money."

"Well, if the Court will permit me to go back a little, my father was studying for the Episcopal ministry when he met my mother . . . and she persuaded him he would have a greater congregation in the theater than in the Church, so he became one of America's greatest playwrights and carried his message throughout this nation, and when motion pictures came along I was enabled to carry on through his teachings . . . he read to us every night ... a chapter of the Old Testament and New Testament and a chapter from American History. ..."

The witness estimated that about eighty million persons would see the picture, not counting "at least forty million who are not picturegoers, or theatergoers, and who don't read the movie columns or movie magazines."

"Upon what do those people depend for their recommendation as to pictures they should see?"

"On religious magazines, on the preaching from the pulpits, but most of all on the word of mouth that this picture is not an ordinary movie but carries a message they should hear."

Upon cross-examination the opposing attorney referred to DeMille's pictures as spectacles.

The witness flushed. "I challenge the statement."

"How would you describe them?"

"How would I describe them?"

"Yes."

"As works of art."

"They were also, let us say, spectacular pictures, were they not? Spectacle pictures?"

"Your definition of a spectacle, I am not sure what that would be. If you will tell me what you mean by spectacle I can answer that."

"What I am trying to get at is this: you have scenes with four or five thousand people, haven't you?"

"We used to be able to use four or five thousand, but we can't any more."

"You can't any more? You can't use that many?"

"No, sir, prices are too high."

"Would you go this far with me? In 1947 your pictures were well known in the trade and had assumed a more or less standard pattern?"

"Well, sir, I once made a picture for Ina Claire for $9,000. You say a standard pattern?"

"Well, these Biblical pictures have assumed a more or less standard pattern, haven't they?"

"Well, I don't think the Bible story follows a standard pattern. You have the Old Testament, you have the New Testament."

"In this instance you have followed the pattern of the Bible as you see it?"

"I follow the pattern of the Bible as it is written."

"Is there any difference in these pictures generally, their general character, general make-up, general production, as in these other Biblical pictures you have produced?"

"Yes, sir, the Bible story is different."

"I know it is different but you know what I mean, the general theme, the general treatment of it, the general approach to it is the same, is it not?"

"No, sir, I do not know what you mean. I am sorry."

"Well, this picture *Samson and Delilah* is completely different, you think, from the other Bible pictures that you have made?"

"From *The King of Kings,* yes. It is a different story."

"It is a different story but is the treatment different?"

"Yes, the treatment is totally different from *The King of Kings.*"

"In what way?"

"Well, *The King of Kings* is the difference between the Old Testament and the New Testament."

"Now, as I understand your testimony on direct examination, it is that the religious theme and religious treatment and religious angle are, I think you put it, quite near to your heart. Is that your position?"

"Yes, sir, very near to my heart."

"And you want the largest number of people possible to see this religious theme so they can be benefited by the religious teaching of the picture?"

"Yes, sir."

The questioning turned to the role of Delilah, played by Hedy Lamarr.

Q. Now, Miss Lamarr has been cast and featured in pictures quite foreign to the religious motif, hasn't she?

A. Yes, I would think so.

Q. Would you call her a seductive star?

A. Seductive?

Q. Yes.

A. Delilah was a very seductive lady.

Q. This is a story of seduction, isn't it?

A. Story of seduction? It is a story of faith.

Q. Well, is it a story of seduction?

A. No, sir, it is not.

Q. It is not?

A. No, sir.

Q. *Samson and Delilah* is not a story of seduction?

A. No, sir, it is a story of triumph over seduction, it is a story of faith, of faith in God, of a man who, as I said, did not have vision until he was blinded, who yielded to the world of the flesh and the devil and in making his escape he was able to save his people. . . .

Q. All right, you said *Samson and Delilah* was not a story of seduction. Did Delilah try to seduce Samson?

A. And succeeded.

Q. And Hedy Lamarr, you think, is well fitted for that role in the picture?

A. She gives a very fine performance.

Q. Are the pictures which you have got connected with your petition here, are they correct showing as to how she is garbed?

A. Yes, sir, except that the breasts are bare in the one picture and we covered them.

Q. Well, you had to get by the Board of Censors somehow, didn't you?

A. We had to follow the rules of good taste and decency.

Q. And that is why you did that?

A. Why we always follow them in my pictures.

Q. Who is Victor Mature? Is he Samson in the picture?

A. Yes, sir.

Q. He has been cast in roles somewhat foreign to religion— that is true, isn't it?

A. Yes, sir.

Q. He has a large feminine following of movie fans?

A. I hope so.

Q. You knew those things when you were casting, didn't you?

A. Of course I cast the most popular man that was suited for the part.

Q. And you cast the most popular actress suited for the seductive part, didn't you?

A. No, sir.

Q. Well, you did cast her?

A. Yes, sir.

DeMille won his case, and the saga of the Jewish strong boy and the Philistine temptress played extra weeks in the Windy City.

In reality, the story was as clearly a drama of seduction as any could be. DeMille knew it as well as the attorneys, but only the incorrigibly foolish would have expected the boss at a public hearing to cast aside one of his most basic precepts—that a thing is often no more or no less than what you represent it to be.

DeMille was convinced his appearance at the Chicago hearing left much to be desired. Opposing counsel had irked him greatly, and the replies which he had been forced to make fretted on his memory. He was furious over a reference to the hearing that appeared a few days later in a Chicago daily, and subsequently reprinted in the *New Yorker* magazine, his arch enemy.

The item in the *New Yorker*, under the caption "Furthermore Department," read:

> From the Chicago *Daily News:* The film is a work of art, of great interest to people of religious faith because it is a Biblical story, DeMille said on the witness stand in Federal court here Wednesday....
>
> "All denominations commend the picture," he said. "It will draw 40 million people who don't usually go to movies. My father studied for the ministry and read the Bible in our home, and this picture is near my heart. Furthermore, we have to take in $7,000,000 on it to break even."

The transcript of DeMille's testimony revealed no statements in that juxtaposition. DeMille called in attorneys and ordered them to demand retractions from the editors. They refused even in the face of strong hints of legal action. No suits were brought, and once again DeMille's convictions about "the big city press" were rekindled.

3.

DeMILLE'S testimony in Federal court that day would have attracted much wider interest had he revealed his real attitude toward the Samson story—the attitude he set forth nearly four years earlier when he gathered with writers for the first time to outline the mood and spirit of the Biblical story.

That session took place on July 19, 1946. Like all of DeMille's opening story conferences, it was an occasion long awaited. The writers marked the day because DeMille would give them the first word on how he expected the story to shape up. What he said would become a sort of blueprint, a master plan for the coming months. His ideas at these opening conferences were set down in shorthand, copies thereafter distributed, to be consulted and referred to when a writer, unwittingly or not, strayed from the original theme.

On this occasion DeMille held an Old Testament on his lap, the page turned to the Samson chapters in the Book of Judges; he read aloud from the Great Book, stopping after each verse to give his interpretation of what it meant. Biblical scholars might have shuddered at the swift analysis of the episodes, and the ease with which DeMille supplied links between unlinked occurrences. DeMille began:

I really got part of the idea for Samson and Delilah from an old Hindu story about a courtesan who loved a priest. She was the mistress of an emperor and when the emperor found out about the priest he had the courtesan's feet, hands and breasts cut off and he threw her on a dung heap outside the city, and then the priest came and sat with her.

And there was a certain man of Zorah, of the family of the Danites, whose name was Manoah; and his wife was barren, and bare not.

And the angel of the Lord appeared unto the woman, and said unto her, "Behold, now, thou art barren, and bearest not; but thou shalt conceive, and bear a son."

And the woman bare a son, and called him Samson. And the child grew, and the Lord blessed him.

Actually Samson's mother swore him to be whatever it was—a Nazarite?—to be clean from birth, to touch no liquor or women, but he didn't live up to that, apparently.

Then his father and his mother said unto him, "Is there never a woman among the daughters of thy brethren, or among all my people, that thou goest to take a wife of the uncircumcised Philistines?" Samson said unto his father, "Get her for me, for she pleaseth me well."

Samson says, "Get her for me, for she pleaseth me well." You can see his father saying, "Listen, Samson, my boy, why do you have to go over to the other side and choose a daughter of our enemies? Well, you can have many beauties right here in our own neighborhood. Look at Sam Jones' daughter down the street. . . ." But Samson says, "Look, Dad, I like this one. Get her!"

Brethren is better than Israelites or Jews. As much as possible we will remove all mention of sectarianism. Use *people* as much as possible and as little of *Jews, Israelites* and *tribe of Dan.*

So his father went down unto the woman; and Samson made there a feast; for so used the young men to do.

Evidently the bridegroom gave the first banquet . . . seven days . . . wow! A feast seven days long! They knew how to throw a feast in those days. A little later on in the story there's a second sister. She's the younger sister of the girl Samson wants to marry. Now keep the younger sister in mind because she's quite a bitch. The older sister apparently was a bit of a scheming dame like women sometimes are. The little girl, well she is determined to split that marriage if she can. Samson is at this feast of Philistines, and he has proposed a riddle to the guests, and made a wager with them, but they can't guess the answer. They want to, because they're wild to put this rube, this country boy, in his place. He's stepping pretty high, this punk from the hills, coming in there and marrying a high-born Philistine girl. So the younger sister sees something here, a way to break up the love match. Her sister, she figures, can get the answer to the riddle out of Samson if anyone can. The younger sister has no motive in the world, except from the bottom of her feet to the top of her head, her body tingles when she sees him, and she wants him. She's never had a man but, boy, she's ripe—and she wants that Samson. Now there's nothing in the Bible about all this, but it could give us the motive we need. So this scheming little dame goes up to the Philistine guests—all big tough bruisers, they're the soldiers—and she teases 'em. "Why don't you get the bride to find out the answer to the riddle?" She says to George, "You know her quite well. I've seen you behind the apple bush. Why don't you . . ." Well, they like the idea. "We're not going to let a country bumpkin come in and make suckers out of us." Nobody has picked a fight with Samson, but he's a strange figure sitting there. The little girl has been pouring and serving, with eyes for no one but this man.

And Samson's wife wept before him and said, "Thou dost but hate me, and lovest me not; thou has put forth a riddle unto the children of my people, and has not told it me."....And Samson's wife wept before him....

You can see this dame trying to wheedle the answer to the riddle out of him.

And she wept before him the seven days ... and it came to pass on the seventh day that he told her, because she lay sore upon him; and she told the riddle to the children of her people.

And she wept before him... In other words he was having a helluva time, and the little sister was saying, "Boy, it works!"

... because she lay sore upon him... either she plagued the life out of him or she twined her beautiful body around him. You can interpret that any way you like. So she double-crossed him. This was his wedding present, this is how he got it. The whole damn thing turns into a frightful tragedy.

... If ye had not ploughed with my heifer ye had not found out my riddle ...

That's what Samson says when the guests tell him the answer to the riddle, and he is mad as hell. Every time the Spirit of the Lord comes upon him he goes out and rips about ninety people apart. He just got mad as hell, and when he got mad he was strong as hell. Well, they had the riddle, so Samson lost the wager and owes them thirty garments, one for each of them.

... and slew thirty men of them, and took their spoil, and gave change of garments unto them which expounded the riddle. And his anger was kindled....

In other words he said, "Oh, you came in here to get my wife. That's the kind of people you are. You want your thirty garments? I'll get them for you." He kills thirty people and brings back the garments and says, "Gentlemen, the bet is now paid." Now here's the rough part. When he gets back with the garments he finds that they have given his wife to her old beau, a Philistine like herself.

But Samson's wife was given to his companion, whom he had used as his friend.

The friend is the head Philistine, who has been in love with the older sister. They may even have had an affair together. Samson was just a country sucker—he'd just landed in town.

Remember that we haven't yet brought in the little sister in the
Bible. She is the dominating force of that feast. She knows of
the affair between the friend and her sister. You have to be
careful you don't lose this younger sister for all time. She loves
Samson, but if she knows Samson is being tricked, being hood-
winked, lied to, made a clown . . . and she loves him and that's
why she's doing it. Be very careful you don't come up with the
kind of dame in *Children's Hour*. This sister has a great passion
and sees the man she loves being made a fool of. You have a
terrific driving force in this girl's love. It has to be the strongest
thing we have ever seen. It's passion 3,000 years ago. Now, Samson feels it is safe to come back after he killed the thirty gentlemen. You can see the little sister getting ready for this. When
Samson comes back and demands to see his wife, the little one
knows her sister is married—given to the other guy—and the cat
that ate the canary is nothing to this dame. As she looks at this
guy she wants him more than ever, and now is her chance.

*And her father said, I verily thought that thou hadst utterly
hated her; therefore I gave her to thy companion; is not her
younger sister fairer than she? Take her, I pray thee, instead
of her.*

That's the father's offer: take the younger sister who is prettier
than the older sister. Now this is her moment, but he doesn't
pay any attention to the little dame at all. He says, "Those sons
of bitches married my girl off. You connived in it, Papa, and
anything I do in your goddamn city is on your head." Looking
for a minute at the younger daughter he evidently said, "Oh,
nuts! Take that little thing away." So, all the little girl's plans,
her ego, the new dress she had fixed and the manicure and the
headdress—all went phooey out into the gutter. I don't know
what he said to her, maybe—"You little pigtailed rat. I'll give
you to my son." Anyway, it must have seared a white-hot poker
through the kid's soul, so much so that it will motivate everything that follows in our story.

*. . . and the Spirit of the Lord came mightily upon him, and
the cords that were upon his arms became as flax that was burnt
with fire, and his bands loosed of his hands.*

You can see Doug Fairbanks or Superman all tied up.

And he found a new jawbone of an ass, and put forth his hand and took it, and slew a thousand men therewith.

That probably was a helluva fight, a terrific show for drama. Probably the fight has grown. He probably killed three people and by the time it had got to the tribe of Levi it was ten thousand. Now, I want to tell you this. Productions are going up to three and four million dollars. I want to do this picture for two million. This picture doesn't need crowds; they are of no value to it. The ruins are little bits of places. I'm going to get a lot of the effects with painting, a lot of shooting outdoors and up at my ranch without even any transportation charges. The magnificence of costumes. Yes, the magnificence of drapes because that's the setting of the jewel. There's only one big set that I see and that's the temple scene at the end.

Then went Samson to Gaza, and saw there a harlot, and went in unto her.

This is typical Robin Hood stuff. He does a terrific thing, supposedly has a miracle of the Lord and then goes down and finds a whore. You can see them surrounding the house. This guy's in there, and they start edging up to the place. He gets out, then carries off the gates of the city. There's a wonderful drawing of that in Tissaud.

Now, they chase him all over the hills but he keeps getting away. The Lords of the Philistines are pretty shrewd babies; if they can't capture him by force they'll do it another way, an easy way, through a woman. So they go to Delilah. Why Delilah? Now get this, the Bible doesn't name the little sister at the wedding feast who was spurned, and who hates Samson with every fiber in her body. But we'll name her. We'll call her Delilah. See! There's our motive. We can't follow the Bible story because Delilah doesn't enter into it until way toward the end. But if you call the little sister Delilah, then everything makes sense. She's out to get him because he's wrecked her home and burned the fields of her people, and he's spurned her. When the Lords of the Philistines come to her and say, "You knew this man. Listen, you have charm and a beautiful body. You can do anything with any man. Go out and entice him. Find out where his strength is." You can see what her viewpoint is. "Boy, will I! I'll bring this bastard in with a ring through his nose. I'll lead him! The only condition I make is that you won't harm him. He's mine."

And she made him sleep upon her knees; and she called for a man, and she caused him to shave off the seven locks of his head; and she began to afflict him, and his strength went from him.

That's quite a scene. There Delilah has her great triumph and the Philistines come and take him away. Now they'd promised not to touch his skin. Well, they didn't. But they held a hot poker near his eyes and blinded him. When she goes to visit him in the prison house—he's blind! She cringes with remorse. He'll never see her beauty, her lovely body, the things that prompted her to do everything so she could be his, so she could show herself to him, get the satisfaction of the passion from him that she could create. It was all gone! If she was an ugly wench it wouldn't be any different. That's when she falls in love with him. She goes down and sits with him, the great Delilah, the great courtesan, the great mistress of the King, goes down and sits with this outcast, this blinded, ridiculous slave.

Now, there are certain things you cannot do. You can't offend the great house of Israel. I think they regard him as a clown more than anything else. Samson was a whoremonger, a guy who apparently went out and raised hell. He's no fool and yet he's a fool. He goes out and gets drunk and does the shrewdest things.

4.

LATE in November 1939, Paramount purchased the film rights to *Family Portrait* for $35,000, to be made into a movie produced and directed by Cecil B. DeMille.

Anxious inquiries burst from a number of religious quarters.

Was DeMille going to base a story of the Virgin Mary on *Family Portrait* and did he not realize that the Broadway play depicted Mary as the mother of *several* children?

America, the prominent Jesuit weekly, quickly entered the growing controversy. It angrily branded *Family Portrait* as heretical because it denied the divinity of Christ, His Resurrection, the virginity of Mary, and the Immaculate Conception.

A lengthy "open letter to Cecil DeMille" appeared in *The Queen's Work*, the official publication of Catholic Sodalists. *The Queen's Work* was edited by DeMille's old friend, Father Dan Lord. The open letter was signed "The Staff," but was actually written by Lord.

> In this day, when purity is taking such a battering and virginity is treated with contempt, a play that presented Mary, not as a virgin but as the mother of a large family, is more than distasteful to us.
>
> ... You are going to be surprised and probably shocked to find how many followers of Christ bitterly dislike, if they do not actively hate, the mother of the Savior.
>
> Some queer twist of the human mind makes men think that Christ would be pleased with them if they attacked His Mother.... Yours is a heavy responsibility.

DeMille and Father Lord had been talking off the record about the Mary story prior to publication of the letter; now it was out in the open between them.

Father Lord, a peaceable man, hurriedly sent a note to DeMille. The open letter, the priest wrote, had aroused wider publicity than he had intended:

> As you realize, I looked upon it as answer to the many Sodalists who were asking, 'How is DeMille going to handle it, and how about *Family Portrait?*' I felt the letter would reassure ... hundreds of thousands of Catholics interested in your picture. I hadn't intended that publicity ... hope you regard it as entirely friendly and entirely favorable....

From other Christian sects came signs of concern.

But at Paramount, William LeBaron, production head at the time, sent a jubilant note to DeMille: *Hooray for controversy!*

DeMille did not share the sentiment. When it came to publicity he rarely objected, but this was of a kind distinctly not to his liking. Moreover, if *Family Portrait* was useless, a $35,000 mistake had been made.

To his numerous critics, DeMille made soothing reply, announcing that no part of *Family Portrait* would be used in his story.

He said, "We are approaching the hallowed story with a deep sense of responsibility and with the same spiritual and artistic thrill that impelled the making of *The King of Kings.*"

Still, he felt something might be salvaged from the investment in the play. He met with Joseph I. Breen of the Production Code office. The studio go-between at the time was Luigi Luraschi, an amiable, spirited man whose duties, in addition to wrestling with the Breen office, included the checking of scripts for whatever might offend any race or creed outside of the United States (a function which, with respect to material offensive to Americans, did not appear to be vested in any single person at Paramount).

Breen advised Luraschi that the play was not acceptable to large groups of professing Christians. First, the play suggested that Christ came from a large family and that his mother was not the Virgin Mary of the Gospels. Another major objection lay in that portion treating Christ, not as "the Divine Son of God," but rather as a "son of man," gifted with genius possibly, and nobler than his fellows.

Further, should the stage play be adapted for the screen, Breen advised a treatment that would "definitely and affirmatively" establish Christ as the only son of the Virgin Mary and as the Divine Son of God.

If it had come to pass that fate had signaled him out as the world's foremost embattled dispenser of mass religion, DeMille was ready to accept the challenge. He was in no mood to be forced to rest on his Biblical laurels by mere differences of attitude or interpretations. As it was, he had long ago decided on a perfect title for a *King of Kings* sequel—*The Queen of Queens*.

Shortly after Christmas of the same year studio calm was shattered by a memorandum from Albert Deane of Paramount's foreign office. Its contents were indeed exasperating to DeMille, already hobbled by forces he normally could ignore or conquer.

In the British territories, chiefly Great Britain and Australia, a *fairy* or *pansy* is referred to as a *quean*, the memo advised.

True, there was apparent difference in spelling between q-u-e-e-n and q-u-e-a-n, but, Paramount men in London feared, a ribald element might make a play on the title.

DeMille was not inclined to regard this quirk in English phonetics as too alarming. He had a flair for pungent titles, and he had used quite a few that crackled with promise of incendiary pleasure—*Old Wives for New, Forbidden Fruit, The Golden Bed*.

Mulling over the unfortunate co-incidence of *queen* and *quean*, DeMille hit upon another title that seemed perfect: *The Virgin*. It had box-office lure and, moreover, "ends any argument about our using *Family Portrait* and shows we are treating the birth of Christ as set forth in the Bible."

He tested it on clergymen; the results were not good. The title was dangerous and, if not offensive, at least misleading in its emphasis on a delicate aspect of the story.

So, he went back to *Queen of Queens*, now willing to take his chances with ribald Britons.

Paramount heads, always nervous over a DeMille Biblical, feared that this time there was real cause for alarm. They prevailed upon him to postpone further work on *The Queen of Queens* and produce a picture based on a serial then running in the *Saturday Evening Post* called "Reap the Wild Wind."

It was secretly hoped DeMille would forget the Virgin Mary story; the producer was of no such a mind.

He wrote Father Lord of the change in plans on *Queen of Queens* ("and, incidentally, I think I have won everyone over to this title"), adding that he would start on the Biblical picture following completion of *Reap*.

He further told the priest he planned the story of a Mother who gave Her Son for the cause of humanity "as so many mothers in England and France are doing today. . . . The love of mother for son and son for mother is perhaps the purest emotion of which our mortal consciousness is capable. There have been many stories of motherhood that have been successful on the screen, and the story of the greatest of all Mothers should be the most successful."

He disclosed he would have a treatment ready for discussion with the priest in the early fall. "Do you expect to come this way about that time? If not, I shall seek you."

DeMille, an ox for work, personally swarmed over every detail of *Reap the Wild Wind*, at the same time supervising the progress of the Virgin Mary story.

The first draft was being written by brother Bill. Kinship did not alter the usual uneasy DeMille-writer relationship. He had notified Bill that it was up to him to put it down on paper, and that he, Cecil, would outline the story, as well as its mood and temper. Bill would submit his material as he wrote it, then sit back to wait for the explosion. Rarely did he wait in vain. But he was a person of enduring nature and unfailing good humor, and so patiently rode out each storm.

In June 1940, Cecil telephoned Bill—it was the day before the start of shooting on *Reap the Wild Wind*—to report his first reactions to Bill's preliminary draft of the story.

Close at hand, a secretary took down what Cecil said, and later sent a copy of the conversation to Bill for his guidance. DeMille's comments ran in part:

... If we were on Mary's face and could see the whiplash descend on the back of Jesus, and could hear the blows, and the ridicule of the Roman soldiers, it would mean far more to us than to her John saying, "Oh, my, this is terrible."

Where the two lovers come out, Miriam is crying, and Judah says, "You mustn't cry—you'll be ill"—this is plain sloppy. Jesus is about to be crucified and this fellow is worrying because Miriam's eyes will be sore from weeping.

So far, you haven't told us any story that can excite us much. I know the story is there but you haven't told it.

Miriam and Judah: I'd have them watching the cross that's being dragged through the Via Dolorosa. Play different things over that.

Perhaps Miriam grabs some water from a jar or bucket that someone has, and tries to get it to Jesus. She is stopped by Judah who says, "If you do anything—if you try to help Him, they'll kill you." Miriam says, "I don't care—I don't care what they do to me—He raised me from the dead. I want to help Him."

A Roman soldier overhears this and looking at her, says, "What did you say?"

That's the way to get scenes all through the story. As to the Mother at the bottom of the cross, I don't think it is right for her to cry out, "My Son, my Son." ...

DeMille looked upon the Catholic Church as the big stumbling block to *The Queen of Queens*. At the same time he needed a sensitive thermometer of religious opinion. Catholic approval, he felt, would pretty much guarantee the picture a favorable reaction from religious groups generally. The two men he settled upon as official advisors were Father Lord and Bishop (then Monsignor) Fulton J. Sheen, two of the finest Catholic minds.

DeMille was aware now that his story treatment had some extremely touchy areas, chiefly the relationship between the Virgin Mary and husband Joseph.

Hidden away in DeMille's mind was the possibility of staging Salome's famous dance of the veils, to sort of counteract the heavy overburden of piety. If "color" was needed, Salome looked to DeMille like the gal who could furnish it. His preliminary draft brought together Judas and Salome, and there were other scenes which undoubtedly would catch the ecclesiastical eye of Sheen and Lord.

DeMille hoped to do a repeat of a party as lively as the one before the golden calf in *The Ten Commandments*. But this time he would stage the orgy in Herod's court with teasing soubrettes dressed in little more than serves a stoker crew on a river steamer.

It was the DeMille formula at work, and once again he risked getting caught between the hammer of propriety and the anvil of "popular appeal." The Herod's-court sequence, he felt, would prove what the Bible plainly intimated, that there were voluptuaries in those days who liked their drink strong and their women awash with willingness.

Those were the big issues when DeMille sent Bill off with the preliminary draft to see the two priests.

"Remember, you are dealing with Jesuits who have graduated far beyond the kindergarten stage." Cecil cautioned him. He told him not to try to get dramatic criticism from the priests, only advice on church attitude.

See whether we are on any dangerous ground with Catholicism, he wrote in a letter to Bill shortly after his departure.

Then added: *I want to know whether they think our portrayal of the Virgin Mother is "sufficient" in character, ideal and treatment to warrant their approval of our dramatization of their great Heroine.*

Cecil did not think it would be a good idea to leave the draft with Father Lord. His note to Bill continues:

If you can get from him what you want without leaving the draft with him we will be much better off because it will be copied, sent to Rome, and will become the official accepted or rejected version of the story.

Bill must have smiled indulgently at the last instructions—they might have caused him to wonder whether Cecil was intimating the Catholic hierarchy would purloin his bouncy story of the Virgin Mary and institute it as the *ex-cathedra* version. At any rate it aroused new awe for his brother's sprightly egoism.

DeMille's fondness for Father Lord lost some of its edge; the priest's behavior in recent months was causing him to wonder whether he might not have been mistaken in his original estimate of the man.

> If you have to give Father Lord a copy of the draft to study, I would not leave it with him for any length of time. I suggest that you remain there in St. Louis while he studies it, and then take it back. When we have a finished manuscript ... we will be glad to send Father Lord a copy to study.

In previous talks the priest had urged upon DeMille the possibility he was treading on dangerous ground:

> If you do a film on Mary, you run the risk of offending both Protestants and the Catholics. If you present her beautifully, Protestants will accuse you of being pro-Catholic. And if the film has the slightest element that Catholics think unfitting to associate with Mary, you will hear such an outcry that you'll be forced to run for shelter. You see, we Catholics feel we own the Blessed Virgin.

On his arrival in St. Louis, Bill learned Father Lord was out of the city. He proceeded to Washington and sat down with the learned Sheen. The lengthy conference sparkled with a pleasant interchange of ideas. Bishop Sheen's real feelings toward the script were not known; he devoted the entire time to explaining the accepted idioms and rituals. He did not indicate to what extent, if any, he was disturbed by the sensitive portions of the story.

Bill was overjoyed. He reported to Cecil by letter that all had gone famously with Sheen, pointing out, however, he felt the bishop may have been "a bit shocked by the comedy references to the bridegroom's eagerness to get to his bride." It did appear

Bishop Sheen had made an effort to alter the story line, for Bill reported, "He was so interested he began to write the play and make numerous suggestions for added scenes. . . ."

The conference with Father Lord took place two months later.

They spent two days going over the scenario.

"It was completely dreadful," the priest recalled in an autobiography published in 1956, shortly after his death.

> The story focused around the love affair of Judas, this time with Salome. . . . The climactic scene occurred during the dance of the seven veils. . . . Mary is in the garden outside the house of Herod, and the camera is swinging back from the dancing Salome to the suffering Mother in the shadows as she tries to save John the Baptist.

Father Lord was convinced that the Catholic public would raise the roof. His memoirs then disclosed something surprising only to those who did not know Bill.

> Bill DeMille had come to St. Louis chilly to the whole idea of the film. He knew the scenario was hash and a hazard, and though he submitted it to me with objective justice and some show of enthusiasm, the moment I began to take it apart he was entirely in agreement.

Two days later Lord sent DeMille a seven-page criticism, along with a statement of the reasons why the scenario "must not and could not be done," and a prediction of the extent of Catholic anger if the script ever became a screen reality.

Referring to the episodes between Joseph and Mary on their wedding night, he said DeMille "would have to realize that this is delicate ground. Any slightest rough handling of Mary by Joseph would cause a lot of criticism."

He said too much building up of Joseph's "doubt" (as to his relationship with his Virgin wife) would cause mingled reactions in the audience, largely nervous, since the Scriptures say so clearly that Joseph's doubt was cleared "while he slept."

Father Lord wondered whether it would not be better to show Joseph "on worried guard outside Mary's door on their wedding night, followed by a momentary suggestion of drowsing, *then* the light to indicate his doubts are cleared up." This would cover possible Scriptural criticism.

The priest pointed to the Salome-Judas-Herod sequences. They were "new and different," and a problem that had to be faced. He continues:

> If it goes frankly pagan, if there are costumes that are Folly-ish, if the dancing is shown as wild, etc., etc., there will be very unfavorable reactions and consequent headaches. . . . People will go to this film expecting something on an extraordinarily high level. If they get pagan orgy and bacchanal, criticism will be insistent and troublesome. . . . This would hold true about the costumes of the women of the court, and especially of Salome herself. . . . I keep wondering about the possibility of not show-ing Salome's dance itself, but doing it entirely by suggestion— as you did in the famous stripping scene in *The Volga Boatman*.

It seemed to have been somewhat Father Lord's fate to keep films about the Blessed Virgin off the screen. The priest re-counted in his memoirs how he had frustrated the Warner brothers' plans to film *The Miracle*, a story about an eloping nun, as also an effort by Stephen Vincent Benet and Samson Raphaelson.

The autobiography further notes:

> When we were working on *The Kings of Kings*, with con-siderable amusement Cecil showed me a cartoon of himself, labeled "The Man that Nobody No's." Indeed, I had been warned by many that to him you said yes. The one who corrected that was Jeanie Macpherson, who told me that I was to say no whenever the situation called for no. If I made any contribution to his great film, it was my constant use of the word no when I thought the scene simply would not do for the story of Christ. Now I was saying no to an entire subject. In the future when we met, Mr. DeMille regarded me a little sorrowfully and re-

minded me that I had blocked the production of *The Queen of Queens*. Personally, I think that was Mr. DeMille's good luck.

Recalling it in later years, DeMille atttributed the abandonment of the project to the Catholic Church's attitude on "the one big scene I had in the picture, the meeting between the Paragon of Virtue and the Paragon of Evil." Father Lord had told him there was no evidence Mary and Salome had ever met, then added with the air of a man who had suffered much from the limitations of mortal minds, "He said I could not show them together."

The boss's faith in the Jesuit order was revived a little during preparations for *Samson and Delilah*. The big gaps and seeming inconsistencies in the Biblical story were troubling him. It was apparent *someone* had to interpret these Scriptural passages if he was to put a narrative on paper. Dan Lord was mentioned as a possible advisor, but the boss shook his head. Then, at the suggestion of an assistant, a letter was written to one of the bright young Jesuits, Walter J. Ong, of St. Louis University, who already had made a considerable mark in literary circles.

The priest was sent a number of questions about the Samson episodes in the Book of Judges, and a month later there arrived at the bungalow a 70-page treatise on the subject.

It amazed and delighted the boss.

Here was a Jesuit with common sense! The boss telephoned the assistant from Paradise, where he had been reading the treatise, and demanded to know who this Walter Ong was.

"Why," he exclaimed, "that man has a marvelous mind."

"He's the Dan Lord of the future," the assistant joined in, momentarily forgetting that the boss did not share the general feeling toward Lord.

"What!" he shouted. "He's got more on the ball right now than Dan Lord ever had. And I know nothing about the man other than what he has written in this treatise."

Ong's free commentary became an important reference through much of the early story discussions.

A meeting between DeMille and Ong took place several months later, lasting only a few minutes during a train stop in Kansas City. DeMille extended a bit of fatherly encouragement to the young ascetic. "The Jesuits need your kind of thinking," he said; then added sorrowfully, "The world might have had a great document in the Virgin Mary story but Dan Lord wouldn't let me make it."

But there was nothing to indicate Ong would have either.

5.

DeMILLE would outline his concepts to writers, then dispatch them to their typewriters. He expected those ideas to be reduced to writing in a form as dramatic as he felt he had presented them.

This was where the trouble began.

One scrivener spent months on a draft of a story about the Biblical hero Samson, working closely with the boss and assuming that he was doing fairly well, everything considered. One morning, as he passed DeMille in the corridor, he was handed a note reading: *You have just killed the character of Samson.* The writer, stunned, later sought out his employer and told him it might be helpful if they asked themselves what the objectives were that they were trying to reach. "I've told you that in every language including English," DeMille barked.

Millions of words passed between DeMille and his writers over the relationship of hero and heroine. Every shade of reaction and attitude, every variation of human emotion that appealed to their sense of drama in those circumstances, was trotted out, looked at, taken apart, examined, kept or tossed away. Hours were spent in this manner on literally hundreds of concepts that never got into the final script even by implication. For example, the meeting of the triumphant Delilah and the blinded Samson in the gristmill, a fiery meaningful moment in DeMille's mind, occupied them endlessly in the effort to capture the emotions which DeMille felt were there. Then after periodic rehashing of that scene they finally went back to the concept which DeMille had outlined on the *first* day the scene had come up for discussion, *almost two years earlier!*

Another scene, by a water-lily pond, gave DeMille ample opportunity to peer clinically into his idea of an exciting situation:

Writer: Delilah knows Samson wants to marry her sister but she wants him for herself and she is pretty sure she can get him, so . . .

DeMille: The way you tell it, you've lost the story of that struggle completely. It's a struggle between two women really. Delilah says, "Well, the sonofabitch." . . . This great gigantic brute and this lovely little girl who's in love with him, trying to entice him in different ways and getting nowhere at all. . . .

Writer: Then . . .

DeMille: What he ought to do is to take her over his knee and paddle her with the leaf of a water lily. There are twenty totally different treatments you can give the scene that would be right but it has to be a lovely scene. This little girl playing there, doing what she can, occasionally showing her lovely body, getting a water lily caught in her hair, trying to be seductive and getting nowhere.

Writer: He keeps . . .

DeMille: He keeps trying to go and maybe he takes a leaf and whacks her on the batatada (folo) with it.

Writer: Delilah makes it . . .

DeMille: She's going to outwit him terrifically and tragically in a few minutes. She says, "You big ox, I'm not a little girl to be whacked on the fanny. I'm a passionate woman. I love you! I want you! Why do you bother with my sister, that frozen blonde up there when there's something down here that's worth having?" That's what's in her mind.

Writer: But Samson is too . . .

DeMille: Samson is for the big blonde. He wants to thaw her out. His should be the stupid mistake a man makes in telling the girl how beautiful her sister is—and he's just getting Delilah on fire. He says, "After your sister and I are married why don't you come up and visit us sometime?" Delilah has to be the most fascinating thing that anybody ever ran into. They should make a pair that are flint and steel, whereas you have a pair that are rubber gloves . . . you don't get the power of those two characters.

Writer: Well . . .

DeMille: Her body is against him, her cheek against him. He's having a helluva time and she's in seventh heaven with him in her arms. He should say, "I'll have none of you. I know you, you little bitch. I know what you're here for. You've come to try and get me, haven't you? Well, listen. You can take your pretty little legs and feet and ankles and breasts and tie them in a wet blanket and go home for all of me. I'm not going to be caught as easily as that." . . . Then Miriam coming along, the sweet little girl from Samson's own village. Miriam and Delilah. The fight between good love and bad love. It isn't done here on a big-enough plane. The great courtesan and the great saint. You bring them together, you bring Delilah and the Virgin Mary together for a scene and you've got something to get your teeth into. Here you aren't playing with Christianity; but you're playing the great scene of the seductress and the man seduced and she gets burned with her own fire.

At another stage in the writing, he was unhappy over the progress of an episode in which Samson takes refuge in Delilah's tent. Pacing back and forth and gesticulating, he told the writers why he was unhappy:

"This is an emotional, powerful scene that has to squeeze tears out of a stone wall. The characters don't believe what they're doing and neither do we.

"When Samson comes into this wonderful place to take refuge —when she pulls him in, he sees this little girl that he kicked out, the little girl who has run away from home to go to hell. We must play with that situation like a cat plays with a mouse. It's beautiful stuff. She may keep her back to him for a while or needle him for a while or she might say, 'Why are you trying to get away?' And then she turns around. He sees who she is. And he cries out, 'Jesus H. Christ! DELILAH!'

"Does she try to bait him? Does she say, 'Nuts to you'? Maybe she is going to call the guard—and he takes her in his arms and kisses her so she can't talk for ten minutes. She says, 'I've waited a long time for that kiss.' He says, 'You'll wait a long time for the next one.' And she says, 'By God, I will call the guard.' And she goes to call the guard after she's gotten him where he's a little loose in the knees. We can have an audience so delighted and so afraid with a scene like that. We're dealing with liquid fire."

DeMille: What is the situation created at the end of the scene?
Writer: Delilah is frustrated. What she wants to do now is to fulfill her promise to make Samson crawl.
DeMille: Yes, she has a mad on—but does she want to destroy him?
Writer: Before she destroys him physically, she wants to destroy him spiritually.
DeMille: Ummm. . . .
Writer: She wants to make his heart and soul cry out.
DeMille: Why?

Writer: Because Samson is responsible for the death of her father and sister.

DeMille: He brought death and destruction on her family, then laughed at her.

Writer: In the course of the scene she brings him to the point of just—

DeMille: He wants to take her, yes?

Writer: And just as he is about to, she turns him down.

DeMille: He wants to seduce her. She leads him on. She gets him hot, then says nothing doing.

Writer: She tortures him.

DeMille: Up to now I think we have tried to write this scene a little from the grand opera standpoint rather than from two people. You have got to get it down where I believe it. Joe and Mabel down behind the cotton mill by the Los Angeles River. When you get it on that basis, it will be true. An audience will just laugh when she gives him that talk [waving an earlier draft of the scene] about her arms and eyes. If Delilah talks about herself she can't be much. I've never heard Betty Grable say she has a good figure. But if Samson talks about Delilah's legs . . . If he says, "My God, what you have grown into? Even your feet are pretty—"

From the earliest days, DeMille broke sharply with the usual Hollywood method of screenplay writing. He renounced the custom of sending a writer off to some distant retreat with an order to return several weeks later with a complete story draft. DeMille stationed writers in the bungalow and *worked with writers* in the most uncompromising sense of the phrase. He felt he could drive them to greater literary heights if he kept at them. He once told us, "I fracture my writers. I keep at them until they are half crazy and in the end the blood and tears will get me what I want. I rarely accept their first efforts."

What he feared most was a lot of "pretty" conversation between his story characters. "Pretty writing can ruin a picture."

This morbid dread of "talky" pictures was at the core of his turbulent relationships with writers. He kept an eye peeled for any spoken word that might slow down the forward march of his plots; if it did, out it went. Experience of others had made him sensitive to pictures with too much dialogue—"artistic pictures that please the critics and writers and lose money at the box office." This attitude sharply reversed itself when it came to his press agents. They spared no metaphor. Their nouns rarely escaped the typewriter unescorted by a conceited adjective. Their phrases rode atop ideas like a peacock plume on a tam, hopeful that the ornament would obscure the vacuity of the idea. They were talking *about* DeMille pictures, and that was a different matter.

He brought in name authors as well as the industry's ace scriveners, and paid them big salaries—not to write what they wanted but what he wanted. This tendency to exercise their craft independently of him has caused DeMille some of the most agonizing moments of his life. "God protect me from the writer who wants to write." He compared this type to a builder "who spends all his time on pretty shutters and scalloped flower boxes before he has put in the foundation and plumbing."

He once hurled a scathing dictum at a writer who had spent several hours searching for the right adjective: "Your problem can be summed up quite easily. You've impaled yourself on a toothpick. Instead of stepping over it you're screaming with terror."

In one episode for *The Greatest Show on Earth* Frank Cavett, one of the colony's most talented script writers, had a character saying, "Oooh! What I said!" It was the sort of thing that brought the producer out of his office on the run.

"What does it mean?" said DeMille, too busy to keep up with conversational fads.

Cavett told him it was mock surprise, a sort of "throw-away" piece of dialogue.

"Throw away!" repeated the astonished DeMille. "We throw

away nothing in a DeMille script. That line's not only a waste but it means the character is a pansy."

Cavett, whose "Going My Way" had won an Academy award, remained away from his desk for a few days to recover from the shock. Sensitive, like scores of other writers before him, Cavett could not get adjusted to this method of evolving a screenplay, and left after a few weeks.

Melodrama burned brightly in DeMille's mind. If he warred, rather than worked, with his writers it was because he wanted them to feel the scenes as deeply as he did. He constantly hammered at the emotional meaning. Once he cried, "There's terrific power in this scene. You can get the audience so worked up they can't bear it. What I want here is something that would make Shakespeare say, 'Why didn't I think of that'!"

DeMille: This is the best piece of writing thus far but I am still a little puzzled by the motives of the two people. It's very well done but what is it they do? I don't know what the man is thinking. I'm not sure whether she is in love with him or not. He starts out by saying, "You're a vicious little bitch," but I don't know how he finishes. What's she trying to do? You don't reach any climax. You ring the curtain down because you have run out of breath. They're just exactly at the point where they came in.

Writer B: His whole feeling has changed.

DeMille: Where do I get that, except from you? Now he says, "You're not going to do anything to me, I'm getting out." What progress has been made?

Writer A: She breaks him down in the course of the scene.

DeMille: Where? How? Where does she break him down?

Writer A: Page 100. . . .

DeMille (looks over page 100): Nuts! I don't get that here.... He hasn't changed a bit. There's nothing here that changes him. Let me see why he changes. He doesn't just look at the moon and start to drool. What is his emotion?

Writer B: He starts out by being very suspicious of her.... Then she doesn't give him away.

DeMille: Is he falling in love with her? Is he suspicious of her? It's a rambling scene because there is no point of construction.

Writer A: The objective of the whole scene is when he takes her in his arms and tells her where he is going to be.

DeMille: He tells her his hiding place! Why would he do that? If he does he's a goddamn fool. He's suspicious of her, and would he say, "You have pretty legs. I live up in a big cave. You won't tell anybody will you?" He'd never in God's world tell her that. He's a judge, a hunter, a canny Jew. He'd never tell the girl. . . . I don't like this. I don't believe it. If you had three reels leading up to it . . . but to walk into this room with all its finery and say, "I'll tell you all my secrets because you have pretty legs." The last time he saw her he said, "Get out of my way, you little bitch." Now he sees her dressed up in a million dollars' worth of clothes, and says, "Oh, darling, let me tell you all my secrets." Why did you think I'd believe it? You don't. . . . To ask the secret of his strength here is just nuts. I know she's going to find out the secret of his strength. I've read the Bible. It's no great surprise that she's going to cut off his hair. You have to be clever enough to make me believe how cutting his hair off will destroy his strength. I gathered she meant she was going to get this guy to where he was in a state of imbecility over her and then do what women have been doing for ten thousand years. He betrays his people, his trust, everything in the world because of this woman. . . . The main way that women hurt men is to drain them dry. The way you have it, there's no possibility of his falling in love with this girl. He sees a good-looking dame and he's perfectly willing to go to bed with her. That's about all we have now.

A cursory search in Hollywood will flush out at least a score of writers who have angrily stalked out of the bungalow, declaring what DeMille needed was not a writer but a trained seal. His haggling with writers, singly or in sets, sometimes went on for as long as two years before a finished script was evolved. A great deal of personal anguish might have been averted on both sides had DeMille counseled from the start, "Look, I expect to beat your brains out until I get what I want. Please understand, nothing personal. We'll try to do a job, *my way!*" A half-dozen capable, highly paid writers, among them Fred Frank and Jesse L. Lasky, Jr., knew and understood the system. Tactfully and wisely, they put up with it, though sometimes, as both Frank and Lasky concede, at a dreadful cost to their nervous systems.

Lasky, son of DeMille's early-day partner, smilingly recalls: "Every weekend he would go up to his ranch and fortify himself for the following Monday. There he would mull over the sins of writers, how they degrade drama, frustrate common sense and multiply his own labors, and then in a fine wrath he would descend upon us on a Monday morning spitting little balls of cyanide."

No one better than young Lasky, the veteran among DeMille writers, knew how to handle the boss, and in such a way as to reveal no hint of his strategy. "Otherwise, the roof would have caved in on me. DeMille could not tolerate anyone beating him at his own game of manipulating people and talents."

Lasky learned a valuable secret early: "Keep the stuff down to earth." Nothing offended DeMille more than an imposing sophistry or a dashing metaphor, and it was a waste of time to try to slip one into the screenplay.

Frank, a former New York advertising account executive, remembered his first story conference with DeMille. He says he had to struggle to keep a straight face when DeMille issued these instructions: "Write it the way I lay it out and when you have finished, bring it back to me and I'll tell you why you've done it all wrong."

On one memorable occasion a topflight writer, in the midst of agonized efforts to evolve something pleasing to DeMille, felt pretty good about one of DeMille's penciled criticisms— *What I've crossed out I don't like. What I haven't crossed out I am dissatisfied with.* Usually, the writer said, his material bore such cryptic denunciations as: *This is baloney; This isn't the way we talked about it; My God!* or simply a huge NO.

DeMille once tipped off a couple of newly hired hands on how to get along with him; he asked them to look up the 45th Psalm. They did. It read: *My tongue is the pen of the ready writer.* From this hint they soon developed the knack of listening carefully during story conferences to DeMille's plot suggestions and bits of dialogue and later weaving them into a script. He told two other such laborers, "Your job is to please *me*. Nothing else on earth matters."

DeMille took great pride in lines of dialogue which he thought up himself, though there is considerable evidence of struggles with writers intent on changing them. Some even tried to discard them.

For a scene in *Unconquered*, DeMille suggested a line for the heroine—"Nothing for nothing is given here."

It puzzled the writers, so they left it out of their draft of the scene.

DeMille put it back in, and when the writers rewrote the scene, the line was again omitted. Once more DeMille penciled it back in, then took the draft down to them personally and demanded that they explain why they were taking it out. They said they didn't understand it.

DeMille grunted. "It's a perfectly marvelous line and it stays in."

For another bit of dialogue he battled less successfully. It came in the lion hunt scene in *Samson and Delilah*. A snarling beast appears atop a rock ledge, whereupon Delilah hands Samson a spear. "I don't need that. He's only a young lion," DeMille had Samson saying. The Bible itself refers to a *young* lion, but even so the writers contended the remark might provoke a laugh from the audience at a serious moment.

Right after the picture's opening in New York word was flashed to the studio that audiences were laughing at Samson's remark. DeMille wouldn't budge. The line was staying in.

The next day Barney Balaban, Paramount prexy, was on the phone.

"It's ruining the scene," he said.

DeMille wanted to know why they were laughing.

"I don't know, but they're laughing."

"It is a laugh of relief, Barney, relief from too much excitement."

"But the laugh is coming *before* he kills the lion."

"Anticipated excitement, Barney," pursued DeMille.

"I don't know. I don't think so," said Balaban.

"I don't like to take it out, Barney."

"It's ruining the scene, Cecil."

DeMille finally gave in. Authentic Biblical fact was thrown for a loss by what he felt was indecent surrender to the disorderly minds of "big city audiences."

Certain gems authored by him had long and successful careers. "By God, you have courage" was one of his favorites, hurled by the hero at many a DeMille heroine. Its first recorded use was back in 1930 in *The Volga Boatman*, with William (Hopalong Cassidy) Boyd toasting Elinor Fair. Twenty years later Victor Mature tosses the same lively rejoinder at Hedy Lamarr in the Samson story. Another that made a regular appearance was useful as a thrust at the hero's character. In

Unconquered, the heroine bitterly scores the hero, a professional revolutionary, "You haven't blood in your veins . . . you've
gunpowder." With equal wrath the heroine of *Greatest Show on
Earth* charges the circus boss with having in his veins not blood,
but sawdust. Cavett, noted for the fresh vigor of his style, made
a few attempts to substitute another line having no reference
to the circulatory system, but abandoned the effort when it was
obvious he could not break DeMille's staunch affection for his
own material.

During the writing of the Samson story, we trooped up to
DeMille's for a hush-hush screening of the old Rudolph Valentino silent, *Son of the Sheik.* The film's heorine, Yasmin, had the
same trouble as Delilah, apparently; she was forced to hate
the man she loved. Yasman lashes out at Valentino, "I'll hate
you with my dying breath." DeMille, an old hand at dramatizing
classic passions, improved on the line quite a bit. He has
Delilah hissing at Samson in the big love-through-hate scene,
"I'll *kiss* you with my dying breath."

The Sheik himself, to prove his strength, bends a sword which
the son straightens to show he is Papa's muscular equal. DeMille
has Victor Mature as Samson bending and straightening a
sword, in virtually the same motion. He found other things he
liked, patterning Samson's wedding feast brawl after the silent's
night club fight, the central figures in each case using a table as
a shield and hurling lighted lamps at their opponents.

Often without warning, DeMille would test writers for general attitude.

A young man came to help on the story for *Union Pacific.*
DeMille met him in the corridor, eyed him for a few moments,
then said sharply:

"Why do you hate the railroads?"

The writer, a timid lad, was startled.

"Mr. DeMille, I don't hate the railroads."

"Then why did you come to work on this picture?"

Union Pacific was a saga of violent opposition to westward development of that road, a facet of the plot which, in DeMille's view, could not be dramatized unless a writer felt some loathing for railroads as an institution. The writer indicated he would take a firm grip on his emotions and try to dredge up some serious hate against common carriers.

Temperamentally, the more creative writers were unsuited for working with the boss; they soon realized it and left. Such partings were often in the best of humor; others were edged with rancor or occasionally deep resentment. One writer, after six weeks of the DeMille system, left without word that he was quitting. He purchased some fifths of Scotch and for a week went into hiding from his family and friends. Later he told a fellow writer, "It will take me six months to get over the experience with that ——."

The obvious conclusion to be drawn from the outcome of a writing stint at DeMille's is not necessarily a safe one; DeMille's story formula, quarried and refined out of the experience of years, was peculiarly his own, and no force would cause him to change it.

He felt that movies should tell their story without dialogue. "This is a pictorial art and to permit it to become a mere shadowgraph of the stage is simply throwing away our heritage." He was a creator in a different sphere; while writers were shaping subtle little definitions, DeMille was figuratively atop Olympus devising ways to make worlds collide. He made sure he did not commit the mistake of a producer friend, who "lost a fortune because he became engrossed in creating a series of individually charming pictures and forgot to build up a clash of characters." The emphasis on conflict—"the only thing that will keep an audience awake"—caused him to construct a plot in terms of action, often breaking down a story into what he called "pieces of action." A memo tacked on his wall all during the story-writing phase of *Greatest Show* set forth THE FIVE PIECES OF ACTION IN GSOE. In *Samson and Delilah* he envisioned the plot in the same way: 1. Brawl at wedding feast,

2. Fight with Lion, 3. Fight with King's wrestler, 4. Jawbone Fight, 5. Falling Temple. Inevitably his credo of physical upheaval made him a natural prey for the sweeping movement of Biblical history. He once exclaimed, "I can make a picture out of any fifty pages of the Bible," then in momentary self-abnegation, "except possibly the Book of Numbers."

The plot, its mood and pace, were matters upon which he ruled. Suggestions were apt to be risky, at least until the writer had been given some idea of the sort of story whirling about in DeMille's mind. The story of Helen of Troy was once under serious consideration, later abandoned in favor of a remake of *The Ten Commandments*. At the time there was much secret speculation. How was DeMille going to approach the classic Trojan tale? We were not in doubt for long. At luncheon one day he set forth the format, which, incidentally, revealed a good deal of his formula with the old heroics:

"We eliminate all the gods and goddesses in the Helen of Troy story. We think of the characters as people and not as something out of Homer's *Iliad*. Some have dandruff, some have toothaches, some are clean and intellectual, others are dirty and sinful. Some have B.O., others are lovely. They must talk like people yet not like a reporter giving an account of a Dodger-Giant ball game. We caught the spirit pretty well in *Samson and Delilah*. A man may address his god with thee and thou but not when he is addressing a human being. The thing is to give the speech a poetic quality and still not go down to the Dodger level."

Part VI

"B" AS IN BARNUM

1.

PARAMOUNT paid something like $250,000 to the Ringling outfit for the use of its famous motto *The Greatest Show on Earth,* and its circus machinery.

At that point the two assets were just about all DeMille had: equipment and a title. However, he was not worried. He was interested, not in a history of the circus, but rather in a stream-of-civilization plot with a kind of *Grand Hotel* flavor. He conferred at great length with his researcher, Henry Noerdlinger, who went to the books in search of sawdust drama. The rest of the staff was alerted to the problem.

With customary contempt for obstacles, he wasn't exercised at first by our failure to come up with circus plots. He had been without a story before and with his usual convulsive drive he had always churned around and obtained one.

Now some preliminary churning was taking place, with little apparent result. More churning; still nothing. It was strange and a little startling. Then we came face to face with an astonishing discovery; there was very little in the way of circus *fiction,* but a great deal of non-fiction, such as memoirs and on-the-spot observations.

The preliminary work on ideas for a circus story was begun by a writer in late summer of 1949. In the following months his suffering proved to be heroic. He withstood constant hammering from DeMille, who daily reminded him that he was being paid $500 a week—on a long-term basis—to come up with something "acceptable to me."

Five months later a second writer was engaged. His salary was $750 weekly. At first the two writers worked together, then moved into separate quarters, taking time out only for those dreaded conferences with DeMille, whose patience was getting thinner by the minute.

DeMille assigned Writer No. 2 to the task of checking what Writer No. 1 had written thus far toward a screenplay. He advised DeMille that in his opinion it lacked a basis for a story, even though he was aware that DeMille had contributed much to the material thus far. Writer No. 2 was of an independent turn of mind, and we felt as the days wore on that he wasn't going to last much longer.

One afternoon DeMille returned a few pages of copy to the newcomer.

"This stuff is ghastly. What does it mean?" the producer said with a grunt of derision.

A seasoned staff man would have fended off the thrust with a smile, knowing the boss's weakness for this sort of hyperbole. Perhaps he really liked the material but wanted to hear the writer justify his story approach.

Writer No. 2, no apostle of the way of life in the bungalow, put on his coat and departed.

Writer No. 3 was brought in, at $300 a week, to bend his efforts to furthering the story line, while Writer No. 1 worked on the script itself. It was not usual to start writing a script when the story itself was incomplete.

"We've been at it a year now and we still don't have a story," DeMille said grimly, one day.

He remembered a circus classic, the silent movie *Variety*, which starred Emil Jannings. Its plot suited DeMille in every way; it was great drama. The boss waxed lyrical over the old silent movie, like a collector fondling a rare gem.

For weeks we lived on a diet of *Variety*. If only we could hit upon something with the same power. In *Variety*, a husband is one-half of an aerialist team. He's the "catcher." The other half, the flyer, is having an affair with the catcher's wife. This was not prudent. If the catcher finds out, he is in a position to take care of the adulterous flyer. And simply: He can let the flyer fall and assert it was an accident. Occupational hazard!

The husband *does* learn of the affair, and is sharply reminded of it every time he catches the flyer.

"What a magnificent situation!" chortled DeMille, eyes gleaming. "You can feel the tension mounting with each flight through the air. Will he catch him, or let him fall? Remember, the guy is sleeping with his wife and the unwritten law is on his side."

In great torment, the husband makes his choice. He is a trooper. The circus comes first. He accomplishes the killing without artifice. He walks into the flyer's tent and pumps several bullets into the blackguard's hide as he cringes in a corner.

DeMille's antics during this period were not of a kind to endear him to his writers. He flayed them in conference, then openly at staff luncheons. There were moments when he seemed close to panic. Costs were piling up. More than $50,000 had gone into writers' salaries. There were thick stacks of material, conference notes, bits of plots and miscellaneous ideas—but nothing drawn together into dramatic sequence.

One day DeMille thought of Jody.

Jody is his grandson, eight years old at the time. As a rule Jody sat next to his famous grandfather when the family viewed movies at the home, and the youngster's remarks in the course of the evening were carefully noted. DeMille regarded them as valuable clues to the success or failure of a particular film.

"When Jody says, 'That's the bad man, Grandfather,' or 'That's the good man,' I know that all is well with the story." said DeMille. "But if Jody has to ask who the bad man or who the good man is, then I know it is not a good story and probably will have trouble at the box office."

He confronted his writers.

"I want one of you to write the circus story in language that little Jody can understand."

Writer No. 3 was singled out for this undertaking and ordered to work alone in an adjoining office. He produced what became known as "the Jody version," seventeen typewritten pages, single spaced, with roughly 6,000 words. It was an excellent effort and contributed greatly to the final story, largely by tying together loose ends.

It began on an appropriate note: "Once upon a time there was a circus," then proceeds, "and the boss of this circus is a strong, tough young fellow called Brad Gable. Brad lives and breathes circus ... he eats and drinks circus. Brad is in love with Holly, the flyer, but Brad would never tell Holly that he loves her. In fact, he hardly admits it to himself. He knows it isn't good for the boss of a circus to be in love with a performer. When that happens he gets to worrying about her because she might fall and be hurt. She becomes more important to him than the circus, which shouldn't be. . . ."

This evaluation of human life vs. circus was not pursued further, but the Jody version developed a kind of life-and-death struggle à la *Variety*, but without infidelity. The struggle is between Betty Hutton as Holly, and Cornel Wilde as Sebastian, both in the roles of flyers. She goads him into extraordinary feats, figuring that a flyer who has the honor of the center ring ought to be capable of any derring-do. Determined to outshine her, Sebastian goes too far. He is seriously hurt attempting a triple flip through a suspended loop. Now the circus needs a center-ring performer, but the scheming Holly doesn't get the call. Like the hero of *Variety*, DeMille's circus boss is all circus, so he tells the girl he loves that she can't have the center spot; the circus comes first.

Even with the "Jody version" DeMille made it clear he was

far from appeased. He had a story line of sorts but "we should have had it nine months ago. We have a few bones. We've got to breathe life into this carcass."

At this point Writers Nos. 1 and 3 were in our employ, No. 2 having quietly resigned.

Still champing, DeMille brought in No. 4. His pay: $1,500 a week. He was assigned the task of polishing the material written by Writer No. 1.

Here DeMille announced that from then on he and a staff assistant would constitute a two-man team to act as trouble shooters. This meant the team would keep the writers on the right track, at the same time contributing plot suggestions and dialogue.

Meanwhile the story conferences continued.

The staff assistant shuttled between the writers and DeMille, making known the boss's attitude toward a piece of work and seeing to it that DeMille's ideas were not only incorporated into the script, but retained there precisely in the manner outlined by him.

One day DeMille heard about a young writer reputed to have a flair for originality. After talking with him, the boss offered the fledgling $1,500 for one week's work and, should the results please him, a minimum of $20,000 for an eight-week stint.

At the end of the week the young man, Writer No. 5, was informed his services were no longer required.

That winter, 1950, came the sixth writer. At $1,000 a week he was put to work polishing the material turned over to him by Writer No. 4, who was polishing Writer No. 1's material. No. 6 worked at home and came to the studio for the staff luncheons, now devoted largely to story problems.

During this period the non-writing staff members felt reasonably secure. For the time being at least they enjoyed a reprieve from criticism, and could approach the luncheon table with stomachs supple and minds at ease. The boss had his hands too full with writing problems to take more than a casual interest in the doings of his other functionaries.

Our table, an oblong affair, was next to a wall in the Paramount studio café. DeMille sat in an arm chair, back to the wall, in deference to a maxim, probably apocryphal, that in Hollywood one should have his rear protected and if possible both flanks. Always on DeMille's right sat Berenice Mosk, jotting down the boss's comments which might require action. Often a guest was at his left. If there was no guest, a production assistant occupied that chair. The rest, usually about five in number, filled in around the table.

Immediately upon the boss's taking his place he was served a generous bowl of potato chips, which he nibbled on during the half-hour or more prior to our being served. This was of course a gesture to eminence and while nothing prevented the staff from ordering a few chips of its own, no one ever did. Though it may be put down as an affirmation of our fallen nature, this pre-luncheon orgy sat askew on our disposition, not improved by the lateness of the hour at which DeMille preferred to lunch. The *crunch, crunch,* accompanied by digs, often not sly, at the hungry aides for work done or left undone, created a barrier to the healthy flow of the staff's gastric juices, which internists staunchly contend is a requirement of proper digestion.

The weekly cost for writers at this point was $3,300. After almost a year and a half, the script was only two-fifths finished. The date set for the start of filming was only eight weeks away. DeMille announced he expected the remainder of the script within that time.

A seventh man was brought in, at $500 a week, to act as co-ordinator, advisor and general overseer of writers.

In the days that followed, the bungalow's timbers trembled. Never had it witnessed such toil and turmoil, weighing and discarding, joy expectant and hopes dashed, withering sarcasm and open denunciation. One of the writers, harried but nobly unbowed, described the arrangement in crisp military terms: "I'm the 'point' man. The chap next door is the first wave. The one across the hall is the supporting troops and the one in the farther office is the reserves. C.B. and his aides are at the end of the corridor with muskets ready for any signs of defection."

Once, DeMille scanned twelve pages which he had received from Writers Nos. 1, 4 and 6. He ordered them to be reduced to six pages. The writers performed the surgery and a few days later DeMille demanded to know what had happened to certain lines. "The story is not complete without them," he said. They had made the mistake of cutting lines of dialogue thought up by the boss.

By November 1950, only a little polishing remained to be done on the script. The writing cost had reached a total of $113,000.

One scene of *Greatest Show* was squarely within the DeMille idiom. The giant circus, breaking camp and rolling off in its 25-car private train to start another season, filled him with exciting thoughts. It promised crowds, action, the helter-skelter dash of tardy performers climbing aboard at the last moment. The departure scene could also be used to play on the romantic strings of the plot—Holly with flirtatious eyes for Sebastian, the debonair flyer; Brad the boss remaining strong and aloof; Klaus the elephant trainer resenting the way Angel looks at Brad.

DeMille went over these crisscrossing relationships endlessly, trying to get the writers to squeeze every ounce of drama out of them:

DeMille: What is the effect on Brad? What effect on Angel? We have to create a situation between all 5, 6 and 7 characters. Holly and Sebastian have challenged each other—Sebastian has an interest in Holly. He's taken an interesting look at her. Angel has said, "Well, here's my chance, I guess," looking over at Brad. And Brad is busy as hell getting the circus off, and looks around and sees Sebastian either take her hand or 'Can't I help you into the car?' And Angel sees him and you get the little smile on Angel's face. . . . You have Klaus getting his elephants into a freight car, and saying, 'Come, Angel, get away from that thing. What you smile at? Get your stuff and get in here.' And Angel going by with some wisecrack to Brad, 'Well, I see your high flyer's started. Your devil on the ground. . . .' Some wonderful wisecrack she makes.

Writer: I haven't played the reactions on Brad and Angel.

DeMille: We fill the departure of the circus with wonderful stuff. Some little clown who's left something, some midget falls and someone picks him up. During all this hullabaloo the priest is blessing the train—somebody coming by and crossing themselves. Someone says, 'Look out! Your elephant's got his trunk out!' 'Well, he's starting to travel, isn't he?' The departure of the train—if one of the snakes got loose and goes up a telephone pole—but we don't want to use snakes. All those people. The fat woman? How about her? How the hell does she get through the door? Does she have to go into the elephant car? The living skeleton—does he help the fat lady? Is there a romance between them? The bearded lady is terrified of everything—that I know. She's the most timid. She has beautiful feet and legs and lovely breasts, well dressed, a lovely feminine person with a terrific black beard. A mouse goes by and she nearly climbs to . . . All those things converge on this exit. . . . What do bearded ladies carry? She should be knitting all the time, a little bit of a sweater, everybody stops and says, 'Oh?' She looks up at them and smiles with this big bearded smile. . . . The thin man is probably terrifically brave. . . . But the Bearded Lady has to be the most feminine, lovely thing you've got, with black satin shoes and pretty feet. Sebastian stops and sees these lovely feet and you see the look come in his eyes and he starts up and he's just about to make a crack—camera going up with him—and you see his expression suddenly change, this face with this muff! Say her name is Eloise. She should always be crocheting or tatting— no, *needlepoint*. That's very feminine. All queens did it. She should be very attractive. Only she's got a beard! Other women protect their hair in the rain. The Bearded Lady protects the beard. Holds her two hands over it.

Writer: The double doors on the car have been opened for the Fat Lady to get in. Two or three of them helping her in. Could we go right from the loading of the elephants to the loading of the Fat Lady?

DeMille: Sure. The Fat Lady should have the same characteristic. . . .

Writer: She collects romantic novels.

At this point, the writer working on the Jody version comes in, and asks about the aerial contest between Holly and Sebastian.

Jody Writer: If Holly wins the first round, it looks like the duel is over. I think she has to lose the first round.

DeMille: I don't care who wins or loses. She does a wonderful something and the audience applauds and Sebastian applauds. Then Sebastian does 18 hand spins. Then Holly gets ready to do another and the Ringmaster blows his whistle. 'Come on down! You should have been down five minutes ago!' Your point about Holly being put in the center ring is no good. What's the next part of the duel? Who wins that? The next time Sebastian does the same thing and he wins, and the audience says hurrah! and Holly does nineteen spins on one foot and the audience gasps. What are they saying to each other? What are the things that make an audience interested in the scene? What are the reactions of the people below? The audience doesn't know what it's about. To hold your motion picture audience's interest in the duel is what is difficult to write. You see that happen there. Holly does something, you see Sebastian say 'Jesus!' and applaud, and then he does fifty flips. I don't think it makes any difference who wins the first round. If you get over they're fighting a duel, you're damned good. What's going on elsewhere? What's the act—the feature? What's going on underneath?

Writer: I haven't shown the circus yet.

DeMille: I wonder whether your audience is interested, because they think Holly and Sebastian are in a Hollywood studio turning over on invisible wire. That's what they'll think, unless you show the circus.

Before shooting could start on the circus story, a way had to be found to light up the Big Top with enough amperage for the hungry color cameras. At enormous cost, clusters of small "cold lamps" were devised, and hung on the circus poles. They gave the cameras enough light and also permitted them to shoot upward at the aerialists—an angle that was impossible under the old system of Klieg lights manned from catwalks above the sets. Unglamorous though it was, the innovation marked a brilliant technical milestone for Paramount and Technicolor engineers, whose highly sensitive new film made possible for the first time filming of action under the circus tent.

DeMille had to gauge the Ringling circus's production time against his own, arrange players' commitments to dovetail with the circus schedule. These two items alone constituted a small portion of the total agony of detail that staff and technical aides checked up to the boss.

Around Hollywood the private hoots of dilettantes were being heard again, rising from the old anti-DeMille crowd. In the past they had said every DeMille picture was an old story with a new dress, that he hid the similarity behind mass action splashed across a huge canvass. When DeMille made three versions of *The Squaw Man*, the last in 1931, his sidewalk arbiters unleashed a chorus of "I told you so's." DeMille laughed at his critics then, just as he lashed out against Paramount executives who would balk at releasing anew one of his early successes. "You don't throw away a Renoir after you've seen it once," was his usual logic on this point. "You want to see a masterpiece time and again."

With most writers, as with DeMille, a half dozen basic concepts have served for plots, a form of literary inbreeding openly practiced in Hollywood throughout its prosperous days.

DeMille hewed to a distinction between what he called "narrative" and "dramatic situation." "Narrative" could be a string of interesting little episodes, but the latter was something considerably more vital. His idea of a perfect situation—a woman contracts to destroy a man, then falls madly in love with him—came to full flower in the Samson story, but it eluded him in the circus story. It eluded him in the awful succession of weeks that filled the corridor of the bungalow with cajolery and threats. And when it was all over, the plot situation was far below his hopes.

The circus project had one uniform effect—it welded all his critics.

This time, they were convinced, the old man was going to trip over his tripod. One producer, joining these prophets of doom, repeated a remark once hurled at DeMille by W. C.

Fields: "Some day the – – –— is going to be crushed under one of his own epics."

The time was at hand! Hollywood had never made an honest-to-goodness circus picture *under* the Big Top itself *with* circus people.

Technically, it had posed fantastic problems. Dramatically, it would be the sheerest folly; circus stunts like flying and the "iron jaw" routine were usually not to be found in any Hollywood actor's bag of tricks. Thus, it would require too many phony shots—"long" shots of performers substituting for the principals.

So-called circus pictures like *Chad Hanna* (with Henry Fonda) and *Laugh, Clown, Laugh* (Lon Chaney) had merit because they accomplished what they set out to do within narrow limits, but in no real degree did they mirror circus life. This was even true of that granddaddy of circus classics, *Variety*, with Emil Jannings, and such lesser efforts as *Halfway to Heaven* (Jean Arthur, Buddy Rogers), *The Mighty Barnum* (Wallace Beery, Virginia Bruce), and *Sally of the Sawdust* (Carol Dempster, W. C. Fields).

Other producers, sensitive to public taste, also had rummaged around in literary sources only to discover there was precious little to choose from in the way of circus fiction. Like DeMille, they did not want to photograph a sentimental memoir. They saw what he saw in the circus—"A fighting machine, a thing struggling against accident, flood and storm"—but up to this point they had refused or were unable to pay the price a true-life circus drama would exact.

As the following months proved, the diagnostic slurs of critics had not taken into account DeMille's most potent strain, his fighting spirit.

2.

THE sign of the fighting showman went spectacularly aloft in the late summer of 1949. DeMille figured there was only one way to learn about circuses and that was to join one on tour. With a writer, secretary and publicist, he picked up the Ringling Brothers' circus in Milwaukee and took the northern swing, digging his nose in the sawdust, soaking up circus customs and living with the performers. The merger struck quite a number of fancies. In town after town the news that DeMille was with the circus brought out capacity crowds, delighted over what struck them as a first-rate combination—DeMille and Barnum, two high priests of showmanship. The circus's advance men made much capital of the double billing.

The spectators had expected to see a tailored executive, perhaps enthroned in a special box surrounded by servitors. Their gaze met instead a stalking figure in breeches, boots and open shirt, peering through a camera "finder" at Bengal tigers within a foot of striking range. He went around and through the performers, scaling rope ladders to aerialist platforms, often outdistancing his staff, a determined Watson on the search for story clues for his circus picture.

The rapt attention of thousands were fixed on the scampering DeMille at the precise moment aerialists were engaged in death-defying stunts.

DeMille, possessed of a seasoned affection for the masses, was joyfully engaged in a bit of scene stealing!

On the third day out he decided he wasn't getting up high enough for the kind of camera angles he had in mind.

He went to Art Concello, then a big spoke in the circus organization, asked him to rig a bucket seat and pulley.

"I want to see how things look up there," DeMille said, pointing to the dizzy top of the huge tent.

"A birthday caper, eh?" Concello grinned uneasily.

It was August 9; DeMille's 68th birthday was the 12th.

Concello dismissed the request, concluding it was made in jest. What DeMille was asking was to be sent up forty feet higher than the highest aerialist platform. . . .

The next day the citizens of Eau Claire, Wisconsin, witnessed an unscheduled act. They gazed up at a tiny figure in a swaying bucket seat, high against the blue ceiling of the Big Top. Concello kept a nervous watch below. "I was thinking of what might happen." The spectators cheered, and the circus performers themselves joined in—cheering a man with a flair for their special brand of razzle-dazzle, and the energy of a puma.

DeMille came down, mopping his brow and grinning. "Let me give you a piece of advice," he told Concello. "It's 101 degrees up there and you need air in this tent. You can get it by opening the slit in the top of the tent." Each year the Ringling circus bought a Big Top. The next one purchased had an improvement; perforations to admit air.

His pace did not slacken even as the trip wore on. Only a few of us knew the extent of his fatigue when the day was over. On more than one night, at dinner, he slipped into a sort of semiconsciousness. His private secretary Gladys Rosson held up his head to keep it from striking the dishes. When he awoke he went right on with his meal as if nothing had happened. With five or six hours of sleep he was set to spring back into action.

This was the first time the circus had been stalked by a man of DeMille's vigor. It was no stranger to stress, whether from man or the elements, which may account in some measure why the folks of the 3-ring circus, aerialists and roustabouts alike, found themselves drawn to him, and why they soon began calling him "the fourth ring."

Nor had the prophets of doom reckoned with DeMille's talent for inducing stars to risk their high-priced necks for their art, or at least their art as portrayed by the dashing producer in puttees. When Betty Hutton elected to try her hand at flying, DeMille promptly and gleefully assigned as instructors two "catchers" and two of the best women aerialists in the field, Lynn Couch and Antoinette Concello of the once-famed Flying Concellos.

The vivacious blond star went into two months of training on Paramount Sound Stage 3, generously hung with rigs and pendulous trapeze bars like stalactites in Carlsbad Caverns. Betty's daring gymnastics startled her trainers; almost daily they entreated DeMille for help to rein in his star performer before something serious happened. Long before she took her turn before the camera, with remarkable grace in the key flying scenes, Betty was the talk of the Paramount lot. Understandably, the press received, if not with contempt, at least with vast cynicism the reports that the star would do her own flying in the picture. Her aerial accomplishments did not make the columns until she staged a special exhibition, convincing the doubters that the glowing rumors were not spawned by zealous publicists.

Gloria Grahame, too, caught the fever in her elephant-girl role. She consented to a piece of bravado that might have turned easily into disaster had the animal been startled as he lowered the bulky paw to the tip of Gloria's nose. DeMille merely suggested the scene, left it entirely to Gloria to make up her mind; he would not place loyalty above possible disfigurement.

DeMille took the affair in stride. He had affectionate memories of similar demonstrations. Years ago, Gloria Swanson permitted him to arrange a scene in which a lion placed a paw with uncut claws on her bare back. On that occasion DeMille, pistol in hand, shouted encouragement from a high platform nearby while a trainer goaded the lion with flicks of a long whip.

Miss Swanson's father watching the scene shook his fist in helpless rage at DeMille. Miss Swanson never budged a muscle while the lion roared at his heckler.

A half hour later the delayed reaction hit her. She broke down and burst into DeMille's office, crying hysterically.

"What's the matter, young fellow?" he asked. He always addressed her by that nickname.

"I-I'm tired!" she bawled. "I can't work tomorrow!"

DeMille smiled. "I've been waiting for this. At last you've shown you're a woman, not an automaton. Here, take anything you like."

He pulled out a tray of jewelry from one of the most exclusive shops in Los Angeles.

"I picked out a gold-mesh evening purse with an emerald clasp," Miss Swanson relates, "and immediately felt much better."

Miss Swanson in later years reflected upon it as "the greatest thrill" of her film career, comparing it with another type of experience, the thrill she received "when they first put my baby in my arms." DeMille was pleased to note the comparison; there was no doubt as to which event he considered the more important.

For her feat of flying, DeMille gave Betty Hutton one of his "medals," a memorial half-dollar, "for spunk above and beyond the call of duty," and another to Gloria Grahame for her gameness with the elephants.

The coin was one of a small number minted in 1937 in observance of the 350th anniversary of Walter Raleigh's colony on Roanoke Island. DeMille bought 2,000 of the issue. Selectively, he handed "DeMille Medals" to the pluckier of his players who did not flinch from the hazards of a DeMille script. Among the donees was Franklin Delano Roosevelt for the permission to film the story of Navy Commander Corydon Wassell, World War II hero of Java.

DeMille lived to rue the gesture to the President, breaking sharply with the administration's labor-union policies. His irritation cropped out unexpectedly in the direction of the President's dog, Fala, during the making of *Unconquered*. In one scene Gary Cooper pats a small wire-haired pooch with the remark, "Hi! fella." DeMille ordered it struck from the script. "Someone," he said, "might think he said, 'Hi! Fala!'"

DeMille went about the making of *The Greatest Show on Earth* with his usual *joie de vivre*. He led a troupe of some 200 players and crewmen to the Ringling winter training quarters at Sarasota, Florida, for a 2-month location that convinced the local gentry that here was a new and formidable force in circus life. The situation had in it the elements of a first-class struggle—two vigorous societies, Hollywood and the circus, with widely divergent habits and mode of living. Circus folks are of a suspicious bent, their pride admittedly not the product of Cadillacs, 6-figure salaries or servants-in-waiting. When the DeMille entourage moved in, the toilers under the Big Top were agreeably surprised. The stars and the rest scampered about in jeans and slacks, indistinguishable from the rank-and-file of the circus. Before departing Hollywood, DeMille had issued a strong edict: "Don't put on airs. We are joining *their* way of life." The warning proved unnecessary; in no time at all we all were caught up in the magic of the spangled world.

The Sarasota location was two weeks old when DeMille took stock of our progress. The results were alarming—a great deal of activity but little finished footage to show for it.

"This thing is costing us $20,000 a day," he told his top aides. "We'll be here ten years at this pace." DeMille shared a percentage of the production costs with Paramount. At this point he was on the books for 10 per cent of 2 million dollars plus 5 per cent of three-quarters of a million, or a total in excess of $200,000.

Fresh efforts were directed at the mysterious slowdown in the next few days. Ringling personnel were at our disposal but the two groups weren't meshing. Precious hours were wasted in waiting for a workman or piece of equipment. DeMille was growing desperate. "Maybe I should give them a million dollars and get the hell out of here."

Roy Burns, DeMille's durable business manager of many years, struck at the problem realistically. "We can't expect these circus people to pitch in with the same vigor as our own crewmen. We're down here on their grounds, taking over the winter quarters. I think we ought to pass around a few gratuities to show how much we really appreciate their co-operation."

The per diem cost of the location was astronomical; DeMille could well afford to adopt a beneficient attitude. Good-will offerings were made, $1,000 here, $5,000 there.

To a skilled key man, Burns handed a check for $25,000. There was nothing untoward about the offer or its acceptance; it would be worth the price to have the Sarasota stay shortened a few days by effort beyond what might be reasonably expected.

The following evening this key individual appeared in De-Mille's suite at the Ringling hotel. He handed the producer the check for $25,000, saying it might not be wise to keep the money as it might be construed in the wrong light. The check was torn up in the visitor's presence, and he left.

DeMille, his face cast in worry, turned to Burns.

"Roy, we're in trouble."

"But we saved $25,000!"

DeMille shook his head. "I cannot agree. That man turned his back on $25,000. No one does that. Take my word for it, we're in trouble."

DeMille kept a sharp eye on the man, expecting some devilish plot. He insisted that a mind that could reject such a sum of money could be capable of enormous evil.

Nothing dastardly took place, and when we moved out of Sarasota, still unpunctured by some occult treachery, the perplexed DeMille marked the occasion as historic. Hollywood had always evaluated people in terms of dollars. Here it had failed for the first time in memory.

He had called Samson "a story of the power of prayer."

On the sets, on tour, the "tag" became a motto. For such tags and labels DeMille possessed a rare sensitivity. He had a way of reaching right into the heart of a situation and coming up with a phrase that seemed to expose the story's inner meaning.

The Greatest Show on Earth was, to most of us, an actionful circus picture, but to DeMille it was an institution of co-operative creeds and races—"a sort of United Nations that works." At every turn he pelted audiences and press people with the concept.

This, and every other picture of his, had to be sold on a theme, and we knew that his "United Nations under the Big Top" idea, while a nice editorial thought, was not dramatic enough. DeMille knew it, too, and almost daily let it be known he was expecting one of us to come up with another key theme for *Greatest Show*. With the hundreds of production details we knew he was grappling with at the moment, this problem would remain with him, a small nagging voice, until he or someone unearthed the answer that satisfied him.

"Why did I make this circus picture?" he kept asking. Almost daily two or three replies flowed from our typewriters into his office. This went on for quite some time. Abruptly one day we were advised by memo that the boss himself had the answer. "Mr. DeMille has the idea which will keynote the entire publicity and exploitation campaign. . . . He decided to make *The Greatest Show on Earth* because it is a HAPPY PICTURE. . . . He made it to lift hundreds of millions of people out of the worries and tensions that beset the world today—hanging over their heads like the sword of Damocles. . . . This tinsel and spun-candy world will make the farmer forget his crops, the housewife forget her dwindling budget, the head of the house forget the headlines. . . . As Lincoln said, when the wounded soldiers paid more attention to Barnum than they did to him, 'Laughter is the best medicine!'. . ."

It seemed a first-rate approach, hitched shrewdly to the post-World War II miseries and restlessness! We knew that in time we would be called upon to speak out on the merits of the happiness theme—one of those dangerous situations that called for advance thinking. "Yessing" the old man could, in this situation, evoke some new tensions. The staff was not sure the theme was right; it had none of the characteristics of DeMille's past movies, steeped in thunder and foul play. We remembered the sign he had posted in the writers' conference room: WHAT IS THE CONFLICT IN THIS STORY? We had heard Frank Cavett, that gentlest of writers, smilingly repeat a comment uttered by his ten-year-old boy: "My dad is working for Cecil B. Demolish."

The happiness theme had not so much a false ring as an unlikely one, a pretty concept that sat askew on the brow of the maker of spectacles.

The showdown did not come in the usual way. Some time later a full-page advertisement carrying DeMille's signature was placed in *Variety*. It was the first public expression on the picture, and read: *My compliments to those stars and players who took great personal risks on the high trapeze, in the elephant acts, in the train-wreck scenes, and with the gorillas and other jungle animals while making* THE GREATEST SHOW ON EARTH.

More than a half a million dollars was spent on the film's advertising and promotion, but not a cent on the happiness theme! The staff felt it had been navigated safely past a dangerous shoal.

The New York office had eleven months in which to plan the premières and general release of *Samson and Delilah.* For *The Greatest Show on Earth,* time was all too short; no more than six, possibly seven, months.

The picture had not yet been unveiled to Paramount's New York brass—a key moment in our lives. Nevertheless, certain policy decisions had to be made, and to subject them to high-level thinking a conference was set up with the Paramount bosses.

Top Sales was there. As also Top Publicity, Top Advertising, Top Distribution, Next-to-Last Word, and Final Word, the last two being occupants of the highest Paramount echelon. Their appearances at conferences of this kind, though infrequent, left imprints on the course of future action that were deep and sacrosanct.

"May and June are consistently bad months for business," said Next to Last Word. He was more active than Final Word and took the intiative in deciding lesser-type details. "The third of July would be about right to release G.S.O.E."

Mr. DeMille expressed concern that Metro-Goldwyn-Mayer was about to release *Quo Vadis,* also a spectacle. Would they hurt each other? The others had no such concern.

"They are in contrast to each other," said Final Word. "Big contrast. There is no choice between them. *Quo Vadis is* big spectacle, a big picture but it hasn't the heart of G.S.O.E. They are not alike. You don't compare them."

"We would release G.S.O.E. whenever we are ready," chipped in Next-to-Last Word, putting the issue to rest. *Quo Vadis* would not be in opposition to it."

Top Sales said we would not need months to cultivate the public, that there had been a lot of pre-selling done already.

"We've done two years of pre-selling," said Top Publicity.

Mr. DeMille was still worried about *Quo Vadis*.

"Where you have two spectacles," he asked, "would you rather be the first to release, or follow the other?"

Top Distribution said there was room for fifty good ones any time.

Top Sales agreed. "Twentieth Century-Fox is benefiting with *Bathsheba* from our handling of *Samson and Delilah*. But with *Quo Vadis* and G.S.O.E. you have two Hope diamonds."

Top Publicity did not believe we would get much by previewing the picture in Sarasota. It could cost too much to bring in the press and it would be too much of a local project to benefit the picture nationwide.

"If we are hasty about these decisions we may lose," Top Sales put in. "We want to get started on G.S.O.E. but we have to see the picture and we have to decide what is best and then do it."

Next-to-Last Word felt there was a distinction, "With *Samson and Delilah* you had to be convinced of what you had. With G.S.O.E. you don't have to be convinced. We are thinking right—saturating the country and getting a complete fast liquidation."

"And we don't need any prestige engagements," said Mr. DeMille quickly. "And we don't underestimate the circus fans of America. They are a very large and influential group . . . they know their stuff. They can't be taken lightly."

"Should our terms be 50-50 from the first dollar, and sell to any exhibitor who is willing to pay 50 per cent from the first dollar?"

Top Distribution was happy to see this matter come up. On *Samson and Delilah* the exhibitor charge remained unfixed for nearly four months.

"A 50 per cent deal might look cheap to them after what they're going to pay for *Quo Vadis*," said Next-to-Last Word reflectively.

Mr. DeMille thought it would be wonderful not to have to raise admission prices.

"Our thinking is along that line," said Top Sales.

Top Publicity pointed out that *American in Paris* was coming out at advanced prices and a percentage basis, *Streetcar Named Desire* was asking $1.30, *Quo Vadis* was anybody's guess, G.S.O.E. would look awfully attractive at 50-50 and no advanced admission prices.

Provided, DeMille spoke up, the exhibitor does not think the picture is bad. "He'd have to believe that we were offering him a very attractive deal. I think the way to handle it is for me to make the announcement, in an interview, that I object to any raise in admission prices, that this picture was made for every man, woman and child in the world, that it is a picture they will take to their hearts—and I might even say it is a good piece of merchandise."

Top Publicity picked up the thought.

"If a newspaper has a big story on Page One it doesn't raise its price to seven cents, so why ask the public to pay more to see a great piece of merchandise in the form of a picture?" then adding, "We would give it to Louella Parsons or some other important outlet perhaps two weeks before our opening sales date, to make it part of the campaign."

The wording on circus sketches prepared by New York refers to "their spirit, sweat and supreme courage."

Mr. DeMille thinks *sweat* is not a good word; it is offensive to him. This would be checked.

Top Publicity suggests huge posters be held aloft during all future circus performances with wording to the effect *This picture soon to be shown on every screen.*

Mr. DeMille objects.

He feels there will be a kick-back from circus spectators who have just paid $4 each to get into the circus and are hit with an advertisement to see the same show in a movie.

"A circus atmosphere must be created—in dry goods stores

and theaters," says Top Publicity with feeling. "Theater ushers in clown suits, colored sawdust in the lobbies, spun candy, balloons, penants, whips, hats. . . .

". . . . on New Year's Eve, at 11:55 P.M., from every window on the lower floors of the Paramount Building and from offices on both sides of Broadway from 40th to 49th streets we will release balloons with G.S.O.E. on them—START THE NEW YEAR WITH G.S.O.E."

Top Publicity feels Mr. DeMille should be the principal speaker at the convention of the Variety Club in Las Vegas. The Club would like to have him.

Mr. DeMille hesitates. Top Publicity is given permission to have the invitation issued to Mr. DeMille. Mr. DeMille will await committing himself until he learns who is going to receive the Club's annual Humanitarian Award, as Mr. DeMille wishes to make sure that he would be happy to appear on the same program.

Now . . . let's see . . . Top Publicity and Top Publicity assistants have given a lot of thought to it . . . a traveling ambassador visiting towns and cities before G.S.O.E. is released.

Dorothy Lamour did such a fine job as M.C. on *Place in the Sun* and on a Crosby picture. . . . We want to send her out to forty cities as "Special Assistant to Cecil B. DeMille in Charge of Public Relations on *The Greatest Show on Earth.*"

Top Publicity feels strongly as to the wisdom of this arrangement.

"She would have a fully prepared and fully rehearsed script —and our idea is for her to tell America what she saw with her own eyes. She could bring in things like Jimmy Stewart who, with a wife seriously ill, still went on, a real Pagliacci act. Like her taking her own children to the Sarasota location, what it meant to them, their reactions."

Top Publicity thinks Miss Lamour would be terrific on this type of picture.

"She knows all the answers and is very quick on a comeback," Top Publicity confides.

Further, were we aware that Omar Rainey of the Cleveland press—"who has not been a friend of ours on every occasion—is a circus fan from way back."

Mr. DeMille nods approvingly.

". . . And Rainey is trying to sell articles to magazines like *Saturday Evening Post, Life* and the *New Yorker?*"

Mr. DeMille stiffens at the sound of these names. He is biting his finger tips, the mannerism escaping those who do not have access to his confidential moments. The sudden crisis might have dissolved by itself, except that Top Publicity presses on.

"We're in contact with a writer who has a firm commitment from *Saturday Evening Post* for a six-part article on DeMille and also a book commitment to do either a biography of DeMille, or help DeMille with an autobiography. This writer has had two books published in the last two years."

The crimson flush creeping up his neck, Mr. DeMille enumerates the reasons why he thinks it a waste of time to give the man the time he would need—two years of undivided time to do a book properly.

"In the end," DeMille concludes, "the six-part commitment would end up as a one-part commitment, or not be published at all."

Top Publicity, surging on, suggests they were ripe for DeMille on the cover of *Time* magazine.

"And a profile," he adds, brightly.

Time magazine! It was like a thousand wounds being reopened, a harsh cry redolent of the whiplash of the first review printed by the old *Life* magazine on February 10, 1921, under the custody of Robert E. Sherwood, who was not yet a name on Broadway.

Three times a year DeMille sends forth a new picture con-

taining a batch of multimillionaires who are just a little multier than the last, Critic Sherwood wrote in the first review for the new Silent Drama department, sounding an anti-DeMille note which he replayed down through the years, until it was picked up with orchestral fervor by the *New Yorker* magazine.

If only Sherwood and the *New Yorker* had been *for* DeMille; there were moments when the boss seemed to admire the beauty and volume of their literary assaults. It was not to be. A few years before his death the *New Yorker* plunged another rhetorical dagger into DeMille in its *Samson and Delilah* review:

> Perhaps DeMille's survival is due to the fact that he decided in his movie nonage to ally himself with God as his co-maker and to get his major scripts from the Bible, which he has always handled with the proprietary air of a gentleman fondling old love letters . . . he has never taken a step backward . . . he has never taken a step forward, either. . . .

The seeds which Top Publicity was attempting to sow on behalf of *Time* fell on spectacularly barren ground. . . . Mr. DeMille feels that in his opinion *Time* is bent on being destructive, and he cannot believe it now wants to be constructive. He is willing to let *Time* treat G.S.O.E. in its regular Cinema column. . . .

The conference is not going well at this point. Mention is made of a Hollywood première for G.S.O.E., at which Mr. DeMille begins biting his finger tips again.

"We'll première in the Chinese Theater on the very day the theater opened twenty-five years ago with *The King of Kings.* The stars are all in Hollywood and they're easy to get. We have 400 correspondents around, too, and the cost certainly would not be excessive. We are very enthusiastic about doing this."

Mr. DeMille does not share this enthusiasm. "There are people in Hollywood who are not partial to me and my picture," he says in a firm but polite retreat from what has been to him one of life's oldest problems.

Top Publicity goes quickly into the matter of buying promotion. . . .

"If we have an August 1 release date, and a half-dozen prerelease engagements in late July, we will want to start in May with several key locations in twenty or twenty-five cities and towns where we will post, and we really mean post, twenty-four sheets. Our thinking is along the line of what you'd expect a circus to come in and do. In June and July we'd post 2,500 or 3,000 billboards from coast to coast, on important highways, going into towns and cities. Is Paramount to pay the usual 50 cents for every dollar spent by the exhibitor? On *Samson and Delilah* Paramount's share of this came to $427,000. Of course we will go into the national magazines just as strongly as with S. & D. We figure the cost on G.S.O.E. will be about the same. We want four-color stuff and *good* drawings for the national mags. One page in four colors runs about $200,000. Maybe $230,000. The first week of 1952 we are going to run a 7-day teaser on the front page of the *Hollywood Reporter* announcing: 1952 IS HERE WITH THE GREATEST SHOW ON EARTH. Nice line, eh?"

3.

ONE of the more difficult periods for the staff invariably developed during negotiations with the Hays (later Breen) office and the Catholic Legion of Decency on matters of propriety.

The boss liked zest in his plots, peppering the dialogue with tingling aphrodisia. The censors in his life were almost as formidable as the critics; he had little use for either.

On *Greatest Show* it appeared for a while we might get off with few censor problems. The Breen office had objected to a remark by a girl performer—"I never was thrown out of bed like that before!"—as being "unacceptably sex-suggestive." We could have kept the line in the script but New York warned it might be ordered out by state boards, and it would be much less expensive to delete it at this point.

Eight lines of dialogue were censored and subsequently removed from the script. Fortunately for the writers, all had been contributed by Mr. DeMille.

Nor did the Breen office cotton to scenes in the girls' wardrobe room. We were told the Breen office "naturally assumes that where any of the girls are changing their clothes or performing other functions of their toilet, such as washing, etc., they are not to be clad in only shorts or bras—unless it clearly appears that these are *rehearsal* scenes, and not underwear. If the wearing of underwear is desired, then the girls should also have on dressing gowns or negligees."

A remark by Betty Hutton to Jimmy Stewart, as the clown—"Maybe you killed someone because you loved her too much"—was ordered changed; it implied a justification of euthanasia, or mercy killing.

Further, there might be repercussions by the Legion of Decency, we were advised by the Breen office. The Catholic Church's opposition to euthanasia was well known to all of us. We were also aware of the boss's bland indifference to censors while in the process of preparing a script; he preferred to fight those battles later, should they arise.

The Legion of Decency quickly spotted "the insinuation of euthanasia," as Father Thomas F. Little, an executive of the Legion, put it in his letter to Mr. DeMille.

Father Little's letter dropped like a bomb in our midst. It

contained an almost sweeping denunciation of Mr. DeMille's *happy* picture, made, as we so often held it forth, for every man, woman and child in the world.

The boss read the letter, once, twice, three times, then concluded that Father Little and the Legion had lost their sacerdotal buttons. "I used to feel that someday I would be a Catholic," he remarked at luncheon, "but the Catholics will have to get rid of at least three priests before I join up—Dan Lord, Bishop Buddy down there in San Diego and Father Little."

DeMille, more perhaps than anyone, realized the importance of a favorable rating from the Legion of Decency. What would his old critics say? DeMille can't make even a *circus* picture without sex; that sprightly, innocent world basted with suggestive juices! And a show especially for kids!

The Little letter, dated December 11, 1951, stated in part:

> ...We realize what the circus means to the youth of this country in every hamlet, village and town. It is assuredly an integral part of our American culture...as a youth and priest we have enjoyed [its] drama and entertainment...
>
> ...we wish to express our objection to several morally offensive elements in the film.
>
> ...while the circus is both adolescent and adult entertainment it is primarily and essentially a product for the youth of this country and the world. It is regrettable and unfortunate that you deemed it necessary to use offensive material.

The objectionable dialogue, according to the letter, centered around the character of Sebastian (Cornel Wilde), "repeated time and time again without necessity to establish his character." Since the letter did not set forth any samples, we hurried to the script for possible sources of the irritation. It was possible Little had eyed the moonlight haystack scene. Here, Sebastian says to Holly (Betty Hutton), "You are beautiful, exciting, like wine. You know women are like wine. Some are like sweet Sauterne, some are warm like Burgundy...." He classifies her as "champagne—sparkling, tantalizing. You make a man's head spin," admitting, "Oh, I have wandered a little—but how else could I appreciate what I have found now?"

In the scene Sebastian, skillful on the ground as in the air, draws the girl near, murmuring, "My heart beats fast, like yours. That's the magic of it—you love me."

There are other danger spots in the script, such as the contention between Holly and Angel (Gloria Grahame) for the hand of Sebastian.

ANGEL

Sebastian! I don't care if you break him up for firewood. He asked for it, playing around with you. But Brad is on the level. . . .

HOLLY

Brad hasn't got time for love.

ANGEL

I'll take Brad the way he is.

HOLLY

That is, if you're his type.

ANGEL

Who you callin' a type! Maybe I have been over the course a few too many times, but I've got a heart under this costume and there's only room in it for one guy. You've busted him apart, and I'm gonna pick up the pieces. He'll never miss you, Sugar. I've given him more than you ever could.

HOLLY

Maybe so, you've had plenty of experience.

Father Little's letter was hard for DeMille to accept. Just a short time before, he had shown the picture to a small group, and afterwards a producer had remarked, "More entertainment than I have ever seen in two hours." Later, recounting the evening to us, DeMille was inclined to reinterpret the producer's remark. "What he was really trying to tell me was that it was a great picture because of its *spiritual* power."

The climate in the bungalow grew more oppressive each day for those of us who, being Catholics, remained silent on the issues. DeMille, furious with Father Little, became more articulate, bringing the entire framework of Catholicism into the range of his observations.

At one point he likened the power of the Catholic Church to world communism, then eyed the Catholics on his staff for some sign of reaction. They managed a smile, a kind of gentle, understanding smile that recognized the boss's anger and that actually he did not really mean half of what he was saying.

"Father Little's attitude is purely political," he fumed. "One of those men who have the power to say 'Thou Shalt Not'!"

He said his daughter had told him of her plan to send her son, Jody, to a Catholic school, but he had advised her to think a little before doing that—"Then I told her all about Father Little."

The emotional blood-letting did not diminish. For the next week a member of the staff worked on what DeMille said would be a strong reply to the Legion of Decency. The letter might even be made public as part of an attack on the Legion, should the controversy compel his taking so drastic a course. He felt deep within, however, that the Legion surely would withdraw from its position.

The first draft of the reply was very strong and was toned down, but the final letter left little doubt that DeMille was heatedly inviting a head-on clash with the national censoring body whose recommendations come to the attention of the majority of the million and a quarter Catholics in the United States.

Mr. DeMille's letter charged Father Little with being "the first and only person to raise an objection to the picture on moral grounds." He denied Sebastian's character was offensive, and "I cannot by any stretch of the imagination conceive that the soul of any human being, young or old, could be corrupted by his dialogue."

The letter goes on to say:

> I conceived him [Sebastian] as a light, airy, flirtatious character, full of wit and fancy. I am sorry if you personally take offense to the fact there are in the world men like Sebastian and that people in the world discuss their foibles and failings. I might join you in wishing that all men were saints. I could not agree with you, however, if you would deny to any form of art . . . the right to portray the world as it is, so long as such portrayal does not bring about that corruption of human souls which the Legion of Decency properly and vigilantly guards against.

Mr. DeMille then quotes Cardinal Newman, one of the Church's most distinguished converts: "It is a contradiction in terms to attempt a sinless Literature of sinful men . . . you will seek for it in vain . . . take things as they are, not as you could wish them."

Nor did he agree that Miss Grahame's costuming was "suggestive," inasmuch as it was the same worn by the regular Ringling performers.

Quoting St. Paul, he adds:

> All things are clean to the clean. I think you will agree that what one person finds "suggestive" may be perfectly innocent to another. . . . I suppose that there are a few individuals so morbidly prurient that looking at someone dressed in a circus costume might constitute a moral danger for them. Such unfortunate persons should go to see a psychiatrist rather than *The Greatest Show on Earth*. . . . I am sure you will not accuse the children or the youth of America of having minds like that.

After a lengthy rebuttal of Little's claim of euthanasia, DeMille continues:

> I will not bandy threats with you. . . . Since you will not, I think, lay claim to infallibility I ask you to give equally serious

consideration to my reasons for thinking you have sincerely erred in this instance.

Before mailing the letter, DeMille called us in, one at a time. Most of us confessed later to reading the letter with shock, though taking care not to show it at the time. DeMille asked what we thought of it. One said he felt there might be another safer and more productive way to handle the matter than by the letter—perhaps an off-the-record meeting with Father Little, but this suggestion was angrily brushed aside. The boss was in no mood for tactical negotiation; the epicmaker was on the march, storming the bastilles of censorship.

The letter was sent, and our position was clear: we would change nothing as a result of the Legion's request.

As was feared, the reply from Father Little was firm and unequivocal. He did not take kindly to what he had read. He repeated his concern, "shared by the personnel of the Legion," that the picture by its very nature would appeal particularly to youth, still judging it to be "potentially harmful to the moral well-being of the young."

The danger in respect to Sebastian's "unsavory" character was felt to be even greater because "he is both a leading and sympathetic character."

And may we note, my dear Mr. DeMille, that besides the Sebastian character there were other items in your film which we judge to be rightfully considered as "suggestive."

. . . We recall to mind, for instance, one of your own pictures entitled *The Sign of the Cross* and particularly to a dance sequence that was included. We would remark in passing that this was one of several pictures by various producers that led directly to the formation of the National Legion of Decency.

Father Little tallied a quote of his own, from St. Augustine, "Hate the sin and love the sinner." As far as Miss Grahame's "suggestive" costume was concerned, he pointed out that a spectator at a regular circus performance does not get the same "intimate impression" of costuming that is provided the movie-goer by Mr. DeMille's camera close-ups!

The Legion of Decency gave the picture a "B" rating. There was only one lower rating—"condemned," reserved for films that violated the canons of marriage or morality. Most frequent of such offenders are carnal tid-bits often tagged as "art films."

The "B" rating was bad enough. It meant that DeMille's happy circus picture, *The Greatest Show on Earth,* was "morally objectionable in part for *all* persons."

The boss was dumfounded.

"It's a lot of— —hogwash. Morally objectionable to boys and girls! This is a picture with clowns, elephants, fliers in the air, horseback riders. . . ."

He shook his head wearily.

"With those Catholics a little euthanasia goes a long way," he said.

The two Catholic members of the staff were ready to concede that whatever aspirations the Catholic Church may have had toward DeMille as a convert were now dashed, irrevocably.

The hurt caused by l'affaire Legion was salved to some extent in a totally unexpected manner, and from the strangest of sources—the Academy of Motion Picture Arts and Sciences, donor of the annual "Oscars."

No Oscar had ever been voted a DeMille picture. The Academy always passed the elder showman by, with marvelous unconcern for his half century in the craft as well as for the public's preference that reflected itself in his dazzling record of boxoffice championships.

Three honors went to *Greatest Show* on the night of March 19, 1953, the occasion also observing the silver anniversary of the Academy. To Mr. DeMille went the Thalberg Award for eminence in the profession, which, coupled with the "best picture" and "best screenplay" awards, made it a memorable evening for the bungalow. The boss was moved by the gesture; how deeply it cannot be said. Perhaps it had come too late; too often he was passed by, too little had been said when the occasion called for much to be said.

A numbing chill swept his critics.

The award to the picture was not expected. Many who had cast their ballot for the year's top grosser were quick to make it known that it was a mere courtesy—"after all the old man has been around a long time and has done a lot of good."

However DeMille may have felt inwardly, he viewed rebuffs from colleagues with devilish amusement. Profit and the masses were on his side and he saw no reason to change his belief in the ultimate judgment of the people. He liked to think that that judgment was the most intelligent, too.

4.

THE sex-happy 1920's had sharply widened the powers of censorship, the natural hand maiden of public indignation. The screen was crowded with dancing mothers, speakeasies, petting parties, flappers, cake eaters.

Censors lurked behind every corner, moving in swiftly to deliver sudden and savage attacks. Just when Hollywood felt it had proved that wolf-whistling and the ardent embrace were inevitable products of man's fallen nature, along came the state censor—a hydra-headed monster spewing purity and morality.

DeMille took note of the new menace. He was at the peak of his "bathroom period" in 1923 when he issued a pre-Christmas statement to the press, damning censorship as "the most pernicious influence in America today."

He didn't feel it was Hollywood's duty to protect the public from awful truths like the existence of evil women. "The censor's mind is the eye of the needle and the great story minds of the world are the camels trying to pass through." He was sufficiently wroth over the issue to add: "This civilization is riding to a fall just as Rome did."

For DeMille, the wars with censors went back to *Joan the Woman*, his first epic, and provided him with the first in a large repertory of border incidents to illustrate the low quality of the censor mentality. *Joan the Woman* was tabbed by critics and patrons alike as worthy of a place with the finest half-dozen films of the era. It had another distinguishing feature. It was a silent yet it starred the most renowned dramatic soprano of her day, Geraldine Farrar. Goldwyn and Lasky had hired the Metropolitan Opera beauty for a kingly sum to appear in not one but three silent pictures. All racked up splendid grosses, leaving a distinct impression among observers that the era was so golden that even errors in judgment paid off.

DeMille took *Joan the Woman* to New York for a showing to censors and ministers.

The screening over, a minister said he did not see anything offensive in the picture.

A woman censor disagreed.

"Yes, there is one thing that has to come out," she said. "It's the line where Joan says, 'My God, my God, why hast thou forsaken me.' "

DeMille asked the woman whether she knew who had first spoken that line.

"It doesn't make any difference who spoke it. It means that God would forsake someone and it has to come out."

One of the ministers intervened.

"My dear lady," he said "I wonder whether you are aware that those words were said by Jesus on the cross!"

As a matter of fact, those words of Jesus are a quotation of the first line of Psalm 21, which is a prophecy concerning His own passion, thus placing the woman censor in a not too implausible position.

There were times when DeMille found the edicts of censorship tiresome, refusing to pause in his labors even long enough to challenge them. But hotly contested points drew him and the staff into lengthy dispute.

Some years back Jean Arthur did a portrayal of the swashbuckling frontier gal, Calamity Jane, in one of the best of the DeMille horse operas, "The Plainsman."

In the course of a scene DeMille has Calamity reviling a female rival.

Calamity calls her a "mopsy."

The Hays office, checking the script prior to filming, sent word to DeMille that he couldn't use the word "mopsy" because it meant "prostitute."

"Mopsy" did not mean that at all, DeMille retorted, and set his office to work searching for definitions. The staff came up with a few—"term of fondness applied to a little girl," "a pet appellation for a lap dog." But there was evidence it also could be applied to a "slattern."

It appeared DeMille was losing the battle of dictionaries, when his researcher chanced upon a popular child's book entitled *Flopsy, Mopsy, Cottontail and Peter.* It was all about four rabbits of unquestioned virtue scampering in the woods. DeMille was ecstatic. He asked the Hays office to designate which rabbit was of ill repute. Hays was not willing to put the brand of shame on this Mopsy, and withdrew his objection.

Calamity Jane caused other trouble. The script called for a scene in which she puts her arms around Hickok's neck, holding him tight, then pulls his head down with a sudden effort and kisses him full on the lips. He pulls her arms down and wipes his lips with the back of his free hand as Calamity exclaims, "You four-flushin' mule! You ain't wipin' it off—you're rubbin' it in!"

The Hays office labeled the shot objectionable because Hickok's reaction to Calamity's kiss "tends to build up the flavor of her being a prostitute."

The censors thought it detected other signs of promiscuity in Jane, such as Hickok's remark, "She didn't care much who got her scalp, she didn't care about anything," and "You weren't so touchy last night," a remark uttered by a vagrant.

Once more the Hays office backed away upon DeMille's contention that Wild Bill Hickok was not a ladies' man and he would wipe off *any woman's* kiss, no matter what the condition of her morals.

One of DeMille's more challenging encounters with censors took place with *Carmen* back in 1915, when prints of the picture were sent to all state censor boards then in existence—twenty-seven in all.

The results seriously impaired DeMille's happiness for months. "Each of the twenty-seven censors found something objectionable, but no two censors objected to the same thing. They asked me to make cuts in twenty-seven different scenes!"

There was concerted eyebrow lifting in the Hays office over the *Story of Dr. Wassell* script.

Hays would not approve a GI on Java chasing a Javanese girl because it indicated "illicit sex."

A reference to "chop suey" was ordered out; it might offend the Chinese.

DeMille was advised to handle carefully the scenes of Wassell "bathing, toweling and putting on his pants."

Also, "the location of the wound in the woman's leg should

not be used suggestively in connection with Johnny's remark 'Can I help?' "

DeMille had an untamed weakness for injecting little surprises in his movies, often causing both innocent observers and censors to fall into exasperating traps. He numbered among his choice tidbits such seeming blunders as Roman soldiers shooting dice, Joan of Arc using a safety pin, Scottish Highlanders in kilts lifting the siege of Ft. Pitt.

In a transport of secret joy, he sent to Hungary for a replica of the famous bent crown for the player who portrayed King Nicholas in *The Crusades*. As he predicted he received indignant letters calling attention to, as one writer put it, "the old second-hand crown with the bent cross."

H. B. Warner literally felt the weight of this fondness for authenticity. Portraying the Christ in *The King of Kings* he was called upon to carry a cross weighing 160 pounds, just a few pounds lighter than the original.

DeMille was rhapsodic over one revelation by Dr. Corydon M. Wassell. In the film a brown-skinned character named Tremartini does a native dance which smacked more of Harlem than Java, where the customs are largely pre-Moslem. DeMille set his critics straight. The character was authentic, being an exact counterpart of a Javanese nurse. As to her outlandish hula-hula dance, Dr. Wassell was the authority: "Java girls do a sexy hula as a result of having seen Betty Grable pictures."

DeMille was unhappy over the chronic refusal of censors and critics to take his pictures at face value. What one saw in a DeMille picture one could believe, a motto of the DeMille office which the public never quite raised to the dignity of a maxim. Through the years he had demonstrated an academic fervor far beyond the needs of the moment, spending thousands of dollars tracking down these bits of historical lore. He would complain moodily, "I spend $100,000 on research but along comes a critic who has just read a paragraph out of some encyclopedia and which the encyclopedia probably paid $10 for. Will the critic say I am right? No, he'll turn his back on my $100,000 worth of research and say, 'That's Hollywood for you.' "

Shakily we would commit a picture to the care of the censors and critics. When the reaction was hostile, DeMille was able to suppress a homicidal desire to strike back.

Probably the boss's longest stretch of silent suffering started in 1921 and continued for fifteen years. And no doubt longer, had not the magazine gone out of circulation.

The culprit was Robert E. Sherwood, playwright and presidential speech writer, film critic of the old *Life*. Sherwood's monographs on DeMille were chock full of witticisms, his humor edged with telling observations. Once installed as reviewer, Sherwood lost no time in getting to his target. His first swipe at DeMille was a backhanded compliment on *Forbidden Fruit*.

For once DeMille has had the sense to subordinate the sex appeal and pay a little attention to the story, Sherwood wrote.

The following week Sherwood, dipping his pen in tabasco, turned to *The Affairs of Anatol*, based on the Arthur Schnitzler play.

The review struck up an imaginary conversation between Sherwood and a man seated next to him at a showing of the picture:

But who is that?" asked my friend in a startled tone, as the picture began.

"That is Wallace Reid, who is playing the role of Anatol, a young, 100 per cent American millionaire."

"But—"

"Hush" I cautioned him. "You are drowning out the organ."

"Whose bare leg is that?" he queried next.

"It belongs to Gloria Swanson (Mrs. Anatol). In a moment the rest of her will appear."

It did. . . .

"Listen, my friend," said my inquisitor, querulously, "I saw *The Affairs of Anatol* on the stage, but I remember no such occurrences as these. Who is that rustic youth—and who is his companion?"

I smiled patronizingly.

"That 'rustic youth' is Monte Blue, after whom the Blue Ridge Mountains and the Blue Grass State were named. The lady with him is Agnes Ayres, who is supposed to be his wife. She has an affair with Anatol."

"I remember nothing of the kind in the play," he murmured.

Followed a period of silence.

Again he spoke, in a voice that was hoarse and barely audible.

"Who in heaven's name is this?"

The fellow's ignorance appalled me.

"That, my man, is Bebe Daniels. She is now making an assignation with Anatol; that is, she is making an assignation in every state except Pennsylvania."

"But the play," he gulped.

"Oh, forget the play—everybody else has."

"But the public—will they countenance this monstrosity?"

"You bet they will! What is more, they'll pay good money to countenance it, and the local exhibitors will wax richer and fatter."

"Then there must be something terribly wrong with the public."

"There is.". . .

He rolled a glazed eye in my direction.

"I'm Schnitzler," he gasped. "I'm the man who is supposed to have written that play—"

He sank in a limp heap.

The picture remained on Broadway for weeks and each week Sherwood kept his readers advised with paragraphic tidbits. "(The picture) should be enormously popular, especially with those who think Schnitzler is a cheese." (It *was* enormously popular, earning better than a million dollars over its cost.)

Merrily, Sherwood continued his clubbing of DeMille's films.

Early in January, 1922, he went after *Fool's Paradise*, contending that Leonard Merrick's story had been "mutilated, deformed, truncated, disfigured and beaten to a pulp . . . offensive to the eye, to the aesthetic sense and frequently to the digestive organ. . . . A sordid, distasteful theme."

But *The Ten Commandments*, released two years later, rocked Sherwood back on his heels; it was a good picture.

Sherwood admitted it, but soon was gaily back at the old stand. "It is a source of genuine regret to me that I must return to my old policy of roasting Cecil DeMille's pictures. Some time ago I met him face to face, and he seemed like *such* a nice man."

These continued attacks were one of the most sorrowful aspects of DeMille's life and in view of his success the most puzzling. He had established early that he was on the side of the common people, or possibly that they were on his side. Having pleased vast numbers of filmgoers, he found himself in the trying position of facing the critics with this dastardly achievement. He often took the view the conflict was between the critics and the masses. "What the critics are telling the world is that if the people had any sense they wouldn't enjoy a DeMille picture."

It was our practice to search newspaper reviews of DeMille films for comments stating in effect that, despite its low quality, the picture would probably make a huge profit. At least a half dozen such verdicts were rendered by major critics on every DeMille hit. On one picture the boss anticipated the usual critical reaction, grinning as he remarked to a visitor, "This picture stinks but it probably will be enjoyed by millions." Some key reviewers said just that, in one way or another, and the *Samson and Delilah* picture went on to post impressive boxoffice returns. A quarter of a century ago the old New York City *Post* tagged DeMille's *Volga Boatman* as a "bore . . . silly and vulgar," adding, "It is almost certain to make a barrel of money."

The New York Times assessed *Samson and Delilah* as a

"movie for DeMillions if there ever was one," and went on to say "it has more chariots, more temples, more peacock plumes, more beards and more sex than ever before."

In time DeMille inverted the precept; when a writer who had helped on the script told him the picture would receive good notices from the critics, DeMille drew back in feigned shock.

"Just a minute!" he cried, "I've got a lot of money tied up in this thing."

"The critics say my pictures are full of hokum. Well, what is hokum? It is pure and simple emotion. Christ making the blind girl see, I suppose, is hokum. They say my pictures are spectacles. Was the crucifixion a spectacle? That had a lot of people. Was Guadalcanal a spectacle? There were a few in that one, too."

This philosophic note crept into his thinking as he became hardened to criticism of this type. He was impressed with the possibility he may have inherited this tribulation. A few years back he showed Frank Freeman, Paramount studio head, a review written by a Chicago critic. Freeman read it and said he was puzzled, that he did not recall DeMille having made a picture of that title. DeMille was entranced. It wasn't a review of one of *his* pictures but of a play written by his father. "They treated him just the way they're treating me, and his plays were always successful."

However he may have felt deep inside, the money-making potential of his pictures was a soothing balm. The hostile arrows of critics broke harmlessly on the armor plate of golden box-office returns; and not even the critics cared to contest his skill for giving the public what it liked. Of all the bolts hurled by newspaper literati and the slick magazine gentry, only those of the *New Yorker* cracked DeMille's apparent indifference. In 1949 the magazine ridiculed DeMille, and riddled *Samson and Delilah*.

An assistant approached DeMille with a copy of the *New Yorker* review, and was questioning its logic when DeMille turned on the aide with sudden fury.

"Do you think for a moment the *New Yorker* crowd cares whether *Samson and Delilah* is good or bad! This is a political attack against me, against my beliefs! It has nothing to do with the picture."

The ashen-faced assistant nodded, as if comprehending the reasonableness of the view, and quickly withdrew.

Something of the real depth of this feeling came to the surface with a gesture uncommon to Hollywood. The *New Yorker* was sharply critical of Metro-Goldwyn-Mayer's new version of *Quo Vadis*, produced under Mervyn Leroy. DeMille, who had not seen the picture, called Freeman and urged that the motion picture industry unite against the magazine.

"Mervyn Leroy is young and can't take this sort of thing," he cried. "I've been through it and I'm used to it."

DeMille was not one to let a conviction lie fallow, especially when it was backed up by studio associates. Support of the boss's views too often had little meaning, in view of the fact that it was hard not to agree with him.

He set out his belief that there was a world conspiracy attacking him through his pictures. The declaration won approving nods. From then on, staff members were sent on missions of considerable secrecy, usually to ascertain the political stripe of an offending critic.

During this troubled period Bosley Crowther made a visit to the DeMille office.

The noted film critic of *The New York Times* had already rendered a lukewarm verdict on *Samson and Delilah*.

Crowther, a White Plains conservative with a dazzling grasp of the classics, had no inkling of what awaited him.

DeMille began by saying that he seemed to see a parallel in Samson's destruction and the present state of the world.

"The free world has a Samson that is pulling the temple down on its head," the producer pointed out, adding that the menace was Communism.

Crowther smiled goodnaturedly.

DeMille observed that the opposition to *Samson and Delilah* appeared to him to be entirely from Communist sources.

"I can't agree with you that only Reds disliked the picture," Crowther said quickly, smiling. "Perhaps *I* didn't like it."

The interview ended on a decidedly frigid note and as soon as Crowther was gone DeMille called in one of his staff.

"*The New York Times* review says *Samson and Delilah* is in bad taste," he said.

The aide frowned.

"You seem a little uncertain. It does say the picture is in bad taste, doesn't it?" DeMille persisted.

"Well, I don't seem to recall it. . . ."

DeMille brushed the remark aside.

"I think you will find that other papers around the world pick up what the *Times* says—Australia, Paris, Belgium, London. I have noticed that the foreign reviews say *Samson and Delilah* is in bad taste. They are a Communist ring and if you can check the foreign critics I know that's what you'll find. It's a Red band circling the earth, and this is one of the ways they're fighting me."

DeMille instructed the assistant to read every *Samson and Delilah* review in this country and abroad, then check the politics of those critics who refer in any manner to the picture being in bad taste.

For weeks the assistant pored over scores of reviews and was unable to uncover that specific reference in *The New York Times* or in any other American paper.

There were, however, a few in foreign publications. In Paris, *Figaro,* a De Gaullist extreme rightist paper, stated:

> *DeMille has at the same time surpassed the Himalaya as a champion of bad taste.*

The conservative *Hufvudstradstrladet,* in Helsinki, described the film as "a Biblical luxury rigged out more expensively than tastefully," while Stockholm's *Dagens Nyheter* called it "a strongly colored mausoleum of DeMille's vitality and vulgarity." The highly conservative London *Daily Telegraph* pointed to "moments of beauty," and scenes "with a deal of bad taste."

As far as the assistant was concerned, the project was proceeding badly.

He came into the office of a fellow assistant one afternoon.

"I could be in a lot of trouble," he said.

"Why?"

"The boss is trying to prove he's being chased by Communists who have infiltrated the movie sections of newpapers . . ."

"Well . . ."

"Well, I don't seem to be able to prove it. Anyway I'm writing my report today and tomorrow all hell will probably break loose." He was operating as best he could on the no-matter-what-you-think, your-troubles-are-over-if-you-please-DeMille philosophy, and on this basis he was in some peril.

By the bungalow's standards, his report was courageous. He advised the boss that he was "unable to sense any world-wide subversive pattern in the bad reviews."

He pointed out that in several of the large Eastern dailies, "the critics leave no doubt that they consider sitting through one of your pictures a major ordeal for one so sensitive to art values as a critic. These writers are a very small minority, however, and ninety per cent of the criticisms run from inspired to enthusiastic. I might mention that even the two Communist papers, *Daily People's World* and *Daily Worker,* gave you slightly better treatment than a few of the art-for-art's-sake boys."

The *New Yorker* never relented. A few days before DeMille's death on January 21, 1959, the magazine published a 2-sentence review of a remake, *The Buccaneer*, concluding:

> If that much manpower had been as conspicuously wasted in Russia as it is here, all hands would now be in Siberia.

5.

SHARING with him the tensions of one crisis after another, we felt it was part of DeMille's nature to be in a state of constant motion. He kept up a staggering pace and never seemed to be happier than when chaffing under some mighty dilemma.

The one great battle he lost was the one he wanted to win most—the famous dollar controversy, longest and bitterest of his life.

It began in the fall of 1944. At that time he was a member of a radio union, the American Federation of Radio Artists, and for eight years had been master of ceremonies of the Lux Radio Theater at a salary of $98,000 a year.

While others were responsible for the actual production of the Lux shows, including the selection of stories and actors; DeMille was able to invest them with the aura of his special showmanship. He was a fitting ornament for a showcase featuring the royalty of Hollywood. Thirty million persons listened to the show each week, its Crossley rating rising high above that of any then current dramatic offering.

On August 16, 1944, the program's even, happy tenor came to an abrupt end.

DeMille and the other 3,000 members received a letter from the Los Angeles local of the American Federation of Radio Artists. It asked for $1 to help finance the union's campaign to fight a proposed state amendment called Proposition 12.

If the voters approved Proposition 12 in the coming election, the open shop would go into effect in California, and thereafter membership in a union would no longer be a requisite of employment.

AFRA, therefore, was bending every effort toward its defeat. The letter requested "immediate payment of the assessment," warning that "failure to pay will result in suspension."

It was not a good time for a letter couched in strong terms. For months there had been conflict among movie unions over jurisdictional issues, leading to violence in the streets. Not far from the bungalow, around the corner at the big RKO lot, pickets carrying bludgeons had clashed with workers.

DeMille took the Union letter to a few close associates. He told them how he felt; he favored Proposition 12 and did not want to contribute his money—not a dollar or a cent—toward its defeat. It was the sort of talk studio executives liked to hear at the time; they were weary of the warring locals at their gates, and viewed the prospect of making motion pictures without multicraft complications with a pleasure almost too great to bear. The success of Proposition 12 held the promise of great reward.

Y. Frank Freeman, studio boss, was known not to have sympathetic leanings toward the present brand of union leadership. DeMille also sought the counsel of the late Bill Jeffers. Once a rail worker, Jeffers' rise to the presidency of the Union Pacific had in it all the elements of a Horatio Alger plot, of the sort calculated to produce extravagantly pro-union sentiments. In this instance it visibly did not. Both Jeffers and Freeman urged DeMille to make a stand for individual freedom and, in De-Mille's words, "every man's right to oppose political coercion in any form."

Few issues of the period were more inflammatory. The controversy was certain to attract wide attention if on no other basis than DeMille's great prestige. To his advisors there was another encouraging factor; they knew what a fighter he was, for up to that time or since, no Hollywood executive had made bold to take so vigorous a position publicly.

Around the country, supporters of "right to work" legislation were jubilant; already a few states had passed such laws, forbidding union membership as a *condition* of employment. A DeMille success in California, a key state, would jolt unionism and something that unionism had to have to stay alive, collective bargaining.

In mounting an anti-union crusade DeMille gave solemn thought to his own losses should AFRA rule him off the air. He would lose his weekly contact with a vast audience. The feeling of varied union members who populated every movie set would inevitably worsen. He considered public reaction. He wondered about the millions of union families who attended the cinema.

Moreover, he had come to love the Lux show, showering much care upon his part in it. So much so that on one occasion he harried a writer who was trying to prepare a suitable tribute to the filmdom's star moppet, Shirley Temple.

DeMille felt the man wasn't putting forth his best efforts.

The writer thought he was, and finally lost *his* temper. He demanded to know what on earth anyone could say about Shirley Temple.

"That's for you to figure out," snapped DeMille.

"If you'll tell me what you have in mind I'll try to do it."

"Just this," replied DeMille. "I want to say something about Shirley Temple that people will remember forever."

It was not unthinkable that AFRA might back away, being unwilling to project so important an issue with so worthy an opponent. Indeed, prestige was viewed by AFRA officials as the strongest weapon in DeMille's arsenal.

The union notified him that he had until September to pay the dollar.

The election was held. The proposed open-shop amendment was defeated by California voters.

But DeMille still owed the dollar. The union eased the deadline for payment to December 1.

On the eve of that date DeMille sat down with his wife. He wanted her feelings on the matter. Should he pay the dollar?

In the years ahead, from many and varied speaker platforms, he was to tell audiences what her reply was.

"She told me I had no choice, that if I paid the dollar I would be telling the world I placed money above principle. Besides, she said she was a partner in the firm and would not pay her half of the dollar."

On December 1, the union gave DeMille ten days in which to pay the assessment or be suspended from the air. His public-relations director and executive utility man at the time was Bill Pine, later to join up with Bill Thomas in the production of less costly pictures. Ironically, they were called "The Dollar Bills," a comment only on their small-budget productions.

Pine had just returned from a long location. He went quickly to DeMille, observed how tired and drawn he was. "Bill, can you get me out of this mess?" he said, wearily.

DeMille's dilemma planted a fascinating little seed in the publicist's mind.

They talked for a long time and Bill told him he might have a way out for him.

DeMille's reply to this was that he himself knew of a way out —pay the dollar—but he was not going to do that.

"I can get you out without your paying the dollar," Pine said mysteriously.

"How?"

"Never mind, I can do it. Just trust me."

Pine's plan was simple. *He* would pay the dollar, one of his own dollars in fact, thus removing the curse of submission inflicted by payment from the boss himself.

A day or so later a frightening thought struck DeMille. He hastily called in Pine.

"You weren't thinking of paying that dollar yourself."

Pine admitted he was.

"That's out," exclaimed DeMille. "It would make no difference *who* paid it. I will never pay the dollar and no one will ever pay it *for* me."

The day Lionel Barrymore was to replace DeMille on the Lux program, in February, 1945, the producer was given one more chance to pay the dollar; if he did, all would be forgiven. DeMille's reply was a declaration of intent; he would, if necessary, take the case through every court in the land, quoting Thomas Jefferson:

"To compel a man to furnish contribution of money for the propagation of opinions which he disbelieves and abhors is sinful and tyrannical."

The speaker's rostrum now beckoned. Invitations poured in, and letters flooded the DeMille office. A few letters contained rabid dissents but by and large the writers urged him to fight on, many also enclosing contributions—silver, currency and checks.

He was now deep in a battle far more demanding than any he had staged for the cameras, a modern-day Crusader with a siege of Acre of his own.

The next step was inevitable—an organization to spread his philosophy. With himself, Freeman, Jeffers, Frank P. Doherty, Lloyd C. Douglas and a few others as incorporators, the DeMille Foundation for Political Freedom came into existence in late fall, 1945. The articles described the Foundation as "non-political, non-partisan, non-profit and non-sectarian," with its main purpose being the defense of any individual deprived "of the right to earn a living because said person . . . refuses to pay . . .

dues or assessments to support or oppose any political party . . ." or "for publicly opposing any employer or union."

Hollywood had by now grown accustomed to the framework in which DeMille was wont to move. It had observed him long enough to know that predictions as to his behavior were never safe. One might have expected a man, no matter how stalwart, to give in to judicial opinion. DeMille did not take to cover when first one court, then another, ruled against him. He suffered three lower-court defeats.

Next, the United States Supreme Court declined to take his case, a refusal which meant that in the court's view DeMille's individual guarantees under the Constitution had not been prejudiced by AFRA.

DeMille did not waver in the holiness of his cause. If anything was amiss it was a judiciary capable of rendering a verdict that deprived a man of his right to work, and "therefore his right to life itself."

The courts had said that AFRA in levying the assessment had not interfered with DeMille's right of suffrage or discussion. He could *vote* for the measure, even though his dollar was working *against* it. DeMille pooh-poohed the distinction; his dollar nullified his vote, he insisted.

Apart from the fact his stand was four-square on a matter of principle, it could not be denied that a single vote influenced by the union's use of the DeMille dollar would have the effect of voiding DeMille's ballot.

Judge Wilson of the Los Angeles Superior Court in ruling for AFRA said the circumstances do not permit a complaint by anyone who is still permitted to vote as he pleases.

On the issues, the editorial writers of virtually every major newspaper went to work with considerable gusto. They were about evenly divided on the court's logic but almost all saw a danger in political assessments of this variety. The *Saturday Evening Post* reflected the majority thinking by posing a shrewd and interesting question. "Suppose the assessment had been ten dollars. Would it be reasonable to force a man to cast ten votes against himself on the ground that he was free to cast one on the other side?"

By temperament an expert in the sweeping broadside, De-Mille searched for a dramatic key to his predicament. His cause was just; now to devise a strategy that would expose his evil oppressors.

He was now morbidly certain that Communist influences were at work against him.

At luncheon one day he said he had spoken with the ex-Communist, Louis Budenz. "He told me the Communists had gotten me off the air but they couldn't get Fulton J. Lewis, Jr. off."

He reflected on the possibility of Red infiltration into the AFRA board of directors but a check of their background revealed nothing even slightly encouraging. Frequent conferences with FBI agents sur-charged the air in the bungalow, and missions veiled in the greatest secrecy were entrusted to staff members.

Judge Medina's heroic demonstration of patience and justice in the celebrated Communist trial in New York was closely followed, and the staff cheered when the eleven hooting, howling Reds were convicted.

Reading a newspaper account to the trial, DeMille exclaimed, "I feel the country is swinging to my side. I sense it!"

For the moment, his attention was diverted. An open dispute developed with the Catholic bishop in San Diego, Charles F. Buddy, who hurried to his typewriter whenever DeMille wrote a major article on AFRA, freedom, or rights of man. This flow of rebuttal appeared in the San Diego diocese paper, *Southern Cross*, and the Jesuit publication, *America*.

The unsolicited ripostes from the priest were skillfully thought out. The boss was needled by them. "There are Communist sympathizers in the Catholic Church," he said one day. "I know one, Bishop Buddy," and repeating a favorite lament, "I'd like to become a Catholic someday but I can't make up my mind about an organization that allows a man like Buddy to belong."

It was, all of it, a strange quest much out of keeping with his character, an eerie bit of witch-hunting which sought to inflict the Communist stigma on those who merely disagreed with him.

He told us there was no telling what organizations had become Communist sounding boards. When he was asked by the United States Lawn Tennis Association to permit the honorary use of his name, he ordered a check made of its politics. "We just can't be too careful," he said.

Of the several opposed concepts of DeMille, the impression of him as the "father of the American film" has taken on almost legendary proportions. After-dinner speakers placed DeMille on a pedestal enjoyed by few distinguished Americans, pairing him off with Lincoln, General Marshall, Belasco, Barnum and Billy Rose. In most instances the comparisons pleased DeMille. However, on one occasion a zealot likened Franklin D. Roosevelt's Americanism to DeMille's, a shock which the veteran producer never quite overcame.

It was difficult for the boss to keep from placing much of his woe at the doorstep of Roosevelt New Dealers. At this time, some six years after his AFRA defeat in the courts, he was conscious of how really big was his sacrifice. He was not only off the air permanently but also banned from television. Forgetful persons who sought him for a radio or TV appearance had to be told he could not appear without special permission from AFRA. On our premiere tours across country a few stations did obtain AFRA's consent for local appearances but in most instances the invitation was withdrawn.

In August, 1950, he told J. P. McEvoy of *Reader's Digest:*
"It has cost me at least $800,000 to date because I refused to pay that $1, and I am willing to spend every cent I've got until every American has the right to work when he pleases, where he pleases, for himself or whoever wants to hire him. What becomes of those inalienable rights of man—life, liberty and the pursuit of happiness—if you haven't the right to work?"

Part of our job was to be alert for little inconsistencies that might be uttered by the boss, often too busy in the heat of battle to take note of academic trifles. His remark to McEvoy about the constitutional guarantees of "life, liberty and the pursuit of happiness" was not quite right, according to the Constitution.

A memo to him the next day called attention to the specific reference in the 5th amendment: "nor shall any person be deprived of life, liberty or property without due process of law."

He returned the memo with a notation reading, "It's the New Dealers. Now they have passed laws whereby one can be deprived of property. . . ."

The political climate in the bungalow changed sharply in 1950 when James Roosevelt sought the governorship in California against the incumbent conservative, Earl Warren. Normally, talk of politics was in a light vein.

This time DeMille issued a warning to all staff members within earshot:

"Anyone in this office who votes for Roosevelt can pack his bag and head for the door."

New Deal policies, however, did find a kind of acceptance in a remote corner of the DeMille operation. Up at Paradise ranch, the deer from nearby wooded arroyos gathered on the lawn in front of the main house for a daily meal of potatoes, a deer delicacy. They were "New Deal" potatoes, bought from the government surplus stocks at 5 cents for a 100-pound sackful. The sack itself was later sold for 17 cents. The results were twofold—contented deer and a nice profit, a situation which DeMille attributed to New Deal bungling of the law of supply and demand.

6.

IN the fall, 1950, Hollywood was caught up in one of those "brush fire" controversies which, in the highly emotional community, filled the air with bitter argument. Outsiders were charging that the film colony was a hotbed of communist sympathizers and actual party adherents, and old movie scripts were being dusted off to show how, unwittingly, the studios had produced movies that parroted the "party line" as set out by tainted writers.

Fiery disputes licked hungrily in every direction. DeMille felt there was something to the charge, and so advised fellow directors, friendly ones like George Marshall and Al Rogell. He was at the time a member of the board of Hollywood's strongest and most influential group—the Screen Directors Guild—and what better way to demonstrate the Guild's Americanism than to pass a resolution requiring every director to take a loyalty oath?

While much of this behind-doors activity was going on, the Guild's president, Joseph L. Mankiewicz was traveling abroad. And while he was still away, the Guild's board, led by DeMille and "a few other conservatives like myself," enacted a bylaw calling for the loyalty oath.

This, the Board felt, would silence the industry's accusers so far as the directors themselves were concerned, and put to rest rumors that the Guild was dominated by Commie dupes.

Upon his return to the States, Mankiewicz (in no sense a DeMille adherent) sharply criticized the Board's action. Then he learned something that prodded him into immediate action; a petition was being circulated among Guild members calling for his recall as president.

Now, the lines were formed, and the issues joined—DeMille and his followers against Mankiewicz and those who felt a loyalty oath was an affront to every American.

The membership was aroused and, 500 strong, trouped to a meeting in late October.

Arguments raged for five hours. At midnight the battle was still on.

Mankiewicz made it clear that he was unalterably opposed to an open ballot, a blacklist, and a mandatory oath. He said all three procedures were un-American.

Before he had finished his hour long opening speech it became apparent to most of the members present that, as one observer put it, "the DeMille-Rogell-Marshall faction had attempted to ride the wrong horse."

DeMille defended the position of his faction. As the debate wore on and he began to sense the size of the opposition, he turned his fire on what he alleged to be the questionable politics of his opponents.

Without referring to anyone by name, DeMille charged that most of the twenty-five directors who had tried to stop the recall of Mankiewicz were affiliated with leftist or subversive organizations or theories.

The meeting, according to *Variety*, started to hiss and boo him. "John Cromwell, Don Hartman, Rouben Mamoulian, Herbert Leeds, William Wellman, John Ford, among others, bitterly assailed DeMille's statements."

One director asserted he was "sick and tired" of being required to defend his Americanism every time he expressed an opinion in opposition to DeMille.

Another said he was "wallowing in the muck of Bastogne at the time that DeMille was defending his capital gains in Hollywood."

Rogell and Leo McCarey tried to side with DeMille but their efforts were brief and ineffectual.

Scores of reporters maintained a watch outside the doors of the meeting room, trying to pry pieces of information from members who emerged for a few moments' recess.

Near three A.M. DeMille's loss of ground was evident. He was asked from the floor to retract his charges against the twenty-five directors. He refused, asserting that his statements were true. John Ford then made a motion asking the resignation of the entire board. The motion was seconded by Walter Lang—and the board was out.

For the knot of reporters outside the meeting room, it was a long vigil.

As the evening wore on, they began to view it as a contest in uresis. They began checking the names of directors who took one recess; everyone in attendance had made at least one trip, some more.

Everyone, that is, except DeMille!

It remained for Tom Pryor, then Hollywood bureau chief of *The New York Times*, to deliver the memorable comment, "There's no doubt about it, DeMille has the greatest courage in town and the strongest kidneys."

At luncheon the next day we could tell important events had transpired. The boss's manner was deeply contemplative. For minutes the only sound was a muffled crunch as he fished an occasional potato chip from the bowl in front of him.

His eyes went slowly from one staff member to another, coming full circle to the secretary at his right.

Then, he said quietly, "If you don't think our country is in danger you should have been at last night's meeting."

A weekly series of syndicated articles with DeMille's by-line began to appear in newspapers under the heading, CECIL DEMILLE SPEAKING. At one period, the articles were being published by more than sixty outlets, reaching an estimated 20 million readers. This occasioned a real sense of triumph in view of Hollywood's traditional practice of feeding the press with great quantities of material free of charge. Through the syndicate, General Features Corporation, the client newspapers were paying us for the articles. We were the envy of rival press agents, who assumed we would use the columns to "plug" our own movies, but this was rarely done.

For material, we dug deep into Mr. DeMille's past film activities for anecdotes and humorous episodes, for it was on that basis—light, airy articles—that we were able to sell the idea of a series to General Features. Now a new upheaval threatened, induced by the AFRA and Guild conflicts.

Mr. DeMille made it clear that he wished to strike a blow for freedom through the weekly series. In New York, the Syndicate was disturbed over this proposal; political articles would not be advisable, and would we please communicate that thought to Mr. DeMille. When we did, he said no one was going to tell him what he would write and would we please communicate that thought to the Syndicate.

There were weekly deadlines to meet, and in shuttling between the two parties, we continued writing memoirs for the boss. With each submission, he inquired about the political articles until their preparation could be put off no longer.

DeMille had suggested a series of three articles on the AFRA controversy. Once more Robert Pearsall, the Syndicate's general manager, strongly objected; he said espousal of any cause, political or otherwise, deviated from our original understanding.

The first AFRA article began, "Lost causes are won by men who won't give up the fight," and went on to detail DeMille's sentiments on "right to work" and his part in events that led to the passage of the Taft-Hartley law. There were immediate inquiries from editors, some papers withholding the article from publication. We hastened to tell DeMille that these actions were not a comment on the merits of the AFRA case; it was simply that their contract with the Syndicate called for articles *about Hollywood* from "Mr. Hollywood" himself.

If Mr. DeMille enjoyed haggling with his staff, he should have been at this time in a divine ecstasy. A hot glow of dissension enveloped the bungalow. Writers on the circus story were coming and going. The hunt for possible Red influence in journalism was hard on the heels of sources that referred to *Samson and Delilah* as a story reflecting bad taste. And now along came the Syndicate's opposition to articles designed to deliver a ringing defense of man's right to work.

Within the bungalow the taste for the weekly series was waning. Mr. DeMille withheld approval of articles over long periods, rejecting one after another. The career of each draft grew more stormy; deadlines became a problem as the Syndicate peppered us with appeals for more articles.

To avoid further delay, we began to rely more and more upon DeMille's own suggestions for articles; usually these were promptly approved.

There was no way of knowing just when a future article would pop out of his conversation.

He was saying one day how fate could be pretty capricious with people.

"Years ago we were making a picture with Claudette Colbert and Herbert Marshall on the east coast of Hawaii in thick jungle country, and the only sign of civilization was an asylum for the insane sitting up on a high hill. A path ran down the hill from the asylum past the spot where we were shooting and we supposed it was used by the asylum. In that picture we had a great oriental idol more than fifty feet high, which we had made in the States and shipped in pieces to the Island. Well, it was assembled right there and it looked pretty grotesque, sitting in the jungle before a small clearing. Matter of fact it was outright eerie. The idol was put up and we shot our scenes, and then we all left for a location a few miles away. That evening two inmates came strolling down. They saw the idol and froze in their tracks. Where had this monstrous thing with a face like a gargoyle come from? They did not approach it but turned and fled. When they reached the asylum they hurried to the office of the superintendent with the news. The superintendent received the story with a dubious shake of his head. A few days before he had given these two men the freedom of the area, thinking their minds were back to normal, but now it appeared he had made a mistake. Certainly anyone who sees a giant idol in this remote jungle ought to be checked a little closer. The inmates insisted they weren't nuts, that there really was an idol out there and they could prove it if he would follow them. The superintendent nodded his head, obviously humoring them, and promised he would go with them in the morning, as it was getting dark.

"That very evening Roy Burns and his crew returned to the location, dismantled the idol and placed it aboard a boat for our new location. We had promised the local government not to destroy trees in the area, so Roy and his men were careful to clean up the spot and remove all debris. The next morning the two inmates, now plainly worried about whether they really had seen an idol, returned to the spot with the superintendent at their heels. They rushed here and there, but no idol! And the more they talked, the more the superintendent shook his head. There was only one thing he could do, revoke their right to move around the area and confine them to the asylum."

Mr. DeMille said he had learned the story from one of the Paramount people who had talked to the superintendent of the asylum. The tragic, ironic note of the story appealed to him greatly and he wondered why it would not be suitable for our syndicated series of articles. We agreed, but the ending was a little weak. Now of course if a new ending could be tacked on . . .

The little wheels in the boss's head began to whirl. "Here are these two poor guys who really aren't crazy at all. The superintendent thinks they are, and they are beginning to wonder. Did they see something that wasn't there?"

Ideas were tossed back and forth until we came up with an ending with justice triumphant. Though confined to quarters the two men were granted permission to see the weekly movies shown to most of the inmates. Months now have passed. The idol incident has caused severe psychological damage, and their progress has been greatly retarded. Then one evening they attend a movie, one by Cecil B. DeMille, and they see the coast of Hawaii, and, lo and behold, a giant oriental idol! The two men rush to the side of the superintendent, who is there, too, and the men are vindicated and their rights restored.

With a little reworking it made a wonderful, heartwarming little episode that somehow fit in with the boss's philosophy toward historical drama—"I am interested in people, not dates." The article went into sixty newspapers and millions of homes and the letters received at the bungalow gave us the feeling the boss had wrought a charming and joyful tale.

The Syndicate's insistence on articles of a non-political nature spelled the end of the series. Upon DeMille's instructions it was canceled in September, 1951.

Before the boss had made the decision, we suggested that perhaps another writer might take over—perhaps someone with a fresh viewpoint. Though DeMille promptly brushed the suggestion aside, it was a suggestion that we felt should be made, in view of a comment DeMille had written on the face of a rejected article: *I thought I had an interesting life until I began reading your articles.*

7.

ONE of the fee-simple tenants on the DeMille ranch Paradise was a peacock named Henry. He was not the only one of his species; years ago scores had been imported to the mountainous retreat by DeMille. Soon there were hundreds of the vain creatures strutting about, for Henry and a few compatriots of equally sturdy drumstick were not fettered by any foolish notions of celibacy. Henry measured up to every romantic obligation—with the result that the region teemed with his issue. In fact so magnificent were his feats of paternity that the lineage became obscured, and there were occasions when offspring would pass without so much as a nod at their great sire.

Henry had other marks of distinction, in recognition of which fate one day was to set him out as a marked peacock.

Mr. DeMille's interest in the bird of legend went back a long way. As a boy his appreciation of peacocks was encouraged by the family's Sunday visits to the art museums in New York. The elder DeMille may have directed Cecil and Bill to the old masters for more aesthetic reasons; still, Cecil could not help observing the gorgeous peacocks in the background of many a famous painting, particularly the outsized one atop the stable in Fra Angelico's "Adoration of the Magi." It appeared, however, that the first real spark of his admiration was struck years later when he ran across a copy of the London *Journal* containing a color photograph of a shapely lass in an all peacock-feather gown.

It was on that day that Henry's destiny was inexorably shaped.

In proper season, Henry was a moulting fool. Sometimes De-

Mille himself, but more often the workers at the ranch, stalked the vain bird up crevice and slope to retrieve the magnificent "eyed" feathers that fell from Henry's sturdy frame. These were carefully preserved for the day when Mr. DeMille would encounter a heroine worthy to wear a creation ornamented with the iridescent plumes.

Thus Henry's burnished feathers were stored for years.

In time the DeMille flock dwindled to a mere handful but no marked change could be observed in Henry. He ruled with the air of a monarch conscious of the comparative weakness of his subjects. As a Don Juan his performances were incendiary, his chivalry *à outrance*. Peacocks are accustomed to roosting alone. However, on nights when the moon was high and the spirit of amour was afield, he took to a high limb with his harem, usually two or three awestruck females. Henry rarely was observed in the gloaming with fewer than five peahens in attendance. As if rallying attention to himself, he would let out the shrill peacock cry, sending small fowl into frightened refuge among the shrubs. It is a startling cry to ears that have never heard it, a harsh piercing scream as of mortal distress. It could not be interpreted as distress in Henry's case, for no one would contest Henry's mastery, no matter how aggravated were the demands upon his powers in the course of a single evening. The love season found him the center of a circle of admiring peahens, meek and myopic little creatures, their garb as drab as sackcloth. He staged these exhibitions in the plot of grass west of the main house, and when his audience was large enough and possibly deferential enough he would spread his great fan, then turn slowly about with a kind of deliberate majesty. This, too, was a facet of his understanding nature, for it provided something other than a rear view for the spectators on the porch.

DeMille, sensitive to things that bespeak showmanship, was of the opinion Henry would have been an unbearable prude were it not for one thing. "He would strut around until his eyes fell upon his ridiculous feet and his pride would suffer a complete collapse." He once likened Henry to the actresses who came to his office. "Ninety per cent of them have beautiful faces, bad voices, and ugly feet."

After more than a decade of feather gathering, DeMille decided to make his move. He felt he had found the heroine equal to the honor, no one exceptionally less than that Biblical flapper, Delilah, as portrayed by a woman of even greater beauty, Hedy Lamarr. It is not easy to say what fowlish emotions stirred Henry's soul at the thought that his feathers were to play such a soft and silken part in a mighty epic, or to what extent his composure was shattered by the news that the sum of $10,000 would be spent on Delilah's peacock cape, of turquoise velvet lined with gold lamé, under the direction of Paramount's frequent Academy Award winner, chief designer, Edith Head.

It came about that a blow was struck at Henry's pride.

DeMille was dissatisfied with the color of the "eyes" of the feathers.

They weren't bright enough.

So he set to work a row of some twenty women, in assembly-line fashion, touching up the "eyes" with metallic paints. With pinpoint brushes the painters were at their tasks for several weeks to complete the renovation of hundreds of feathers—an incomparably rare instance of two earthly forces, DeMille and DuPont, setting themselves about to improve on God's handiwork.

While it is sad that Henry's little saga did not end on a note of complete personal triumph, there was considerable symbolism in it to those who interested themselves in the complexity of Mr. DeMille's personality.

In Henry, they found a key to a gentler aspect of the showman's nature—his pursuit of beauty in every form.

DeMille heroines were more dazzling, their ornaments more breath-taking, their living more pleasurable. The people of his post-World War I social dramas moved in an atmosphere of ermine, marble swimming pools and plush footmen. He purchased a $15,000 mink coat for Gloria Swanson to wear in a picture, explaining, "The audience will love it and Gloria will be enchanted. How could she fail to give me a good performance?" No cost was spared if it meant such elegance as flowing drapes, gowns of spun silver bought by the pound in Egypt, or gold goblets purchased from an European treasure house. "The audience," he had said, "little knows what treasures there are in my pictures." If, as his critics cried out, his people were unreal, there was no lack of reality in the things about them, down to the smallest details—real fruit, real wine, real roast pheasant (a distressing problem on our sets was the disappearance of edibles; many a feast prepared for a Roman orgy 30 B.C. was consumed piecemeal by Americans circa 1930 A.D., requiring the posting of guards). Once the boss learned that a head photographer, Whitey Schafer, was applying a kind of lacquer, known as "sex oil" around the lot, to the face and arms of one of his principals, Carol Thurston, to create a sort of glow. It impinged on the boss's concept of natural feminine allure and word was dispatched to Schafer—"Mr. DeMille asks that you stop putting canned sex on Miss Thurston."

Many observers of the DeMille complex accepted what they saw at its face value. One phrase was both obvious and irresistible: "a Dr. Jekyll and Mr. Hyde." This dual temperament at one time or another has baffled virtually everyone, even intimates. They were never sure what kind of human being he really was down deep. After Mr. DeMille's death a staff member of fourteen years of close association wrote for the press that he was "essentially a sincere and humble man," while another observer a few years back regarded him as "a charlatan, trickster, and a man of no real resource."

The editors of a film magazine sent a writer on an interesting mission in the summer of 1930. They asked him to clear up the

DeMille paradox. Before the interview the writer searched the
records, emerging more confused than ever. The records held
DeMille to be "the worst slave driver of all the directors," "the
most considerate man in Hollywood," "merciless," "a man who
likes to be considered a king," "modest and conservative,"
"feared by his associates," "loved by his associates."

The writer arrived on a day DeMille was inspecting a parade
of exotic frocks worn by models. He waved them all out of the
room, "moved a charming old Chinese bronze out of the way
and sat silently, fixing me with very intense eyes."

The writer spoke first: "What kind of man are you anyway,
Mr. DeMille? Are you really Dr. Jekyll or are you Mr. Hyde?
And if one of the characters people give you is false why do
you make no attempt to correct it? Why have you allowed this
two-edged legend to flourish all these years?"

Showman DeMille smiled. "If I told you positively, people
could only talk about me once instead of twice as they do now.
That would be a real calamity, for they might stop going to see
my pictures. I can't answer you. You'll have to guess for yourself."

While the writer could draw nothing more out of him, De-
Mille utilized the occasion to add to his own legend. "He showed
me an amazing collection of curios and gorgeous unset jewels,
and then amidst all this display of wealth and luxury, he
would be interrupted by calls from his brokers, giving swift
answers like 'Buy me so many shares at the market. . . .'; 'Sell.
I don't like their last statement'; 'Yes, I'll endorse her note. She
once played for my father.'"

Lewis Jacobs, a film analyst, contended DeMille had never
made a fine film, "only pretentious ones." Robert Sherwood in
a more contemplative mood tagged him "the Zeus of Hollywood," pointing out that his training under Belasco accounted
for "the form of hokum which was to make him famous and
rich." To Jim Tully he was "the first man in such a position I
have met who knows the mob without thinking on their level.

He has the weakness of those who have tasted power and the mentality of those who realize its futility."

Editorially, the *Saturday Evening Post* judged that "if De-Mille has accomplished nothing else he has at least enriched the English language, for his name is commonly used to describe such things as the Grand Canyon, the Mississippi flood, an onyx bathroom or a Palm Beach debutante party." Almost on the day this estimate went into American homes, a world poll of movie exhibitors placed DeMille far and away at the top of his industry. The writer and consultant to stars, Rufus Blair, was on a DeMille set one day and within earshot when a scenarist was repeating from a script an order given by George Washington to a Virginia militiaman. DeMille asked whether Washington had given such an order. The scenarist said no. "Then," said DeMille, "take it out of the script. You can't change Washington's biography. It's like giving Jesus of Nazareth a new line in the Gospels." Upon departing Blair voiced what for the moment may be a reasonably apt summary of this lofty temperament. "He's a weird despot with a fundamental contempt for the human race, a great genius with marvelous skills, basking in the warm rays of his own personal sun."

He could allow no scene to pass ungilded. His mind, basically theatrical, saw great epochs in terms of episodes of ornate melodrama connected by a thin cord of narration, like pearls on grocery twine. No human actor ever rose above the majesty of a DeMille spectacle, unless it was DeMille himself. It was impossible for many to see his pictures without sensing his presence.

It was as a melodrama-maker that he became an exhibitionist of astonishing stature. He turned the spotlight upon himself with a boldness never equaled in Hollywood. Will Rogers called him his own biggest epic. Carl Sandburg told him he had seen every one of his pictures but that DeMille had never read a single one of his poems. DeMille regretfully agreed. Robert Benchley devoted column after column of inspired invective to DeMille and his pictures, then visited the producer at the studio and watched him trumpet like a chained elephant as he directed a mob scene. Afterwards DeMille received the eminent humorist with open-armed affection, thanked him for keeping his name before the public. Benchley went away a staunch DeMille supporter.

On the day the million-dollar theater opened its doors in downtown Los Angeles, featuring the debut of a DeMille picture, the spectators gasped at sight of an airplane circling the flagpole atop the theater dome. The pilot was DeMille. He received more publicity than either the opening or the picture.

His forays into exploitation were foolproof. He shunned the infantile and made sure that there was enough sense in an exploit to gain it public acceptance. A lapse in this custom occurred in the 'Twenties, when the studios faced an odd racial problem. Every movie gangster was detectably of Italian extraction. The Italians objected, whereupon the villains began looking like Germans, and the Germans complained.

Showman DeMille's instincts were astir. He set out in his yacht, Seaward, and upon his return a few days later announced that he was negotiating for the purchase of the Cedros islands off the California coast. Henceforth all the villains in his pictures would be Cedrans. He told friends that he was going to put the entire island population of several hundred people under contract with a yearly retainer of $10 per capita. There would be enough villains for every studio, at the usual guild rates. Nothing came of the idea other than a gleeful reception by the press.

The Dutch Government decorated DeMille with the Order of Orange-Nassau for bringing to the screen the story of Corydon Wassell's almost singlehanded evacuation of wounded Navy men from Java to Australia during World War II. The world first learned of the Arkansas doctor's heroism through one of

President Roosevelt's fireside chats. DeMille, never particularly attentive to the New Dealer's pronouncements, did not listen to the speech. That night, he received a late call from his capable public relations director, Ted Bonnet, whose first novel, *The Mudlark*, written after he had left DeMille, became a best seller and later a motion picture.

Ted ascertained the boss had not heard the President's broadcast and proceeded to recount the Wassell exploit.

"It's a perfect story for us," Bonnet exclaimed.

"Check with me in the morning and I'll talk to Paramount about it," said DeMille.

"It will be too late then," Bonnet insisted.

"What do you mean?"

"By tomorrow morning every studio and independent producer in town will be on the phone to Washington."

"Well, what do you suggest, that we call now?" It was then past midnight.

"Yes," said Bonnet quickly.

A half-hour later the Secretary of the Navy, Frank Knox, was startled by a caller in Hollywood saying, "I want Dr. Wassell and the United States Navy."

By now fully awake, Knox gently reminded DeMille that the United States was engaged in a major war.

"I can give you Wassell but we'll have to hold off letting you have the Navy for the time being."

"Do you agree that I will have the first chance at Dr. Wassell?" persisted DeMille. The official agreed.

As Bonnet had predicted, a score of applicants eager for the film rights to the Wassell story besieged the Navy Department the following day.

Dr. Wassell was in Australia when the Navy instructed him to proceed immediately to the West Coast and await further orders.

Wassell was worried. He had undertaken the evacuation from

Java without specific instructions, in an emergency that called for swift decision. He hoped he had done the right thing but he was disciplined in the Navy's rigid chain of command. It struck him that the Secretary might now be acting on his behavior, with perhaps even a court martial in the offing.

Wassell was met in Los Angeles and told to go to the office of a film director named Cecil DeMille.

Though considerably relieved, Wassell was puzzled when he took a chair in DeMille's office.

"You are going to be the subject of a motion picture," DeMille said.

The obscure medico from the Arkansas hills rose from his seat, his face flushed.

"A what! Motion picture! I don't care to be in a motion picture."

"Not exactly you," said DeMille, gently. "You will be played by Gary Cooper, if we can sign him up for the part."

Wassell was not impressed. Cooper or no Cooper, he didn't like the idea.

DeMille was sympathetic; he realized what the doctor had been through, but he owed it to America, the Navy, the President and the Secretary to demonstrate to the world the caliber of our men in service.

It was inevitable that the course of the Wassell film would not be smooth. Wassell looked intently to Navy protocol, while DeMille sought to keep his ear attuned to boxoffice values. When the picture was premiered in Washington, officialdom waited expectantly to hear DeMille call Dr. Wassell onto the stage during the opening ceremonies. Not Wassell but Cooper was summoned before the capacity audience. As a showman, DeMille knew the danger of destroying an illusion. "Gary Cooper is the hero of Java in our film," DeMille explained to his staff later. "Cooper *is* Wassell. That's what the public must believe."

8.

IN the forty-six years he spent behind the cameras, he created a wide and impressive assortment of images of himself, some as vivid as the heroes who thundered out of his scripts. In his multiple forms, this last of the great pioneer directors left behind much for his critics and followers to chew on—DeMille the Sound Stage Tyrant, DeMille the Thirteenth Apostle, DeMille the Bathtub King. These and other bouncy titles were not always spoken in jest, yet they glanced harmlessly off his armor. He learned to live without the acclaim of colleagues, always aware that Hollywood disapproved of his firebrand tactics, his Barnumesque settings, his preoccupation with display, and particularly his irritating habit of deriving enormous profit from subjects that were supposed to spell financial ruin.

He had to be the boldest of competitors in order to survive nearly a half century of Hollywood's chancy climate. No one cared to contest the fact that he had proved himself the most durable and tireless of them all. Associates were wont to ponder whether he was mortal and fallible, perhaps even inexplicably immune to the laws of natural tenancy. Not aware of this special dispensation, Hollywood periodically set about writing his epitaph. More than twenty years ago Louella Parsons announced his retirement, speculating on how he was going to spend the 40 million dollars which she estimated he possessed at that time. DeMille emerged from these premature wakes with twice the energy of his would-be mourners and, like a prophet of old, continued to strike miracles from the rocks of Hollywood. He accepted challenge joyfully and knew the uses of adversity, once remarking to his old railroading friend Bill Jeffers, with devilish intonation, "I am the arch ogre of Holly-

wood." To the very end his career bristled with combat, in a
medley of conflicting legends swirling around him like match-
sticks in an eddy. He created a number of these legends himself, only to deny them stoutly in late years when the mantle of
world prestige rested comfortably on his shoulders.

To those far removed from the Hollywood scene, the life of
this fabled man will seem unreal. Some may find it hard to
accept the existence of such a wildly unfettered temperament.
Yet this brilliant self-promoter, this modern-day Renaissance
prince surrounded by obedient mercenaries was the man who
produced pictures that thrilled millions of persons all over the
world. A few years ago an able writer was commissioned to do
a serious biographical study of DeMille. DeMille read it, angrily hurled it into the wastebasket. On its title page he had
written, "I get the impression I have never had a pleasant moment in my life—except when torturing someone."

His own staff never really understood the scope of his efforts
to achieve the extraordinary. On one occasion an aide was asked
what he thought of an episode in the Book of Esther, which
DeMille was considering as a film story at the time. The aide
remarked that the Biblical tale had interesting possibilities. "Interesting possibilities!" the director lashed out. "Why you've
missed the whole point. Think of it, one thousand virgins standing in the courtyard, and the King of Babylon has his choice!"

Again, trying out a story idea on a couple of new writers:
"This is not a religious story, it's a Bible story, but above everything else it's a love story. There is a great message in it, a human message of love. It's not a message that has to do with any
sect. It's not how the Jews were rescued by Moses. It's a story
of human relations of two people. It's just a damn good hot tale,
so don't get a lot of these, thous and thums in your mind."

He was aware that his staff found life fraught with anxieties
and tensions and, like Nero's lieutenants, remained with him
because of the prestige that came with serving him. He did not
expect the staff to approve of his methods, once admonishing an

assistant who was having trouble with a writing assignment, "Don't worry about whether it's good or bad. Just please me and your troubles are over."

His boundless energy and explosive fury made the miracle of his kind of bigness possible, achieving his grandiose purpose with the best of the mortal timber available to him and the air of a person called upon to moor a ship with a thread. He put boredom to flight by sheer pyrotechnics, and in gentler moments enthralled the shopgirl and housewife by his sensitive eye for finery and elegant trappings.

As a ritualist with attentive acolytes as his aides he sought an ideal world. When he did not find it he made one of his own, reduced it to his will and whim. The last twenty years of his life were spent in the narrow confine of studio and staff. In that period Hollywood, hopelessly gregarious, saw nothing of him socially. Here and there was a DeMille intimate but the rest were relationships rather than friendships. In those years he was an unwilling partner with the film colony. Like nature, he developed protective tissue deflecting the jests of the rude and the taunts of the ignorant. If Hollywood was frigid, he was thrice frigid, deriving his strength from what was viewed as the most nutritional of all Hollywood vitamins—big returns at the boxoffice. When the industry made a shortsighted show of bravery a few years back, pretending that a new thing called television was no menace at all, DeMille blandly declared that Hollywood's fate rested on the new medium. It was the sort of prescience that had stood him well. The outraged cries of betrayal from Hollywood executives forced him into an agonizing silence, depending as he did on the purse of others for his productions.

The tantalizing riddle of Cecil DeMille was his remoteness from an industry of which he was the main attraction. No crown from colleagues rests on the head of the fabled Hollywood virtuoso. Probably the most incisive of these reflections on DeMille was destined to be uttered by Mrs. DeMille herself, a most gracious and serene woman.

The occasion was an Academy Award dinner in 1942, and among the notables was the Chinese ambassador to the United States, Dr. Hu Shih, whose country was fighting bravely at the time against terroristic Japanese invaders.

DeMille, introducing Hu Shih, referred to him as "the Japanese Ambassador." He quickly rectified the unfortunate error and amid oppressive silence returned to his seat. Smiling gently as ever, Mrs. DeMille leaned toward her husband. "Cecil," she whispered, "at last you have done something that Hollywood will remember you for."